The Hamlyn Guide to
House Plants

Alan Titchmarsh

illustrated by
Stuart Lafford
Tim Hayward

Hamlyn
London · New York · Sydney · Toronto

FOR POLLY

'The fairest flower that ever blossomed on ancestral timber'

W.S.G. *H.M.S. Pinafore*

Line artwork on pages 10, 16, 21, 22 by Norman Barber

Colour artwork on pages 31, 49, 51, 53, 77, 87, 91, 93, 97,
99, 101, 103, 105, 109, 113, 123, 141, 143, 149, 151, 153,
155, 161, 163, 179, 185, 195, 213 and 253 by Tim Hayward
All other colour artwork by Stuart Lafford

First published in 1982 by
The Hamlyn Publishing Group Limited
London · New York · Sydney · Toronto
Astronaut House, Feltham, Middlesex, England

ISBN 0 600 34625 0 (paperback)
ISBN 0 600 30530 9 (cased edition)

Filmset in England by Page Bros (Norwich) Ltd
in 8 on 9pt Linotron 202 Bembo

Printed in Spain by
Printer Industria Gráfica, S.A.   Barcelona
Depósito Legal B. 24356-1982

CONTENTS

ACKNOWLEDGEMENTS

Several people have been of tremendous help to me in the preparation of this book. Chris Brickell of the Royal Horticultural Society's Garden at Wisley in Surrey has given me invaluable assistance in sorting out the nomenclature. Any mistakes which have crept in subsequent to his early blue-pencil work are entirely of my own doing. Peter Edwards of the Royal Botanic Gardens, Kew, helped me to order the ferns, and the Library Staff at Kew have been very patient with miscellaneous requests for information on the origin of plant names. Mike Park furnished me with snippets of information from his ancient botanical volumes, and Bill Davidson of The House of Rochford trudged from the depths of his greenhouses on more than one occasion to corroborate evidence.

However, this book really belongs to the artists, Stuart Lafford and Tim Hayward, whose exquisite artistry coupled with accurate draughtsmanship has brought to life the plants I have written about. To them, and to my patient wife Alison and bemused daughter Polly, I offer my grateful thanks.

INTRODUCTION

HOUSE PLANTS are becoming a part of everyone's life, whatever their feelings towards gardening and the great outdoors, brightening homes, offices and factories. Some plants are expensive to buy and others very cheap, but once acquired they all demand some attention if they are to stay in peak condition and not disappoint their owners.

This book is intended as a practical guide to the identification, selection and cultivation of a wide range of house plants, some of which are common, and a few of which are rather unusual. The book is in no way a botanical study, though I have made every effort to bring nomenclature up to date, as well as including the older botanical synonyms by which some gardeners may still know their plants. Common names are noted too, and the index should enable anyone who knows a plant by the name of Busy Lizzie or Mind-your-own-business to locate it with ease.

Common names vary from place to place and country to country, so the plants are arranged under their botanical names, which are international. I have adopted Stebbins' arrangement of plant families. The ferns are placed before the flowering plants; the latter are divided into dicotyledons and monocotyledons. This arrangement will help the student without intefering too much with the book from the layman's point of view.

Wherever possible the origin of the plant's generic name has been explained. I have located these in various places but I have found A. W. Smith's and W. T. Stearn's *A Gardener's Dictionary of Plant Names* (Cassell) an invaluable help. I freely acknowledge that much of the information given was culled from its pages.

I have grown the majority of the plants described in this book myself and so the details of cultivation come from my own experience. One or two are just acquaintances but I see no reason for leaving them out. In such cases I have relied upon the information of friends and colleagues whose judgement can be trusted.

The first part of the book deals with the routine care and attention that plants need, and it is to this section that the reader should refer for precise details on potting, watering, feeding, propagation and pests and diseases. The bulk of the book deals with the individual plants, describing them and noting their cultivation requirements.

Every gardener must learn from his own experiences, but I hope this book will take some of the guesswork out of growing a remarkably varied and rewarding group of plants.

A. TITCHMARSH
Sunningdale 1981

CHOOSING PLANTS

Nowadays there is no shortage of places to buy house plants – they are sold in supermarkets and chain stores, on market stalls and in garden centres as well as at their place of birth, the nursery. It's easy to be tempted into buying any plant if it looks healthy and has been well displayed, but if you hope to grow the plant well and if it is to fit into your home you should go out knowing exactly what you want.

Plant types There are basically three types of house plant: evergreen foliage plants which form the backbone of any display and are decorative all the year round; the flowering perennials which are good value for money because they can be propagated and kept growing for years, and although the spectacular gift plants such as the calceolaria, cineraria and chrysanthemum will only be with you for a short time, they make up for their brief lives by being especially bright and cheerful. Make sure you know the life expectancy of any plant before you buy it.

Shapes Find out how much room you have to spare before you buy a house plant. If you have a particular spot in mind then take a tape-measure and note down the dimensions. Choose a plant that will fit the space with room to spare for growth. Some house plants are tall and columnar, others are bushy, some make dwarf rosettes that are easy to accommodate, and others climb or trail so you must allow room for the stems to scramble over a support or to cascade downwards.

A plant for every corner Light, temperature and humidity are the most important things in a house plant's life. Each one has its own preferences so it's just as well if you can find one that will enjoy growing in the spot you want to fill. The following lists will give you a few ideas:

For shade *Asparagus, Aspidistra, Asplenium, Calathea, Fatsia, Ficus pumila, Fittonia, Maranta, Pellaea, Philodendron, Plectranthus, Rhoicissus, Sansevieria, Selaginella, Soleirolia.*

For sun *Agave, Aloe, Beloperone, Billbergia, Bougainvillea,* cacti and succulents, *Campanula, Celosia,* x*Citrofortunella, Citrus, Coleus, Hypoestes, Kalanchoe, Pelargonium, Sempervivum, Sedum.*

For unheated rooms *Araucaria, Browallia, Calceolaria, Campanula, Chrysanthemum, Cyclamen, Cytisus,* x*Fatshedera, Fatsia, Hedera,*

Pittosporum, Primula, Rhododendron, Schizanthus, Senecio, Zantedeschia.

For centrally-heated rooms *Acalypha, Aeschynanthus, Anthurium, Codiaeum, Columnea, Dieffenbachia, Dizygotheca, Dracaena, Euphorbia, Monstera, Peperomia, Plectranthus, Schefflera, Sinningia, Streptocarpus.*

For warm bathrooms *Aechmea, Aeschynanthus, Adiantum, Aglaeonema, Begonia, Caladium, Columnea, Cryptanthus, Dionaea, Episcia, Pilea, Platycerium, Pteris, Saintpaulia.*

What to look for when buying Never buy a plant unless you can satisfy yourself that it is in good shape. Make sure that it is not infested with pests or showing any sign of disease, that it is not wilting, and that the compost in the pot has not shrunk away from the sides of the container. This indicates that the plant has been allowed to dry out at some time and growth may be checked as a result. Always pick a bushy plant in preference to one which is tall and spindly – unless that is its natural habit. Check, too, that the leaves are not brown or discoloured, unless the variegation is its attraction. Do not buy plants which have already shed some of their leaves.

When choosing a flowering plant, always select one that has some flowers fully open and some still in bud. If all the blooms are tight closed they may not open properly in the less-than-ideal conditions in your home.

For preference, buy your house plants in spring and summer when growth is fast and they can quickly shrug off any shock to their systems. This is not possible with winter-flowering pot plants which must be bought when in bloom, but make sure these are wrapped up properly and transport them home quickly. Do not leave them in the car where they may be chilled to death.

THE PLANTS AT HOME

As soon as you get a plant home unpack it from its protective wrapping and stand it in the room where it is to be grown. Even if you know that the plant can tolerate bright sunlight, do not be tempted to expose it to the sun's glare for the first two or three days. Let it accustom itself to your house temperatures before it has to speed up its internal processes under the influence of bright light. If the compost is sufficiently moist leave the plant alone, but if signs of dryness are apparent then give it a drink.

Plants vary in their environmental requirements, but there are certain places that none of them will enjoy: do not place any plant in a draught, against a radiator or other heat source, or where it will be knocked by passers-by. Never leave plants between the window and the curtains on winter evenings but bring them into the body of the room at night.

Above all, site your plants carefully, so they will not only thrive but also look their best. Single specimen plants need a plain background to show them off well, and if you use a pot hider or *câche-pot* make sure that it has muted tones that complement the plant rather than compete with it. Choose one that is of a suitable size for the plant, neither too large nor too small. Make sure that it is watertight too or carpets and furniture will soon be stained.

Many plants not only look better when grouped together, but also grow better too. The atmospheric buoyancy that results from a collection of foliage and compost develops healthy growth. There are several ways of grouping plants. They may be simply stood adjacent to one another in their pots or collectively positioned on a large gravel tray (see notes on humidity on page 11). Alternatively, they may be plunged in their pots in a large container of peat, or knocked from their pots and planted together in a large container of compost. The gravel tray and plunging methods are, to my mind, the most satisfactory schemes, for they provide good growing conditions while still allowing changes to be made in group formation. When planted together in a large container of compost the plants will have to be watched especially closely, and any that show signs of deteriorating must be removed and replaced with haste. Remember that plants which are grouped together must all have the same light, heat and humidity requirements. If they are planted together they must have the same watering requirements too.

House plants prefer a slightly humid atmosphere. This can be achieved by plunging the pots in peat (left) or standing them on a tray of gravel (right).

Temperatures Under each plant heading I have indicated the minimum temperature tolerated. To recommend an ideal growing temperature would be a counsel of perfection, but it is no bad thing if you know what the plant you are growing likes best, for then you can position it where conditions are most likely to suit it. I am not suggesting that you should adjust your central-heating system to suit your plants, but rather that you should choose plants which will fit in with your living conditions.

Central-heating thermostats will control the environment very efficiently during the time at which they function, and many plants enjoy the even temperature regime that exists in rooms heated by radiators. But at night (when the central heating in most thrifty households is switched off) temperatures may fall dramatically. This is only likely to happen in winter, and there are a good number of plants that can tolerate (and a few which even require) such temperature variations.

If you do not have central heating then it is a good idea to invest in a maximum and minimum thermometer. This will show you over a period of days the highest and lowest temperatures experienced in your rooms, so you can choose plants that fit in with these extremes.

During summer all temperature requirements are thrown to the wind, for the rooms will not be heated and the plants will have to cope with a natural rise and fall in temperatures. At this time of year make sure that the plants are not kept too hot. None of them will thrive in temperatures much over 27°C (80°F) and it is ventilation rather than heat which will have to be applied in summer. Above all, try to keep daytime temperatures even. Rapid fluctuations are likely to result in checks to the system and even death.

Light Throughout the book I have talked about 'good indirect light' being what most plants require. By this I mean bright light but not the direct, often scorching, rays of the sun. There are plants which insist on direct sunlight and these have been indicated, but the majority will put up with sunshine for only part of the day. Any spot near a north-, east-, or west-facing window will suit most house plants, and up to several feet away from a window the light may still be good. Only plants which will tolerate plenty of direct sun should be stood in south-facing windows.

Those plants described as preferring shade will thrive in corners that receive no sun at all, but beware of putting any plant where the light is insufficient to read by.

Humidity Most house plants enjoy a slightly humid atmosphere and find the air in our rooms too dry for their liking. Cheer them up by humidifying the air around them. The easiest thing to do is to spray the plants daily with a hand mister filled with tepid tap water (or rainwater if you are in a hard water area). This method is fine where large plants are standing on the floor, but it will have an adverse effect on furniture and also on hairy-leaved plants whose leaves may rot if laden with water droplets. In these circumstances a gravel tray is the best solution. Washed pea shingle (as sold by a builders' merchant or at a garden centre) should be spread on a plastic tray or shallow bowl 1 or 2 in deep and kept moist at all times. Stand the plants on the tray and the moisture will evaporate around them and keep them in good health. Alternatively a deeper tray can be filled with moist peat and a group of plants plunged to their pot rims in the moist medium. Not only will this arrangement moisten the atmosphere but it will also slow down the drying out of the compost, so reducing the need for watering.

Watering Without doubt the single most common cause of failure with house plants is overwatering. Many people seem to believe that the plant will die of thirst if the compost is not kept saturated at all times. There are perhaps two plants that will tolerate this state of affairs – the rhododendron (azalea), and cyperus – the former likes a very moist and peaty compost and the latter normally grows in boggy conditions.

Most house plants are happy if they are watered well as soon as the surface of the compost feels dry. Rub it with your fingers and if it is a little dusty, in the case of the soil-based potting composts, it is dry. If it has as much moisture as a wrung-out flannel then it does not need watering. Peat-based composts are different; if these dry out they will shrink, so when they feel as moist as a wrung-out flannel it *is* time to apply water.

Plants such as cacti do not need to be watered until the compost is really bone dry.

In winter, all plants need less water than they do at other times of year as the compost will stay moist for longer. Only plants which are flowering in winter need to be fed at that time and watered relatively freely, all others will be resting in the cooler temperatures and so should be kept barely moist.

Plants wilt when their compost is too dry, but they also wilt when it is too wet. The first condition is known as incipient wilt, and once the compost is soaked the plants will pull round. However, if they wilt due to overwatering they will never recover.

There are two ways of watering. Most plants can be watered from above – which is why it is important to leave a gap between the surface of the compost and the rim of the pot. When the compost looks dry fill the pot to the brim with water and leave it alone until the surface is dry once more.

Plants such as African violets (saintpaulias) and cyclamen have a rosette of leaves that is often difficult to penetrate with the spout of a watering can or the lip of a jug. For these you will have to develop a different technique of testing for dryness. Get used to the weight of the potted plant in your hand and learn to tell when it is dry by the relative lightness. Alternatively wait until the leaves are just a little limp, then plunge the pot in a bowl of water almost up to its rim and leave it there for half an hour. By then the compost will have taken up all it needs and the plant can be put back in its usual place. Test for dryness every day in summer and twice a week in winter. I have referred to summer and winter throughout the book and given little mention to autumn and spring. At these times of year the plants are either going into their resting period or coming out of it so common sense must dictate how much water the plants need; the same goes for feeding (see below) which should only be carried out when the plants are in active growth.

There is considerable argument as to whether rainwater should be used in preference to tap water where house plants are concerned. In soft water areas it really does not matter, but where the water is excessively hard and white deposits form on the leaves and surface of the compost then it is worth collecting rainwater. I have never seen a plant die from being watered with cold water straight from the tap, but it is always as well to give tropical and sub-tropical plants tepid water to prevent shocks to their systems. Always use tepid water when spraying the foliage.

Automatic watering Gardeners who cannot master the craft of watering will find hydroculture units a real boon, as will those people who often have to be away from home. With this system the plant's roots are established in a perforated plastic container full of a light-weight aggregate. This container sits in a handsomely disguised reservoir of water which is kept topped up according to a little indicator. Soluble plant food is placed in the reservoir at intervals. Plants can grow in these units for many years, being shifted into larger-sized inner pots and reservoirs as necessary. Conversion kits are available to transfer compost-grown plants into hydroculture units, but success is most likely with young plants. Many difficult species will establish themselves in the home with no trouble at all when bought in a hydroculture unit.

Self-watering pots are quite different. Here plant groups grow in compost and absorb their water by capillary action from a reservoir at the base of the unit. Choose your plants carefully for this kind of container – they must enjoy a fairly moist compost at all times. I have yet to see a really healthy collection of plants in such a container, but where time is short and the plants are unattended for days on end, as in offices and factories, these units have their advantages.

Feeding Plants only need feeding when they are in active growth which is usually from some time during spring until late summer, though winter-flowering pot plants can be fed while they are in bloom. Use a liquid fertilizer sold especially for use with house plants and apply it at the intervals recommended under the individual plant entries. Dilute all feeds strictly in accordance with the manufacturer's instructions – do not add one for the pot. Flowering pot plants can benefit greatly from feeds of diluted liquid tomato fertilizer which contains plenty of magnesium and potassium to promote flowers and fruit. It is successful in bringing African violets into bloom and gives many winter-flowering pot plants a boost. Use it on mature plants at the strength recommended for tomatoes, but on young plants apply a half-strength dilution.

Newly potted plants will not need to be fed for some time; allow eight weeks to elapse before feeding plants potted in peat-based composts and twelve weeks for plants in the more nutrient-retentive soil-based mixes.

Alternatives to liquid feeds are soluble granules which can be scattered on the surface of the compost to release their nutrients over several weeks, or the new 'spike' type of plant food which is pushed into the compost and again releases its nutrients gradually. Foliar feeds are diluted in water and sprayed over plants with a hand mister. Use them only on glossy-leaved plants and bromeliads. Contrary to popular belief house plants *can* be overfed, so do not be over-generous. Apply all types of food when the compost in the pot is moist – then they can go straight into action through the roots.

Potting Sooner or later any house plant is going to exhaust the compost in its pot – the container will be filled with roots and all nutrients will have been extracted from the mixture. To keep the plant in good health it is essential at this stage to repot it – moving it into a slightly larger container which can hold some fresh compost. There are one or two plants which prefer to be 'pot-bound' and these are indicated in the text. Move these on only when they force themselves out of their pots.

Never repot into a container more than 2 in larger in diameter than the existing pot, or the plants will start to make root growth at the expense of leaves and flowers. They might also find that the great volume of compost stays too cold and wet for their liking in winter. Almost all plants should be repotted in spring so that they can instantly grow away and establish themselves.

Clay and plastic plant pots are both suitable for house plants; the former have just one drainage hole and so need a layer of broken pieces of plant pot laid convex side uppermost over the hole to prevent blockage by compost if the soil-based mixes are used. Always soak clay pots overnight in water before using them – this rids them of any impurities and prevents them from extracting moisture from the compost after potting. Plastic pots are easy to clean and hygienic and so need no preparatory treatment. They also possess several holes in the base so no drainage layer is necessary.

Many plants prefer a compost with some loam in it, and for these (and for top-heavy plants) one of the heavier proprietary soil-based composts such as John Innes is ideal. These usually come in three strengths and are referred to in this book as basic, standard and rich according to the amount of fertilizer present. Basic compost has the smallest amount present and is suitable for all rooted cuttings and most annual pot plants; standard is slightly richer so is suitable for nearly all pot plants, and a rich compost is best for those that are especially vigorous and greedy as it has the greatest fertilizer content of the three. Recommendations are given under the individual plant entries.

Peat-based or soilless composts do not contain loam. They are for the most part composed of peat, perhaps with the addition of a little sand or some other medium such as perlite or expanded polystyrene. They do contain nutrients, but these tend to be exhausted rather more quickly than those in the soil-based mixtures, and feeding is necessary sooner. Peat-based composts are light and clean to use, but will not give the weight necessary to hold some large plants upright.

Never use ordinary garden soil for pot plants. It is comparatively badly drained when used in a container and has insufficient nutrients to keep the plants going.

Before you repot a plant check that it needs more room. Roots may be emerging out of the drainage holes, and when tapped out the plant will be found to have filled its pot with roots. If this is the case it needs repotting.

Before you repot any plant water it well so that the entire rootball is moist. Place some compost in the bottom of your clean new pot (having put drainage material in place if a clay pot and a soil-based mixture are being used). Knock the plant from its existing pot and stand it on the compost in its new container. The surface of the

Repotting is required when roots can be seen covering the compost (left). The new pot should be only slightly larger than the existing one (right).

rootball should rest between a ½ and 1½ in below the rim of the pot (½ in for the smaller plants in smaller pots; up to 1½ in for big plants in large pots). Fill in around the rootball with compost, firming with your fingers as you do so. Peat-based composts need only be firmed very lightly. When potting is completed the new compost should be level with the surface of the rootball and that gap should be there to allow for watering. Give the compost a good watering and stand the plant in a slightly shady spot for a few days.

Plants in very large pots cannot, for practical reasons, be given larger containers every year. Instead scrape away a few inches of compost from the surface in spring and replace it with fresh. This is known as topdressing and will give mature plants a welcome boost.

Bottle gardens and terrariums Many small and humidity-loving plants thrive in the close and sequestered confines of a bottle garden or terrarium. Here they are sheltered from dry air and draughts and will make an attractive and long-lasting plant feature. Large cider flagons, goldfish bowls, aquariums, sweet jars, clear brandy balloons and cleansed acid bottles (carboys) can all be utilized.

First of all, clean the container with detergent and water, then rinse it and allow it to dry. A 1-in layer of gravel and then a similar layer of crushed charcoal should be put in the base of the container (the latter prevents the compost from turning sour). Then add a 2- to 3-in layer of soil- or peat-based compost. If the jar or bottle has a narrow neck, feed in the charcoal and compost through a home-made cardboard funnel. A teaspoon and a cotton reel each attached to a length of bamboo cane make good planting and firming tools in this situation.

Contour the compost and then scoop out a hole for each plant, drop it into place and firm the compost – using the cotton reel firmer if necessary. Allow the plants a little room to grow – do not plant them too close together. Avoid any rampant species which will quickly swamp slower growers, and do not use flowering plants whose blooms may rot and set up infection.

Water the plants in when the operation is complete – allow the water from a long-spouted can to run down the inside of the bottle, or water a terrarium with a small watering can fitted with a sprinkler head. Stand the bottle garden or terrarium in a lightly-shaded place (it should never be positioned in full sun where condensation will be a problem) and after a few days seal up the opening either with a bung or screw cap (in the case of bottles and jars) or with a piece of glass cut to fit. Watering will be needed very infrequently – say once every four to six months. Steaming up will only be a real problem in bright light, but can easily be alleviated by removing the top from the container and replacing it when the glass has cleared. Replant the container only when it is overgrown.

The following plants will thrive in the comfort of bottle gardens and terrariums:

Carex, Chamaedorea, Cryptanthus, Episcia, Ficus pumila, Fittonia, Maranta, Nertera, Pellionia, Peperomia, Pilea, Pteris, Saxifraga, Selaginella.

Do not under any circumstances use *Soleirolia, Tradescantia* or *Zebrina.*

Hanging baskets and suspended pots Most suitable for trailing plants, both types of container are best filled with peat-based compost which is less weighty than the soil-based types. The suspended pots can be planted up exactly as described for potting; the hanging baskets are wider at the top and several plants can be positioned around their rims so that they are more fully furnished. Use the solid plastic hanging baskets with a built-in drip tray unless you do not mind being showered with water. Remember that both hanging baskets and suspended pots dry out far more quickly than other containers.

The following are all suitable for hanging basket or suspended pot culture:

Achimenes, Aeschynanthus, Asparagus densiflorus, Begonia 'Cleopatra', *Campanula, Ceropegia, Columnea, Episcia, Euphorbia milii* var. *splendens, Fuchsia, Glechoma, Gynura, Hedera helix* cultivars, *Hoya bella, Hypocyrta, Pelargonium* (ivy-leaved cultivars), *Philodendron scan-*

dens, Plectranthus, Saxifraga, Schlumbergera, Senecio macroglossus, Setcreasea, Tradescantia, Zebrina.

Plant care Any large plants are likely to need some kind of support as their stems continue to lengthen. Humidity-loving plants that send out aerial roots in search of atmospheric moisture are best provided with a moss-covered stick into which their roots can penetrate. The moss (or in some cases plastic foam) should be sprayed with water every day so that it stays moist. If it is dry when you get it, soak it for a few hours in a shallow bath of water. Lightly tie the stems (and aerial roots) of the plants to the stake as they extend.

Bushy pot plants that start to flop can either be held upright by short, leafless twiggy branches pushed into the compost among them, or by split green canes pushed in around the pot and linked with several circuits of soft green twine. Single stout bamboo canes will hold up tall, single-stemmed plants – plastic covered twist-ties can fasten stem to stake.

Some plants with tendrils or twining stems are best displayed either on a tripod of bamboo canes pushed into the pot, or on a piece of trelliswork supported at the rear of the pot. Plants such as stephanotis are frequently trained over a wire hoop, but regular thinning out of stems will have to be practised to keep the plant within bounds.

All house plants benefit from having their leaves cleaned once a month. Hairy-leaved plants should never be wetted but can be flicked over with a clean, dry paintbrush to remove any dust, and glossy-leaved plants can be cleaned with cotton wool or soft tissue dipped in tepid rainwater. Add a little milk to the water if you want to bring up a healthy gloss. Use proprietary leaf-cleaning compounds with caution – test them first on a single leaf to make sure the plant is not sensitive to them.

All plants need trimming back and pruning from time to time. Single stems can be removed completely at any time of the year if they have outgrown their space, but generally all hard cutting back is best carried out in the spring, just before the plant bursts into growth. Prunings can often be used as cuttings at the same time.

Always prune with a definite idea in mind, and think what is going to happen to the plant when the stems start to grow – will growth be too congested? Will more thinning be needed later on? Young plants should have the very tips of their shoots pinched out to encourage bushiness, and with certain species this pinching should be carried on all their lives to keep them in good shape.

When cutting out stems, always make your cut just above a leaf – never leave a stub which may rot and encourage fungal attack.

Holiday care The best precaution to take when you go on holiday is to enlist the help of a neighbour who can be instructed on the frequency of watering needed by the plants. If this is not possible, bed the pot plants in plastic trays of moist peat and stand them in a lightly-shaded spot. If watered well just before you leave they will often last for ten to fourteen days without suffering.

Alternatively stand a washing-up bowl of water on the draining board and lead a piece of capillary matting (a fibrous material sold by garden centres) from the bowl into the sink. Stand the pot plants on the matting in the sink. Plastic pots will absorb water from the matting easily, but clay pots will need to be provided with wicks – strips of the matting pushed up through their holes and into the compost to bridge the gap caused by the thickness of the pot. The matting will draw water from the bowl and the plants should be able to take up water supply for quite some time.

PROPAGATION

Raising your own house plants is a satisfying and money-saving operation which need not necessarily involve a great deal of skill. House plants can be propagated in many different ways, but the following methods are the most popular.

Seeds House plant seeds need heat to germinate, and while they can often be sown in pots which are placed above radiators and in airing cupboards, a simple heated propagator is a worthwhile investment. It will cost only a few pounds to buy and be economical to run. It can be used to root all manner of cuttings as well as for germinating seeds. Such propagators usually consist of a plastic seed tray topped with a clear plastic hood and heated underneath by a flat panel which is connected to the electricity supply.

It is best to sow house plant seeds in spring and summer in 4-in plastic pots of peat-based seed compost. Fill the pots to within $\frac{1}{2}$ in of their rims with the lightly firmed mixture, sow the seeds thinly on the surface and then lightly shake over enough of the mixture to cause the seeds to disappear but do not bury them. The very fine dust-like seeds need not be covered at all. When the seeds are sown, stand the pots in a tray of water for half an hour so that the compost takes up the moisture it needs, then transfer the pots to the propagator (or another warm place) for germination. A small piece of glass placed over the pot will keep the compost moist and a sheet of paper will provide the darkness most seeds need to germinate.

Check the pot every day and as soon as the first seedling emerges, bring the pot into the light, removing the glass and paper. If the pots are in a propagator, open the air vents at the top and keep the unit in good light but out of direct sun.

Prick out the seedlings individually into small pots of a basic soil- or peat-based compost as soon as they can be handled. Hold each seedling by one of its leaves, gently lift it out of the pot using a pencil to free the roots and make a hole in the compost in its new pot. Lower the roots into place and firm the compost around them. Water the compost and stand the plants in a warm and lightly shaded place for a day or two before exposing them to full light. Pot on as necessary.

Cuttings A cutting is a portion of the plant which is removed and encouraged to form roots (in the case of stem or leaf cuttings) or shoots (in the case of root cuttings).

Stem cuttings can be taken in spring or summer. They consist of 3-in long shoot tips which have been cut cleanly below a leaf joint and from which the lower leaves have been removed. Just the top two or three leaves are left attached to the stem. Insert five cuttings to half their depth around the rim of a 4-in pot filled with a mixture of peat and sharp sand in equal parts. Cuttings which are difficult to root can have their cut ends dipped in hormone rooting powder (available at garden centres and hardware shops). Water the cuttings in and then cover the pot with a polythene bag or place it in a propagator. Keep an eye on the compost to make sure that it does not dry out, but avoid keeping it soggy. Remove any cuttings which rot off, and pot up the rooted ones as soon as they start to grow away, but beware of one or two species which actually grow shoots before their roots have appeared – quickly push them back into the medium if they are found to be rootless.

Some cuttings root easily in jars of water, but should be potted up quite quickly as soon as their roots are 1 to 2 in long. This transition from water to compost is sometimes difficult.

Rooting bags are a relatively new innovation but they are very efficient at coaxing roots out of many types of cutting. They are like miniature growing bags (plastic sacks of compost) and can be slit at intervals and the prepared cuttings pushed into the compost. Water is poured into a central slit and the bag positioned on a windowsill. When the cuttings are rooted the bag is pulled apart and the young plants potted up.

Always position cuttings in good but indirect light while they are rooting, and pot them up in *small* pots when roots have formed. A basic soil- or a peat-based compost is suitable.

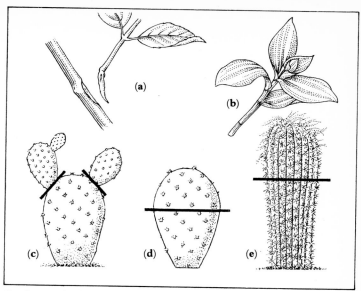

Cuttings A heel cutting is removed with a strip of old wood attached (**a**). Softwood cuttings are the easiest to root (**b**). When increasing opuntia, first remove a pad as indicated (**c**), and then cut again across the widest part to give the largest area for rooting (**d**); allow the surface to dry before inserting in a mixture of sand and peat. Increase other cacti by cutting across the stem (**e**) and treat the cutting as for opuntia.

Leaf cuttings are rooted in a similar way to stem cuttings. Plants such as African violets (*Saintpaulia*) can be propagated by pushing leaves (with stalks still attached) individually into 2-in pots of cutting compost, and keeping these warm and damp. Young plants will soon emerge from the base of the stalk.

Begonia rex leaves can be removed from the plant, laid flat on a seed tray of cutting compost, held in place with small pebbles and the main veins slit open with a knife. Keep the leaf and compost moist by spraying daily with tepid water and a young plant will eventually emerge at each cut. Pot these up as soon as they are large enough to handle. The leaves may also be cut into sections as large as postage stamps and inserted in the compost like gravestones. A young plant will arise from the base of each section if conditions are favourable and the leaf section is the right way up.

The leaves of *Streptocarpus* can be cut into sections laterally and then bedded into the compost like the cut sections of *Begonia rex*. Make sure that they are the right way up – the direction of the sap flow should be from the compost to the upper cut edge, so make sure that the end inserted in the compost was nearest to the base of the leaf.

Some plants can be propagated by taking a leaf plus a short piece of stem to which it was attached and which carries a bud. These are known as leaf–bud cuttings and they can be rooted in the same way as leaf cuttings with stalks.

Some *Dracaena* species produce thick fleshy roots. The ends of these can be removed (cut them off so that they are 2 in long) and bedded into the surface of cutting compost inside a propagator. Kept warm and moist they may form shoots and can then be potted up.

Air layering Tall plants such as *Ficus, Monstera, Codiaeum* and *Dracaena* can be reduced in height and propagated at the same time by air layering. Make an upward incision in a bare piece of stem just below the part of the plant to be removed (the top 2 or 3 ft). The cut should be at an angle of 45° and it should create a 1½-in long 'tongue'. Dust the cut surface with hormone rooting powder. Pad the inside of the cut with damp sphagnum moss (available from florists) and work the same material around the stem a couple of inches above and below the cut area. Bandage the stem with clear polythene and secure it top and bottom with sticky tape. If the stem is weakened by the cut, support it with a stake. Keep the moss moist at all times and as soon as roots are seen (often up to nine months later) remove the bandage, cut off the top plus the new roots and pot up the plant. The remaining stump can be trimmed at the top

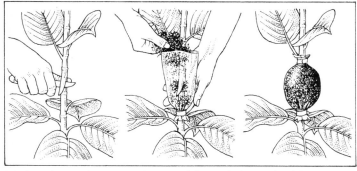

Air layering Make a cut in the stem (left), pack the inside of the cut with moss and then surround the wounded area with more moss (centre). Secure polythene above and below the moss (right).

and may well send up side shoots to improve its habit. Keep both plants warm and shaded from bright sun for a few weeks after the operation.

Division All clump-forming plants make propagation easy. They can be knocked out of their pots in spring and pulled apart into sections – each with some stems and roots. Potted up in good compost they will soon take on a life of their own.

Those plants that form suckers or offshoots (young shoots that emerge at the base of the parent stem) can be relieved of their offspring at repotting time. Cut or prise away these offshoots with as much root as possible and pot them up on their own. Keep them warm and shaded for a week or two to aid establishment.

Plantlets Plants which produce live plantlets make life easiest of all, for these need simply be removed and nestled into the surface of the compost in small pots. Keep them warm and moist in the early stages and they will soon take root. It really is unnecessary to go to the length of persuading such plantlets to form more roots in water, or to bed them in compost before they are severed from the parent (a process known as layering), because they can establish themselves on their own if cossetted for a few days.

PESTS, DISEASES AND DISORDERS

Well-grown plants that are not starved or badly treated are far more likely to show resistance to pests and diseases, but from time to time even the most skilled gardener will encounter some kind of problem. Those that are not caused by pests or diseases are usually termed 'physiological disorders'. They are brought about by faulty management or unfavourable growing conditions. The following are the most common pests, diseases and disorders that the indoor gardener is likely to encounter. Early action can usually prevent the plants from suffering unduly and so quick diagnosis is advisable.

PESTS
Aphids Commonly known as greenfly and blackfly, these pests suck sap, weaken the plant, transmit virus diseases and excrete honeydew which is colonized by sooty mould. They must be eradicated. Rub off minor infestations with your fingers (look the other way if you're squeamish), or wash them off under the tap. Larger outbreaks should be sprayed with a systemic insecticide such as pirimicarb which will enter the sap-stream of the plant.

Caterpillars These fat larvae of butterflies and moths can chew the leaves of pot plants to shreds. Search out the offending grubs (if just one or two are present) and transfer them to the garden where they can feed in peace. Larger outbreaks of severe proportions can be sprayed with derris.

Earwigs These fork-tailed insects are not usually a problem on house plants but they may be brought indoors on plants that have been stood outdoors for the summer. They eat tender young shoots and flowers. Spray bad infestations with HCH or fenitrothion.

Leaf miners These leaf-burrowing grubs are common on chrysanthemums and cinerarias. They make whitish-looking tunnels on the leaves. Spray with HCH. Pick off badly infected leaves.

Mealy bug Sap-sucking pests which colonize many plants including cacti. They surround themselves with white wool. Control as for scale insects, and also by dabbing the pests with a paintbrush dipped in methylated spirits.

Red spider mites Tiny greenish, brownish or yellowish mites the size of pin-pricks. They suck sap and bleach the plant and also spin webs which envelop shoots. A moist environment discourages attack but infestations can be sprayed at weekly intervals with malathion.

Root aphids These insects can infest compost and weaken plants causing general ill health and wilting. If they are found to be present on plant roots, drench the soil with a diluted systemic insecticide.

Scale insects Tiny dark brown barnacle-like insects cling to the stems and leaves of the plant. They weaken the plant's constitution and secrete honeydew. Insecticides have difficulty in penetrating the shell of the pest but outbreaks can sometimes be controlled by spraying three times at fortnightly intervals with malathion. Small plants can be cleared of the pest by rubbing the scales off with damp cotton wool and then spraying with malathion.

Vine weevils Cyclamen and other pot plants may occasionally collapse for no apparent reason, and when the compost in the pot is examined it will be found to contain small white maggots. Discard the plant and the compost making sure that it does not come into contact with any other house plants. Where the pest is suspected but damage is not fatal the compost can be watered with HCH.

Whitefly These dart-shaped white flies colonize the undersides of leaves sucking sap. They fly around in circles when disturbed. Control by spraying with bioresmethrin at four-day intervals over a period of two weeks to catch the adults and the emerging young.

DISEASES
Botrytis A fungus disease which causes stems and leaves to turn grey-brown and rot. It causes 'blackleg' on pelargonium cuttings.

Avoid this disease by ventilating well and avoiding a stuffy atmosphere around rooting cuttings in particular. Remove any faded leaves and flowers which may start up infection. Dust susceptible cuttings with captan.

Damping off This is the term given to the keeling over of seedlings due to fungal attack. Prevent by sowing thinly and ventilating as well as possible. Water seedlings with Cheshunt Compound to prevent attack.

Mildew A white powdery outgrowth on leaves and stems which severely weakens the plant. Spray any outbreaks with benomyl.

Rust Likely to occur on few plants (but occasionally on pelargoniums) rust diseases can be serious. Yellow marks on the upper surface of the leaves are found to be matched by circles of rusty-brown pustules on the undersides. Discard all infected plants and prevent them from coming into contact with others.

Sooty mould This black, felt-like fungus grows on the honeydew secreted by aphids, whitefly, mealy bug and scale insects. Control them and it is unlikely to appear. Where it has already made its mark, sponge it off with moist cotton wool.

Virus diseases These can cause all manner of leaf distortions and discoloration from twisting and elongation to yellow mottling and streaking. They are transmitted by aphids, so control the pest to control the disease. Virus-infected plants will never recover and should be discarded. On no account propagate from them.

DISORDERS

Wilting This state of affairs can be brought about by several causes: the plant may be too dry at the roots, too wet, or too hot. Check to see which is the likely cause. A good soak will remedy a shortage of water, but if the compost is soggy then the plant is unlikely to pull round. If bright sunshine is to blame then find the plant a more shaded spot.

Leaf browning Underwatering, draughts and too high a temperature can all account for leaf browning, as can scorching sunlight, dry air, over-feeding and too little light. Check to see which is the most likely cause and take remedial action.

Leaf yellowing Shortage of light, shortage of nutrients, draughts or overwatering may be the cause of leaf yellowing on a grand scale. If only an occasional lower leaf turns yellow there is nothing to worry about – this is natural as the plant ages.

Leaf fall A check to growth is usually responsible for leaf fall. Make sure that the plant is not too dry or too wet at the roots and that it is not in a draught. Rapid fluctuations in temperature may also be responsible.

Leaf spots Sun scorch, water splashing (especially on hairy-leaved plants), over- or under-watering may all be responsible. Check also for pest or disease attack.

Flower bud drop Underwatering, dry air, lack of light, draughts and movement of the plant may all cause buds to fall before they open.

Spindly shoots When shoots become pale and spindly, lack of light is nearly always to blame, though the pallor can also be brought about by underfeeding.

Loss of variegation Some plants 'revert' and lose their variegation for no apparent reason. Trim off any shoots which are green so that just the variegated ones are left. Variegation can also be lost if the plant is growing in poor light.

Stem rot Though brought about by fungus diseases, stem rot is almost always caused by the compost being too moist. Make sure it is well drained and that the plant is not potted too deeply.

No flowers Plants usually refuse to flower either because they are in too big a pot, because they are starved of nutrients, because they are in poor light or temperatures which do not suit them. If the guidelines for cultivation in the body of the book are followed this should not be a problem. Some plants need short days to flower and will not come into bloom of their own accord when grown in rooms where lights are switched on in the evening. Poinsettias are a case in point.

CHEMICALS
Whenever chemicals are used to control plant pests and diseases, mix them strictly in accordance with the instructions on the container and spray the plants outdoors on a still day. Wear rubber gloves and also wash your hands after spraying. Check with your local garden centre or shop that the product is suitable for the plant and pest in question, and store all chemicals out of the reach of children and animals. Dispose of excess chemicals down the lavatory and do not take the plants back into your rooms until they are quite dry.

METRIC CONVERSION TABLE

Imperial	Metric	Imperial	Metric	Imperial	Metric
½ in	1 cm	5 in	13 cm	11 in	28 cm
1 in	2.5 cm	6 in	15 cm	1 ft	30 cm
1½ in	4 cm	7 in	18 cm	2 ft	60 cm
2 in	5 cm	8 in	20 cm	3 ft	1 m
3 in	8 cm	9 in	23 cm	5 ft	1.5 m
4 in	10 cm	10 in	25 cm	10 ft	3 m

HOUSE PLANTS
ARRANGED IN
ORDER OF
FAMILIES

Selaginellaceae

Tender or hardy evergreen moss-like plants which are closely related to ferns. The single genus is *Selaginella*. The plants are native to the United States, South America, South Africa, Australia, Asia and Europe.

Selaginella (sel-adge-in-*ell*-a) A diminutive of *Selago* - the old name of the fir club moss (*Lycopodium selago*) which selaginella faintly resembles.

Cultivation The selaginellas grown as house plants will tolerate a min. temp. of 10°C (50°F), though growth is much more luxuriant if 21-25°C (70-77°F) can be maintained. Bright light will scorch the fronds, so keep the plants in a relatively shady spot and do not allow the compost to dry out at any time. A daily spray with tepid water in spring and summer will keep the plants fresh and green. Alternatively, grow selaginellas in bottle gardens and terrariums where there is a humid atmosphere. If the plants are grown in containers, repot them in spring into a peat-based compost as soon as they have outgrown the space available. Half-pots or pans can be used as the roots are not sent down very deeply. If the plants are repotted every year there will be no need to feed them. Propagation is simply a matter of nipping off suitable shoot tips (which often have roots already attached) any time during spring or summer and inserting these into a mixture of peat and sand in a humid propagating frame or a pot inside a polythene bag.

THE SPECIES

Selaginella kraussiana (South Africa) Club Moss. A vivid green trailing plant with plenty of feathery fronds. There are also yellow-leaved and variegated forms and other species with tight domes of growth or a more upright habit. All require similar growing conditions.

Sinopteridaceae

Tender or hardy ornamental ferns native to many countries.

Pellaea (pel-*lee*-a) From the Greek: *pellaios* – dark; the leaf stalks are often dark brown.

Cultivation Some of the pellaeas are hardy, but the kinds most commonly grown as house plants need a min. temp. around 10°C (50°F) and up to 18-21°C (65°-70°F) if they are to grow well. Give them good but indirect light or a shady corner and do not let the compost dry out completely at any time. Spray the fronds daily with tepid water from spring to autumn, and feed once a month during the same period. Keep the atmosphere around the plant humid by standing the pot on a tray of moist peat or gravel. Alternatively grow the plant in a hanging pot or basket, but make sure it never dries out. Repot in spring when necessary using a peat-based compost. Propagation by division can be carried out at the same time; pull the plant into pieces, making sure that each portion has roots and leaves. Scale insects can sometimes be a problem, as can mealy bugs.

THE SPECIES

Pellaea rotundifolia (New Zealand, Norfolk Island) Button Fern. Height 6 in, spread 12 in. A rather compact plant with a handsome rosette of fronds which are composed of thumbnail-sized leaflets of dark green.

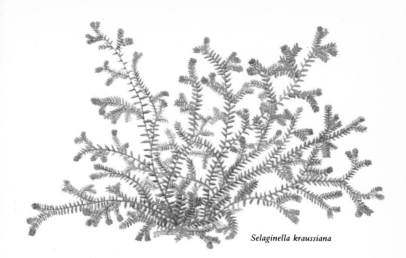

Selaginella kraussiana

Pellaea rotundifolia

Adiantaceae   Maidenhair Fern Family

A single genus of ferns distributed in tropical and temperate areas of the world. All are of ornamental rather than economic value.

Adiantum (ad-ee-*an*-tum) From the Greek: *adiantos* – dry; plunge the fronds underwater and they will still remain unwetted.

Cultivation Adiantum is one of the most difficult plants to keep alive in the home unless you know the secrets of success. First, give the plant good but indirect light. Bright sunlight will scorch the fronds, as will draughts and heat sources such as radiators. Maintain a min. winter temp. of 10°C (50°F) and keep the compost in the pot moist at all times – even in winter. The leaves of adiantum are so thin that they can quickly desiccate and turn brown in a living room, so stand the plant on a tray or bowl filled with gravel which is kept constantly wet. As the moisture evaporates it will keep the air around the fronds slightly humid. Feed the plant monthly in summer and repot it into a basic soil-based compost with a little peat added when it outgrows its existing container. Spring is the best time to repot, and mature plants can be divided at the same time – use a sharp knife to cut the clump into several pieces and pot up the offspring in the recommended compost. Keep them warm and shaded for a few weeks to hasten establishment. Cut off any fronds that do turn brown to prevent them from rotting and damaging other parts of the plant. Badly browned plants can be cut back completely to within 1 in of soil level and grown on again in a warm, humid environment. Avoid spraying the plants with insecticides or leaf-cleaning compounds which may burn the fronds.

THE SPECIES

Adiantum capillus-veneris (Cosmopolitan, including Britain) Common Maidenhair, Southern Maidenhair. Height 9 in, spread 12 in. A graceful clump-forming fern whose shiny black wiry stems display masses of fine, overlapping fan-shaped pinnules (leaflets) of a fresh shade of green. Although a native of Britain the plant is hardy only in very sheltered localities.
Adiantum raddianum (syn. **A. cuneatum**) (Brazil) Delta Maidenhair. Height and spread 12 in. Rather larger than *A. capillus-veneris*, richer in colour and more tender, coming from South America. The fronds are more arching and the pinnules more widely spaced so that the effect is even more delicate than that of *A. capillus-veneris*.

Adiantum capillus-veneris

Adiantum raddianum

Pteridaceae Ribbon Fern Family

A cosmopolitan family of several genera, the most important being Pteris. Many of the plants are of ornamental value, and most are tender in the cooler, temperate countries.

Pteris (*ter*-iss, or *teer*-iss – both are widely used) From the Greek: *pteron* – a wing; the fronds evidently struck the botanist who described them as being winged.

Cultivation Like most ferns, pteris enjoys reasonably good but indirect light (not heavy shade) and a compost which is kept constantly moist but not soggy. Temperatures as low as 7°C (45°F) will be tolerated in winter. Feed monthly in summer, and repot in spring only when the existing container has been filled with roots, using a soil- or peat-based potting compost. Propagation is by division of the clumps in spring. Keep the young plants warm and shaded after division until they are established. Humidity for all these ferns can be provided by spraying their foliage daily with tepid water, or by standing them on a tray of wet gravel, or by growing them in bottle gardens or terrariums. A dry atmosphere will produce brown fronds.

THE SPECIES

Pteris cretica (Tropics and subtropics) Ribbon Fern, Table Fern. Height 9–12 in, spread 6–9 in. A compact little fern with attractively branched fronds that support surprisingly leathery leaflets.
Pteris cretica **'Albo–lineata'.** As the true species but with the addition of a central greenish-cream stripe on each leaflet.
Pteris cretica **'Summersii'.** A very delicate form with much-divided fresh green fronds that are crested at the tips.
Pteris ensiformis **'Victoriae',** Silver Lace Fern, Silver Table Fern. Height 18 in, spread 12 in. Perhaps the most aristocratic of the group, having long, thin leaflets margined deep green and centred with silvery white. The fronds which carry the spores are long and slender, while those which are sterile are inclined to be shorter and broader, forming a well-furnished plant.

Pteris cretica

Pteris cretica 'Summersii'

Pteris cretica 'Albo-lineata'

Pteris ensiformis 'Victoriae'

Oleandraceae Ladder Fern Family

A family of ferns native to the Tropics, Australia, New Zealand and Malagasy. There are 4 genera, of which the most important for the house-plant grower is *Nephrolepis*.

Nephrolepis (nef-ro-*lep*-iss) From the Greek: *nephros* – a kidney, and *lepis* – a scale; the covering over the spores on these ferns is kidney shaped.

Cultivation Good but indirect light or gentle shade will produce the best ladder ferns, and humidity is essential if the fronds are not to turn brown. Spray the plant each day with tepid rainwater and stand it on a tray of wet gravel. Temperatures as low as 10°C (50°F) will be tolerated, but warmer conditions will produce more luxuriant growth. In large terrariums or Wardian cases the plants are seen at their best, for the humidity is much to their liking. If they do become brown and ragged they can be cut down to pot level and encouraged to sprout again if kept warm and humid. Never let the compost in the pot dry out, but conversely do not keep it waterlogged. In greenhouses the plants look good when grown in hanging baskets, but in the home this kind of culture is likely to lead to excessive drying out of compost and foliage. Repot the plants in a peat-based compost when they have filled their existing containers with roots. Spring is the best time to do this, and the plants can be divided into smaller clumps at the same time. Monthly feeds will keep the plants in good condition.

THE SPECIES

Nephrolepis exaltata (Tropics) Ladder Fern, Sword Fern. Height 2-2½ ft, spread 1 ft. A spectacular fern with vivid green fonds that are held upright in the form of a dense shuttlecock.

Nephrolepis exaltata **'Bostoniensis',** Boston Fern. Height and spread 2-2½ ft. A much more arching plant which is more common and has more grace than the true species. This is the form which is sometimes grown in hanging baskets.

Nephrolepis exaltata
'Bostoniensis'

Nephrolepis exaltata

Aspleniaceae Spleenwort Family

Tender or hardy ferns with worldwide distribution. Several species are native to Great Britain. Most aspleniums are grown for ornament but many were previously used in attempts to cure infirmities of the liver and spleen.

Asplenium (ass-*plee*-nee-um) From the Greek: *a* – not, and *splen* – the spleen; an allusion to the fern's supposed medicinal properties.

Cultivation The tender species grown as house plants vary in their temperature requirements (see under individual species) but all prefer light shade rather than direct sunshine which will scorch them. Keep the compost slightly moist at all times and spray the foliage daily with tepid water from spring to autumn. The plants benefit from being stood on trays of moist gravel or peat. Keep them out of draughts. Feed monthly in summer, and repot in a peat-based compost when the plant has filled its existing container with roots. Propagate from spores or by division (where practicable) or by removing the young plantlets and potting them up individually. Keep them warm and humid for the first week or two of their life. Scale insects and mealy bugs can be a problem. Browning of the fronds is usually caused by sun scorch, drought or draughts.

THE SPECIES

Asplenium bulbiferum (Australia, New Zealand, India) Mother Spleenwort. Height 18 in, spread 2 ft. A feathery fern with arching green fronds and dark brown stalks. Young plants emerge from mature fronds and can easily be pulled off for propagation. The plant suits cool rooms for it will tolerate temps. as low as 7°C (45°F).

Asplenium nidus (Tropics) Bird's Nest Fern. Height and spread 2 ft. This bold plant makes a bright green shuttlecock of broad, glossy strap-shaped leaves. It likes a warm room with temps. falling no lower than 16°C (60°F), if possible, and can only be propagated from spores.

Aspidiaceae

Hardy or tender ferns with worldwide distribution. Grown for ornament.

Cyrtomium (ser-*toe*-mee-um) From the Greek: *kyrtos* – arched; the fronds arch gracefully.

Cultivation In milder parts of the British Isles, and in sheltered gardens in general, this plant will often survive outdoors, but when grown as a house plant it is best given a cool room with a winter min. of around 7°C (45°F). It enjoys shade or, at the most, dappled sunlight, and is scorched by direct sunshine. The compost in the pot should never be allowed to dry out completely, and the foliage can be sprayed daily with tepid water in summer. Feed monthly from spring to autumn and repot in spring when necessary using a basic soil- or peat-based compost. Divide in spring or sow spores as soon as available. Mealy bug and scale insects may be a problem.

THE SPECIES

Cyrtomium falcatum (syn. *Aspidium falcatum, Polystichum falcatum*) (Asia) Japanese Holly Fern. Height 2 ft, spread 3 ft. A distinctive fern with bold, sharply cut, dark green leaflets that slightly resemble holly.

Asplenium bulbiferum

Cyrtomium falcatum

Asplenium nidus

Polypodiaceae Polypody Family

The largest family of ferns with over 100 genera. The plants are of cosmopolitan distribution and a great number are grown as ornamentals.

Platycerium (plat-ee-*seer*-ee-um) From the Greek: *platys* – broad, and
keras – a horn; the shape of the fronds tells all.

Cultivation This fern prefers a shady corner which is warm and humid,
but do avoid placing it in a really dark spot where it will not give of its best.
Maintain a min. winter temp. of around 10-13°C (50-55°F) and keep the
compost surrounding the roots gently moist at all times. Although it is often
purchased in a pot and can continue to be grown in a container, it is seen
to best effect when fastened to a piece of cork bark or half a log. It is an
epiphyte in the wild (this means that it grows on trees but is not parasitic)
and if it is removed from its pot, its roots wrapped in moist sphagnum moss
and bound carefully to the bark with wire it will soon take hold with its
roots and grow well. Water the plant by immersing the bark and roots in
a bucket of water whenever the moss feels dry. Hang the bark from a piece
of wire so that the fern is suspended like the hunting trophy it resembles.
Propagation is difficult to achieve without spoiling the plant and it is usually
best to buy a new small plant and grow it on. Never attempt to clean the
downy fronds or the pad. Scale insects may be a problem (touch these
individually with a tiny brush dipped in methylated spirits).

THE SPECIES

Platycerium bifurcatum (Australia) Stag's Horn Fern. Height and spread 2 ft.
There are two kinds of fronds on this distinctive fern. The sterile anchor
fronds form a pad which holds the plant to its pot or bark, and the longer
fertile fronds are divided in the shape of antlers, which gives the plant its
common name.

Platycerium bifurcatum

Araucariaceae Chile Pine Family

Hardy, or more frequently, tender trees native to South America, Australasia, Malaysia and the South Pacific Islands. The plants have a symmetrical habit and possess spiny or scaly leaves and large cones. There are 2 genera; *Agathis* (Kauri Pine) and *Araucaria* (Chile Pine, Monkey-puzzle, Norfolk Island Pine).

Araucaria (a-raw-*care*-ee-a) From the Araucani Indians of Chile on whose territory the Monkey-puzzle Tree (*A. araucana*) was discovered in the late 18th century.

Cultivation Maintain temps. between 10-16°C (50-60°F). Good indirect light preferred but light shade tolerated. Water when the compost feels dry; if it is allowed to dry out the leaves may be shed. Less water will be needed in winter when growth is slow. Provide a moist atmosphere by spraying the plant daily with tepid water, or by standing it on a tray of moist gravel. Feed fortnightly during the summer months. Repot in spring every 2 or 3 years using a standard soil-based compost. Propagate in spring by seeds sown in a temperature of 18°C (65°F); the topmost vertical shoot can be removed from an old plant and rooted in a propagator in spring but the parent plant will be spoiled.

THE SPECIES

Araucaria heterophylla (syn. *A. excelsa*) (Norfolk Island) Norfolk Island Pine. Height 5 ft, spread 3 ft. Grows to 200 ft high in the wild. The upright central stem produces many horizontal branches clad in fresh green spiny leaves. An elegant specimen plant for a cool room.

Cycadaceae Cycad Family

Primitive flowering plants from the Tropics usually having a single central stem topped with a rosette of pinnate leaves. Male and female flowers are carried on different plants. Some of the 9 genera are cultivated for ornament, others for their economic value.

Cycas (*sy*-cass) From the Greek name for a kind of palm.

Cultivation Min. winter temp. 13°C (55°F). Keep in good light but protect from scorching sun in summer. Grow cycads in large pots. Water well when the compost feels dry, then allow to dry out before watering again. Keep on the dry side right through the winter. Spray the plant daily with tepid water or stand it on a tray of moist gravel. Repot in spring every 2 or 3 years, or topdress annually; in both cases use a standard soil-based compost. Feed monthly in summer. Propagate in spring from seeds sown in a temp. of 27°C (80°F) or by removing and potting up suckers during the summer. Scale insects and mealy bugs are common pests.

THE SPECIES

Cycas revoluta (China, East Indies) Sago palm. Height 6 ft or more, spread 5 ft or more. Growth is relatively slow. The thick central stem is covered with dry leaf bases and topped by a rosette of spiny, feather-shaped glossy green leaves, each up to $2\frac{1}{2}$ ft long. The individual leaflets are between 3 and 8 in long.

Araucaria heterophylla

Cycas revoluta

Lauraceae   Avocado Pear Family

Trees, shrubs and climbers native to tropical and temperate countries. There are over 30 genera, the most important being *Laurus*, *Persea*, *Cinnamomum* and *Sassafras*. Most of the plants are of economic value.

Persea (per-see-a) From the Greek: *persea* – the name given by Theophrastus (371– c.287 B.C.) to an Egyptian tree.

   Cultivation Maintain a min. temp. of 7°C (45°F) in winter, and considerably more in summer. The plant enjoys good indirect light but may scorch if positioned in full sun. The habit of growth is rather angular and plants may become ugly if the shoot tips are not pinched out from time to time to encourage bushiness. Water the compost in the pot thoroughly when it shows signs of drying out, but keep it rather drier through the winter months. An occasional spray with tepid water will keep the foliage in good condition, and a monthly feed in summer is essential. Repot into a rich soil-based compost in spring when the plant has outgrown its container. Discard the plant when it becomes too large. Propagate from seeds (stones) by burying them to half their depth (pointed end uppermost) in moist compost; or by suspending them over a jam-jar of water so that their bases are kept constantly moist. Pot up when roots have formed.

THE SPECIES

Persea americana (syn. **P. gratissima**) (Tropical America) Alligator Pear, Avocado Pear. Height and spread may eventually be larger than most rooms can accommodate. Large oval green leaves are this tree's main feature. It produces small green flowers followed by green or yellowish brown fruits in the wild.

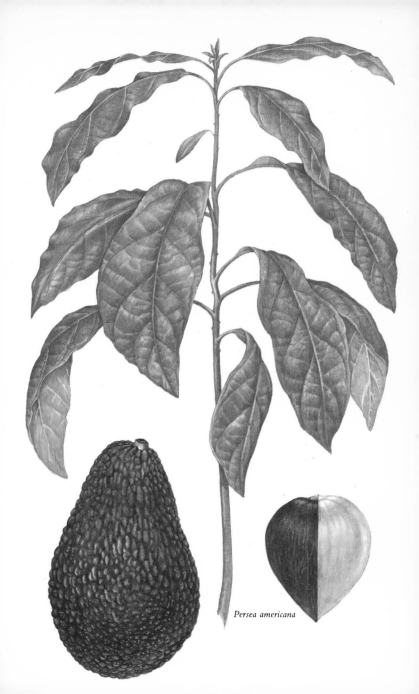

Persea americana

Peperomiaceae Pepper Elder Family

Succulent herbs from tropical and subtropical climates. The most important of the 4 genera is *Peperomia*. Mainly ornamental plants, though some have been used in native medicine and as food.

Peperomia (pep-er-*o*-mee-a) From the Greek: *peperi* – pepper and *homoios* – resembling; the plants look like and are related to the pepper plant, *Piper*.

Cultivation Most of the peperomias prefer warm rooms, though they will tolerate a winter temp. as low as 10°C (50°F) if they are kept rather dry at the roots. Indeed, the plants do better if allowed to dry out considerably between waterings even in summer – soggy compost leads to rotting of the main stem. Good but indirect light is preferred to bright sunshine or heavy shade. In summer spray the foliage daily with tepid water, or stand the plants on trays of moist peat or gravel. Feed monthly in summer, and repot only when absolutely necessary using a basic soil-based compost. Propagate by leaf, leaf bud or stem cuttings in spring and summer (pages 20-2). Nearly all peperomias are good subjects for planting in bottle gardens and terrariums and in mixed arrangements in bowls. The trailing kinds are well suited to hanging baskets.

THE SPECIES

Peperomia argyreia (syn. *P. sandersii*) (Brazil). Height and spread about 9 in. A striking plant with a rounded dome of pointed leaves that are silvery grey veined with green. The leaf stalks are reddish. A difficult species which must be kept warm. The fleshy leaves can be cut into sections and rooted in a propagator.

Peperomia caperata (Brazil). Height 9 in, spread 6 in. A neat plant with dark green deeply corrugated leaves carried on rosy-red stalks. Mouse tail-like flower spikes of yellowish white may appear at any time during the growing season. There is a pretty variegated variety: *P.c.* 'Variegata' whose leaves are edged with creamy white. It is rather more difficult to grow than the true species.

Peperomia glabella **'Variegata'** (Central America). Height 8 in, spread 9 in. A dainty branching plant with reddish stems. The green leaves are pointed and irregularly bordered with creamy white. Occasionally an entirely white leaf or shoot may emerge.

Peperomia griseoargentea (syn. *P. hederaefolia*) (Brazil). Height 6 in, spread 9 in. This plant is rather similar in appearance to *P. caperata* but if the two are compared it will be seen that the leaves of this species are slightly larger and not so deeply corrugated as those of its more popular relative. Instead of being dark green, the leaves are greyish green with darker markings.

Peperomia caperata
'Variegata'

Peperomia caperata

Peperomia griseoargentea

Peperomia argyreia

Peperomia glabella
'Variegata'

Peperomia (continued)

Peperomia magnoliifolia (West Indies). Height and spread 9 in. The rounded leaves are rich green with reddish stalks and extremely thick and fleshy. The plant may be grown upright or allowed to trail, in which case it is well suited to being grown in troughs or hanging baskets.

Peperomia magnoliifolia **'Variegata'**. Of a similar height and spread to the true species, this variety is rather more commonly grown. Its leaves are most attractively marbled with creamy yellow, making the plant highly orna-mental. The variegation is most pronounced in good light rather than shade.

Peperomia obtusifolia (syn. *P. clusiifolia*) (West Indies, Tropical South America, Florida). Baby Rubber Plant. Height 1 ft, spread rather more. A handsome species with dark green, oval, leathery leaves that are edged with deep red. The flowers, when they appear, are white and are carried in the usual spikes. There is also a variegated variety, *P. obtusifolia* 'Variegata', in which the leaves are edged with creamy white.

Peperomia scandens (syn. *P. serpens*) (South America, West Indies). There is a lot of controversy about this plant's name, but the plant normally sold as *P. scandens* is a rather rampant trailer with roughly heart-shaped leaves. It is seen to best advantage when grown in a suspended pot or a hanging basket where its stems can dangle over the rim of the container.

Peperomia scandens **'Variegata'**. This is the variegated form of the above species and it is certainly much more attractive. The leaves are generously splashed around the edges with creamy yellow.

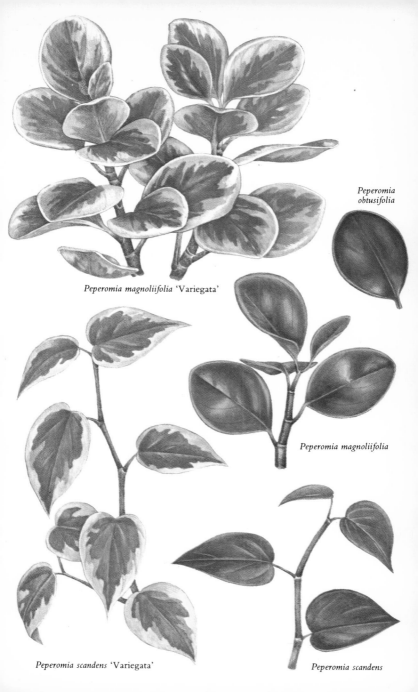

Peperomia magnoliifolia 'Variegata'

Peperomia obtusifolia

Peperomia magnoliifolia

Peperomia scandens 'Variegata'

Peperomia scandens

Cactaceae Cactus Family

Trees, shrubs and perennial plants native to arid areas of North, Central and South America. Some species have become naturalized in other parts of the world. Most are succulent and lack true leaves. Many possess spines and some are epiphytes. There are over 80 genera.

Cephalocereus (sef-a-lo-*seer*-ee-uss) From the Greek: *kephale* – a head, and *cereus* – another genus of cactus; the mature plant has a distinct woolly head at the top of its stem.

Cultivation Cacti need plenty of light so stand them on a bright windowsill. Min. winter temp. 4°C (40°F) but the compost must be kept dry. Bring them into the room at night in winter to prevent frost damage. From late spring to the end of summer, water well whenever the compost looks dry; then let it dry out before watering again. In autumn and winter the compost should remain bone dry – wetted only if the plants show signs of shrivelling. Feed once a month in summer and repot each spring if necessary using a basic soil-based compost with equal amounts of sharp sand. Propagate by means of stem cuttings (page 20) or seeds sown in a temp. of 18-21°C (65-70°C). Mealy bug may be a nuisance.

THE SPECIES

Cephalocereus senilis (syn. ***Cereus senilis, Pilocereus senilis***) (Mexico) Old Man Cactus. Height 10 ft or more. The usually single stem is ribbed and equipped with spines. The long, silky, white hairs smother young plants but are gradually lost from the base. An even larger woolly head of hairs erupts if flowers are produced. These are red and white and open at night.

Epiphyllum (ep-ee-*fill*-um) From the Greek: *epi* – upon, and *phyllon* – a leaf; the plant's flowers appear directly from the stems.

Cultivation Good indirect light and a min. winter temp. of 10°C (50°F). Water when dry in summer; keep drier for one month after flowering and in winter, but give enough water to prevent shrivelling. Support stems. Spray daily with tepid water in summer and feed once a month from late spring to late summer. Repot in an ericaceous compost mixed with sharp sand only when necessary in summer – pot-bound plants bloom more freely. Propagate by cuttings. Mealy bug and scale insects can be a problem.

THE SPECIES

***Epiphyllum* cultivars** (Sometimes sold as *E. ackermanii*) Orchid Cactus. Height 2-3 ft, spread 1-2 ft. Easy to grow with flowers in brilliant shades of red, yellow, orange, magenta and white from spring to summer.

Opuntia (o-pun-tee-a) From the Greek name for another plant that grew in the town of Opus.

Cultivation As for *Cephalocereus* but maintain min. winter temp. of 13°C (55°F). Propagate by seed or by rooting the topmost pads (page 21). Do not keep the plants too damp in winter or the pads may discolour.

THE SPECIES

Opuntia microdasys (Northern Mexico) Prickly Pear, Rabbit's Ears Cactus, Bunny Ears. Height 3 ft, spread 2 ft, less in small pots. The pads bear clusters of minute yellow glochids (hairs) which are painful if they pierce the skin. Yellow flowers tinged red may be produced.

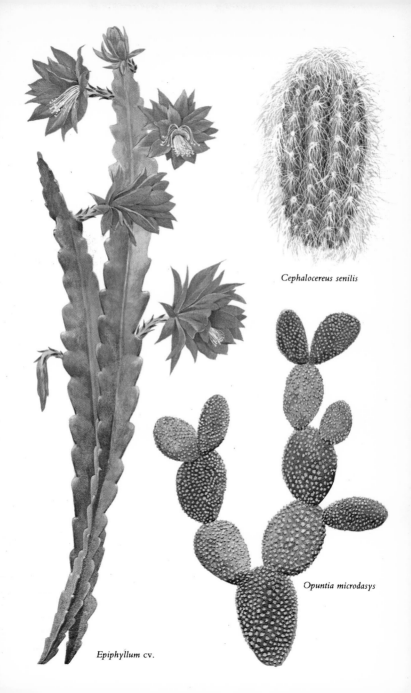

Cephalocereus senilis

Opuntia microdasys

Epiphyllum cv.

Rhipsalidopsis (rip-sal-ee-*dop*-sis) Meaning 'being like rhipsalis'. From the Greek: *rhips* – wickerwork; the plant's stems tend to interweave.

   Cultivation Position in good but indirect light and maintain a min. winter temp. of 10-13°C (50-55°F). Water freely in spring and summer whenever the compost looks dry; keep them cool and drier in winter giving just enough water to prevent shrivelling. Stand the plants outdoors in summer and spray them daily with tepid water. Bring them inside again before frosts threaten. Feed monthly in summer, and repot them each year as the flowers fade, using a basic soil-based compost plus an equal amount of ground bark or peat. Propagation is easy. Snap off stem tips, which consist of 3 or 4 flattened sections, and root these in a propagator or individual 3-in pots of peat and sand covered by a polythene bag.

THE SPECIES

Rhipsalidopsis gaertneri (syn. **Schlumbergera gaertneri, Epiphyllopsis gaert-neri**) (Brazil) Easter Cactus. Height 6 in, spread 1 ft. This is a plant well worth growing for its spring flush of orange-red flowers, held at the ends of flattened, spineless stems. The cool, winter resting period is important if flowers are to be produced regularly.

Schlumbergera (schlum-*ber*-ger-a) Named after Frederick Schlumberger, a Belgian amateur gardener of the 18th and 19th centuries.

   Cultivation Another plant for good but indirect light and temps. which do not fall below 10°C (50°F) in winter. Water well whenever the compost shows signs of drying out between late spring and late summer; keep cool and dry in autumn and then water normally again in winter to encourage flower production. Feed monthly in summer and stand the plants outdoors, spraying them daily with tepid water. Repot after flowering every other year using the compost recommended for *Rhipsalidopsis*. Schlumbergeras are excellent in hanging baskets, where their stems can hang gracefully over the edge of the container. Plant 3 or 4 in one basket so that it is quickly and evenly furnished. Propagation is as for *Rhipsalidopsis*. Flower drop is a common problem if the plants are moved when in bud, or if temperatures or moisture content of the compost are allowed to fluctuate too greatly at that time.

THE SPECIES

Schlumbergera x buckleyi (*S. russelliana* x *S. truncata*) Christmas Cactus. Height 9 in, spread 1 ft. Arching flattened stems will cascade from a suspended pot or hanging basket and in winter (not always as soon as Christmas) will bedeck themselves with magenta flowers that look like ornate trumpets.

Schlumbergera truncata (syn. **Zygocactus truncatus**) (Eastern Brazil) Crab Cactus, Lobster Cactus, Thanksgiving Cactus. Height 12 in, spread 18 in. Rather larger in all its parts than *S. x buckleyi*, and the flowers are nearer to cerise or bright pink with a whitish central tube. The blooms are produced from late autumn to early winter. Recently many new cultivars have been offered for sale with flowers in shades of red, orange, paler pinks and white; all are spectacular when in flower.

Rhipsalidopsis gaertneri

Schlumbergera x *buckleyi*

Schlumbergera truncata

Aizoaceae Mesembryanthemum Family

A large family of well over 100 genera. The plants are all succulent and most have daisy-like flowers. They are native to many tropical areas and are grown for ornament rather than for any economic value.

Lithops (*lith*-ops) From the Greek: *lithos* – a stone, and *ops* – like; the plants look like small pebbles and as such are well camouflaged against attack from browsing animals.

Cultivation Give lithops a spot in very bright light; a south-facing windowsill is ideal, provided the plants are moved off it at night during the winter months. Maintain a min. winter temp. of 7°C (45°F). Water thoroughly when dry from late spring to late summer, but do not water at all in winter. Feed once a month in summer. Repot only when really necessary into a standard soil-based compost mixed with an equal amount of sharp grit or sand. This is best carried out in spring just as growth is starting. Propagation can be achieved from seeds, sown in a temp. of 18°C (65°F) in spring or summer, or by dividing larger clumps at the same time. Cuttings consisting of a pair of leaves can be inserted in very sandy compost in summer and potted up individually when roots have been formed. Do not worry if the leaves appear to shrivel and turn brown in spring, new ones will soon emerge.

THE SPECIES

All are known variously as Living Stones or Pebble Plants, and grow up to 1 in high and as much across.

Lithops marmorata (Namaqualand). The stems are greyish green sometimes with a purplish flush and the upper surfaces are mottled with grey. The flowers are white.

Lithops olivacea (Namaqualand). The stems are olive green to greeny-grey and the upper surfaces a richer colour marked with white flecks. The flowers of this species are yellow.

Lithops pseudotruncatella (Namaqualand). One of the easiest to grow, this species is a greyish colour with darker marbling on the upper surfaces. The flowers are yellow.

Lithops marmorata

Lithops olivacea

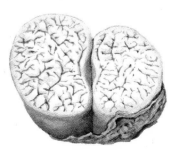

Lithops pseudotruncatella

Nyctaginaceae Bougainvillea Family

Trees, shrubs and herbs native to the tropics. There are 30 genera, many of which are grown as ornamentals, and a few which are used in medicine or as vegetable crops. The most well-known genera are *Mirabilis*, *Pisonia* and *Bougainvillea*.

Bougainvillea (boo-gan-*vill*-ee-a). Named after Louis Antoine de Bougainville (1729-1811) a Frenchman who, after becoming a lawyer, a soldier and a sailor, was sent to establish a French colony on the Falkland Islands. He was the first Frenchman to circumnavigate the globe (between 1766 and 1769), and his name is also commemorated in the largest of the Solomon Islands and a strait in the New Hebrides.

Cultivation Not the easiest of house plants to grow, bougainvillea thrives best in really good light and enjoys bright sunshine. Maintain a min. winter temp. of 7°C (45°F) and remember that the plant does like to be kept cool at that time. It will appreciate more warmth in summer, when the compost can be soaked whenever it looks dry; in winter it can be kept more on the dry side, some gardeners withhold water altogether during this dormant period. Support the stems on a framework of canes, tying them in with soft twine or twist-ties, or pinch out young stems as soon as they are 6 in long to induce a bushy habit. Overcrowding or badly placed stems can be pruned out in late winter as growth starts, and that is when the water supply should be increased. During summer feed the plant fortnightly and spray its leaves with tepid water on warm days. Repot in spring, only when the existing container has been outgrown, using a standard soil-based compost. Propagate the plants from 3- or 4-in long stem cuttings taken in spring and summer and rooted in a heated propagator. Rooting powder will help to get the young plants started quickly. Plants can be positioned in a greenhouse (if available) and brought into the dwelling house just when they are in flower. Mealy bugs can be a problem.

THE SPECIES

Bougainvillea x buttiana (*B. glabra* x *B. peruviana*) (Colombia). Height and spread 20 ft (considerably less when container grown). This is the name under which most of the hybrids of today can be found. The original plant was discovered by Mrs R. V. Butt in 1910, and the cultivar 'Mrs Butt' has magenta-crimson bracts. The flowers of all cultivars are small, creamy white and carried in clusters of three; it is the three leafy bracts around each flower cluster that make the bright spectacle. They are orange in 'Killie Campbell' and 'Orange King'; red to bright pink in 'Brilliant', and orange-yellow in 'Golden Glow'. The cultivar 'Crimson Lake' is a synonym for 'Mrs Butt'.

Bougainvillea glabra (Brazil) Paper Flower. Height and spread up to 8 ft (considerably less when container grown). The shocking pink bracts are rather larger than those of *B. x buttiana* cultivars. Some forms have deeper-coloured bracts, and there is also an off-white cultivar.

Bougainvillea x *buttiana*

Bougainvillea glabra cv.

Amaranthaceae   Cockscomb Family

Annual and perennial shrubs and herbs with cosmopolitan distribution throughout tropical, subtropical and temperate areas. There are over 60 genera, mostly grown for ornament, though a few are cultivated as vegetables or for medicinal purposes. *Celosia*, *Gomphrena*, *Amaranthus* and *Iresine* are perhaps the most widely known genera.

Celosia   (see-*lo*-see-a) From the Greek: *keleos* – burning; an allusion to the brightness of the flowers.

Cultivation   Both types of celosia enjoy good light and can even tolerate a little direct sunlight for part of the day. Cool rooms suit them best as they tend to fade quickly in high temperatures; aim for an average of 13-15°C (55-60°F). Water well when the compost feels dry on the surface, then do not re-water until it starts to dry out again. Celosias kept moist all the time may rot off or wilt and never recover. Feed fortnightly during the summer. These are annual plants that are raised each year from seeds sown in a temp. of 18°C (65°F) in spring. Prick out the seedlings into 3-in pots of a basic soil- or peat-based compost as soon as they are large enough to handle. Give them good light at all times. Pot on into 4½-in pots when the first containers are full of roots, and then grow the plants on to flowering. Discard them once the blooms have faded. The plants can be stood outdoors in summer and are often used in bedding schemes. Whitefly can be a nuisance on celosias.

THE SPECIES

Celosia cristata (syn. *C. argentea cristata*) (Tropical Asia) Cockscomb. Height 6-12 in. A strange-looking plant with oval, light green leaves held closely together on a ridged and rather sappy stem. The flower at the top is of a velour texture and arranged in the form of a curly cockscomb; it is rather greasy to the touch. The flower may be crimson, orange or yellow.
Celosia cristata **'Pyramidalis'** (syn. *C. argentea pyramidalis, C. plumosa*) than *C. cristata* though it is usually the dwarfer strains that are offered as pot plants, these being around 1 ft high. The plume feels the same as the cockscomb but is rather more handsome, and flowers are more likely to be produced from sideshoots as well. Red-, crimson-, orange- and yellow-flowered strains are available.

Celosia cristata

Celosia cristata
'Pyramidalis'

Iresine (eye-ree-*see*-nee) From the Greek: *eireos* – wool; the flowers are woolly.

Cultivation Like most bright-leaved plants, iresine needs plenty of light if it is to retain its shape and brilliance. Give it a spot on a windowsill, and only bring it further into the room at night when frost threatens. Very low temperatures will not be to the plant's liking, so place it in a room which has a winter min. temp. of around 13°C (55°F). The stems of the plant grow quite quickly and should be frequently pinched out to encourage a bushy habit; nip out the tip of each shoot that has reached a length of 4 in. Water well as soon as the surface of the compost feels dry, but let it remain dry rather longer in winter when growth is slower. Feed fortnightly in summer and repot in a standard soil-based compost each spring if the plant is to be grown on. However, it is usual to raise new plants each year from cuttings. Stem cuttings 3-4 in long can be easily rooted in a propagator or a plant pot covered with a polythene bag. Insert the cuttings around the edge of the pot in a mixture of peat and sharp sand. Pot them up individually into 4-in pots of a basic soil-based compost as soon as they are rooted.

THE SPECIES

Iresine herbstii (South America) Blood Leaf, Beefsteak Plant. Height and spread 1 ft, or slightly more. The stems and leaf stalks of this plant are a vibrant wine red, as are the veins which stand out well from the much darker maroon of the leaf surface. Do not think that your plant is deformed if the ends of the leaves possess two lobes and a central indentation, for this is a natural characteristic.

Iresine herbstii **'Aureo-reticulata'** Chicken Gizzard. Height and spread 18 in. This time the leaves are properly pointed, they are green with butter-yellow veins and wine-red stalks. The main stem is wine red too.

Iresine herbstii **'Brilliantissimum'**. Height and spread 18 in. Pointed leaves of dark maroon veined in luminous pink. Perhaps the most spectacular of the three plants.

Iresine herbstii

Iresine herbstii
'Aureo-reticulata'

Iresine herbstii
'Brilliantissimum'

Tiliaceae   Linden Family

Trees and shrubs widely distributed throughout tropical and temperate areas of the world. There are over 40 genera, and while many are handsome ornamentals, such as *Tilia* (linden or lime) and *Sparmannia*, others are valued for timber and, in the case of *Corchorus*, for jute.

Sparmannia (spar-*man*-ee-a) Named in honour of Dr Anders Sparrman (1748-1820), a Swedish botanist and pupil of Linnaeus who sailed with Captain Cook on his second voyage of exploration in the *Resolution* between 1772 and 1775. Sparrman had a puritanical outlook on life for although impressed by Cook's seamanship, he was rather shocked by his bad language! He also accompanied Carl Thunberg in his travels around South Africa.

Cultivation This is a vigorous plant which enjoys good but indirect light and which needs plenty of room to grow. It can withstand temps. as low as 7°C (45°F) in winter, and should be kept relatively cool during the summer. It tolerates a warm room but will not enjoy excessive heat. Water thoroughly when the surface of the compost feels dry in summer, but keep it slightly drier in winter when growth is much slower. In warm weather the plant will drink copious amounts of water. To maintain a well-furnished plant that is relatively bushy pinch out the tips of shoots that are 12 in long. Any drastic cutting back can be carried out in spring or early summer after the plant has flowered. Feed fortnightly in summer and repot each spring until the plant is in a 10- or 12-in pot. From then on simply scrape away some of the old compost and topdress with fresh. For both potting and topdressing use a rich soil-based compost. Propagation is easily effected by taking 4-in long stem cuttings and rooting these in a propagator with bottom heat. Seeds can be sown in warmth in spring. Whitefly seem to like sparmannia and will often colonize the undersides of the leaves.

THE SPECIES

Sparmannia africana (South Africa) African Hemp, African Windflower, House Lime, Rumslind Tree, Zimmer Linden. Height 6 ft or more, spread 4 ft. A really handsome, yet modestly coloured, plant with soft, downy leaves that are carried on vigorous stems. The flowers are delightful – the white petals turn back completely to reveal a central boss of stamens. A fine choice for a large, well-lit room, the plant may also survive outdoors in sheltered gardens when it outgrows available space indoors.

Sparmannia africana

Malvaceae   Mallow Family

Trees, shrubs and herbs of cosmopolitan distribution. There are around 80 genera, many of which are of economic importance including *Gossypium* (cotton). Genera of ornamental value include *Abutilon* and *Hibiscus*.

Abutilon (ab-*yew*-tee-lon) From the Arabic name for a plant like mallow.
   Cultivation An easy plant for a position in good, indirect light where temperatures do not rise too high and with a winter min. of 10°C (50°F). The plant may grow quite tall with the lower half of the stem becoming bare of leaves. For a bushy specimen the shoots should be pinched out as soon as they are 9 in long. Pruning can be carried out in spring, when stems can be cut out completely or back to sprouting buds. Water well when the surface of the compost feels dry in summer but keep the plants drier in winter. Feed fortnightly in summer and repot each spring in a rich soil-based compost until the plant is in a 10-in pot, then topdress annually with the same. Propagate by taking stem cuttings or by sowing seed. Whitefly may be a nuisance.

THE SPECIES

All are variously known as Flowering Maples and incorrectly as Chinese Lantern Flowers (properly applied to *Physalis alkekengi*).
***Abutilon* x *hybridum* 'Savitsii'** (syn. *A. savitzii*). Height 2 ft, spread 18 in. A dainty plant with sharply cut foliage splashed with creamy white. It frequently produces several stems rather than one central shoot. It can be bedded out in summer and brought in before the frost.
***Abutilon pictum* 'Thompsonii'** (syn. *A. striatum thompsonae*). Height up to 6 ft or more, spread 2 ft or more. Fresh green maple-like leaves freely mottled with bright yellow. Growth is angular and vigorous, and the plant may outgrow its allotted space quickly. Pale orange bell-shaped flowers veined with red are produced at any time of the year.

Hibiscus (hib-*iss*-cuss) The Greek name for the mallow.
   Cultivation Hibiscus likes warmth and good light, so maintain a winter min. temp. of 13°C (55°F) and keep in good, even direct, light all the year round. Pinch back the shoots when 6 in long to encourage bushiness. Drastic thinning or pruning can be carried out in spring, always cutting back to a visible bud. Keep the compost moist in summer but drier in winter. Feed fortnightly in summer and repot in a standard soil-based compost in spring when necessary. Old plants in large pots should have some of the old compost scraped away and replaced with a rich soil-based compost in spring. Propagate by taking fairly soft stem cuttings in spring or sow seed. Whitefly, mealy bug and scale insects can be a problem. Bud drop is caused by the compost being too dry or by the plant being placed in a draught.

THE SPECIES

Hibiscus rosa-sinensis (Asia) Blacking Plant, Rose of Smyrna. Height and spread 6 ft or more. A strong-growing shrub with deep green leaves and massive single flowers of rich crimson. The stamens and stigma are carried on a long tube. There are many variations in flower colour as well as a number of doubles and a variegated form. The mashed-up petals exude a black fluid which has been used to clean shoes.

Abutilon pictum 'Thompsonii'

Abutilon x hybridum
'Savitsii'

Hibiscus rosa-sinensis

Moraceae Mulberry Family

A large family composed mainly of trees and shrubs with one or two climbers and herbs. There are 75 genera native to tropical and temperate areas of the world, and many are of economic importance. *Ficus* includes the fig, *Morus* is the mulberry, *Artocarpus* the breadfruit and *Humulus* the hop. *Cannabis* is grown for hemp fibre and narcotic drugs. Many members of the family are grown as ornamentals, and all possess milky sap.

Ficus (*fy*-cuss) The Latin name for the fig.

Cultivation The ornamental figs are a varied group of plants with equally varied requirements. The definite likes and dislikes of any species are listed with the description, but generally speaking all the taller and more shrubby plants like a position in good but indirect light; the creeping types prefer light shade. Keep all the figs reasonably warm in winter, a min. temp. of 13°C (55°F) is ideal, though in an emergency 7°C (45°F) can be tolerated for short periods of time. Water freely in summer, but only when the surface of the compost has dried out, for overwatering is a common cause of death. The compost can remain dry even longer in winter and the plant will not mind at all. Keep the creeping species moist (but not soggy) at all times. Taller species may need the support of a stout cane when their stems become top-heavy. Occasional misting with tepid rainwater will suit all species, as will a monthly feed in summer. Repot in spring when necessary – the large and shrubby species into a standard or rich soil-based compost and the smaller species into basic soil or peat-based compost. Propagate by sowing seeds in spring in a heated propagator, or by taking stem or leaf bud cuttings in spring and summer and rooting these with bottom heat. Tall, single-stemmed plants can be propagated and reduced in height by air layering (see page 22). Scale insects and red spider mites are the only serious pests.

THE SPECIES

Ficus benghalensis (India, Tropical Africa) Banyan, Bengal Fig. Height 10 ft and more, spread 4 ft. A handsome species with a single or a branched stem. The rich green leaves are similar in shape to those of the India Rubber Plant but are less leathery and not at all glossy. A vigorous but often neglected plant.

Ficus benjamina (Tropical Asia) Weeping Fig. Height 6 ft, spread 4 ft or more if given room to grow. Easily the most elegant ornamental fig. The greyish stems arch gracefully with fresh green, pointed leaves dangling from them. This plant often takes a while to settle in to a new home and some of its leaves will turn yellow and fall every time it is relocated. It soon recovers provided that it is given a spot in good light and away from draughts and heat sources. Its growth is rather slow but it makes an excellent specimen plant.

Ficus deltoidea (syn. *F. diversifolia*) (India, Malaysia) Mistletoe Fig. Height 3-4 ft, spread 2 ft. A quaint species with rounded and gently convex, dull green leaves. Round, yellow-green berries are carried all the year round. A slow grower.

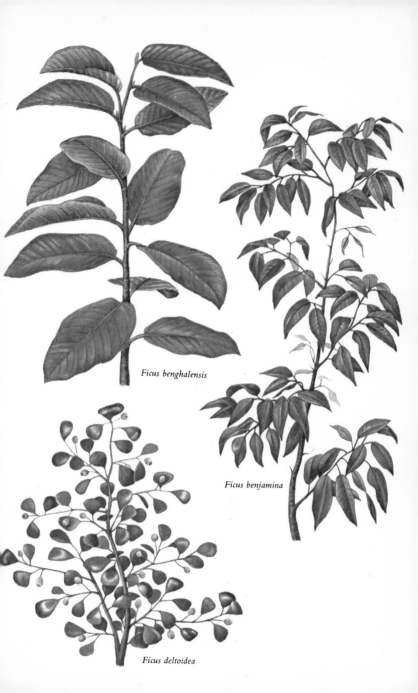

Ficus benghalensis

Ficus benjamina

Ficus deltoidea

Ficus (continued)

***Ficus elastica* 'Robusta'** (Originally from Tropical Asia) Broad-Leaved Indian Rubber Plant, India Rubber Plant. Height 10 ft or more, spread 6 ft or more. Possibly the most common house plant of all. The cultivar *F.e.* 'Robusta' is the sturdiest grower and preferable to *F.e.* 'Decora' which is also widely available. The strong stem is usually, but not always, unbranched, and the dark green, glossy, oval leaves, each with a pronounced point, are carried symmetrically upon it. Cutting out the growing point (always sheathed in a pink protective covering) will encourage branching, and young plants can be pinched out at a height of 2 ft if you have the courage. Very tall plants can be air layered (see page 22) or a central section of the stem can be cut out completely and the top joined to the bottom in the form of a wedge graft. Cut a 1-in deep V-shaped notch into the top of the stump, then cut the base of the upper part of the stem into a wedge that will fit it. Bind the two together with adhesive tape and support the entire new stem with a cane. Soon the two portions of stem will unite and the tape and cane can be taken away.

Clean the leaves of all rubber plants occasionally to remove grime. Few pests and diseases are troublesome, but overwatering will cause the leaves to turn yellow and drop. The yellowing of one lower leaf every six months or so is to be expected with age. Such leaves will fall and should be removed. Brown areas on the leaves indicate that the plant is being scorched by sun, or that it is too near a heat source, or that it has been left bone dry for several weeks.

***Ficus elastica* 'Doescheri',** Variegated India Rubber Plant. Height and spread as for *F.e.* 'Robusta', but growth is very much slower. This can be a difficult plant, but one worth mastering. It requires warmer rooms than its plain-leaved relations, but the extra care is well repaid with a display of gently folded leaves that are generously and irregularly margined with creamy yellow. Whereas *F.e.* 'Robusta' tends to hold its leaves upright, those of *F.e.* 'Doescheri' are rather drooping, giving the plant more grace. Overwatering and bright sunshine will cause the leaves to turn brown. Daily misting with tepid rainwater helps to provide welcome humidity. This is really a plant for the experienced enthusiast.

***Ficus elastica* 'Tricolor'.** Height and spread as for the other two cultivars. This variegated species has rounder leaves than *F.e.* 'Doescheri' and the variegation is more uneven and widespread. There may also be a tinge of pink on the leaf – especially on the midrib. As difficult as *F.e.* 'Doescheri' and in rather short supply.

Ficus elastica 'Robusta'

Ficus elastica
'Doescheri'

Ficus elastica
'Tricolor'

Ficus (continued)

Ficus lyrata (syn. ***F. pandurata***) (Tropical Africa) Banjo Fig, Fiddleback Fig, Fiddle-leaf Fig. Height up to 8 ft or more, spread 2 ft. An exceptionally handsome plant with leathery, rich green leaves that are prominently veined. Single-stemmed specimens are common, but the plant may also branch. This is a greedy feeder which should be given plentiful supplies of compost and a good-sized pot. It also demands a min. winter temp. of 15°C (60°F) if it is not to lose its lower leaves. Generous treatment will produce the best plants, but again be wary of overwatering.

Ficus pumila (syn. ***F. repens***) (China, Japan) Creeping Fig, Climbing Fig. This trailing fig looks easy but can have problems. It suffers in bright sunshine and prefers shade, and its compost should not be allowed to dry out completely or its leaves will turn brown and drop off. The rounded green leaves are about ½ in across and slightly wrinkled. A peat-based compost suits it best and it should be kept warm at all times; aim for a winter min. of 15°C (60°F). Looks good in troughs, suspended in pots or in bottle gardens.

***Ficus pumila* 'Variegata'**, Variegated Creeping Fig. This requires similar conditions to its plain-leaved relation. Snip off any plain green shoots which do not have the attractive white marbling. Both plants can be encouraged to climb if they are given support in the form of a piece of plastic trellis or a tripod of split canes, but they are more graceful when allowed to trail.

Ficus sagittata* 'Variegata'** (syn. ***F. radicans variegata) (East Indies). Another rather difficult fig which is most successfully grown in the warm and humid atmosphere to be found in a large bottle garden or terrarium. Although it is a trailer, like *F. pumila* it can be encouraged to climb if provided with support such as a foam- or moss-covered stick. The oval leaves are slightly folded down the centre and the mid-green base colour is wildly splashed with creamy white. Keep the plant warm and moist at all times.

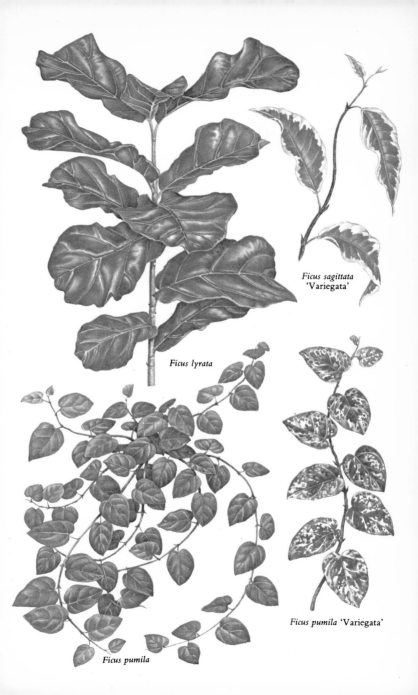

Ficus sagittata
'Variegata'

Ficus lyrata

Ficus pumila

Ficus pumila 'Variegata'

Urticaceae   Stinging Nettle Family

Trees, shrubs and herbs of cosmopolitan distribution. There are around 45 genera, some of which are ornamental, others of which are noxious weeds. Several members of the family yield fibres that are used in textile manufacture, notably *Boehmeria*. *Pellionia* and *Pilea* are the most important genera as far as the house-plant grower is concerned.

Pellionia (pel-ee-*oe*-nee-a) Named in honour of Alphonse Odet Pellion (1796-1868) who sailed with the French navigator Louis Freycinet on his second voyage around the world (1817-1820). Pellion later became an admiral.
   Cultivation Pellionia is a plant for centrally-heated houses. It needs a min. winter temp. of at least 13°C (55°F) and should be kept warm for the rest of the year too. Give it a spot in light shade, though it will also tolerate indirect light, and spray the leaves occasionally with tepid rainwater. Try to keep the compost slightly moist (not soggy) at all times, and feed the plant once a month in summer. Repotting is seldom necessary, for young plants give the best display. In summer three 4-in long stem cuttings can be pushed into a 4½-in pot of peat-based potting compost and rooted in warmth. Once rooted the cuttings will quickly send out plenty of stems to cover the sides of the container. Mature plants can also be divided and repotted in spring. These are good plants for suspended pots, hanging baskets, bottle gardens and terrariums (where they will appreciate the extra humidity). Few problems will be encountered with pests; the main problems are likely to be scorching due to burning sunlight, dry air from a radiator or draughts.

THE SPECIES

Pellionia daveauana (syn. *P. repens*) (Vietnam, Burma, Malaya) Trailing Watermelon Begonia. A trailer with oval, rather succulent leaves which vary in colour from yellowish green to deep green. They are margined either with light bronze or dark green to bronze or brown – the colour varies depending on the amount of light received by the plant. Small green flowers may be produced in late summer but these are rather insignificant.
Pellionia pulchra (Vietnam) Satin Pellionia. Of a similar habit to *P. daveauana*, but here the leaves are corrugated by the deep bronze-purple veins. Both plants lend themselves to being used as infilling material in group plantings, especially in troughs where their stems can cascade over the container's edge.

Pellionia daveauana

Pellionia pulchra

Pilea (py-*lee*-a) From the Latin: *pileus* – a cap; the female flowers have a cap-like covering.

Cultivation Try to maintain a min. winter temp. of 10°C (50°F) for these plants, though they can tolerate lower temperatures in an emergency. The best pileas will be produced in good but indirect light. The plants will also cope with shade though the stems may become a little drawn and spindly as a result. The taller-growing types will benefit from being pinched back when the shoots are 4 in long; this will encourage branching and a bushier plant will be produced. Water well as soon as the compost feels dry to the touch in spring and summer. Allow it to remain dry for rather longer in autumn and winter. An occasional spray over with tepid water will keep the plants in good condition as all of them appreciate a little extra humidity. Repot every spring in a basic soil-based compost, though the plants are best renewed from cuttings or by division every two years or so. Feed fortnightly in summer. Stem cuttings, 3 in long, can be easily rooted in a warm propagator (or a polythene-covered pot) in spring and summer. Red spider mite can be a problem in a dry atmosphere. All pileas are good plants for bottle gardens and terrariums; the trailing species are shown off to good effect in troughs, hanging baskets and suspended pots.

THE SPECIES

Pilea cadierei **'Minima'** (syn. *P.c.* **'Nana'**) (Vietnam) Aluminium Plant. Height and spread 8 in. A most attractive modest-sized pot plant with oval, pointed, glossy leaves that are rich green marked with silver grey. The markings are caused by air pockets under the upper surface of the leaf. The young, emerging leaves are pale bronze.

Pilea involucrata (Panama, Tropical America, West Indies) Friendship Plant, Panamiga. Height 6 in, spread 1 ft. The green or brownish leaves are deeply veined in a herringbone pattern, and the undersides are purplish. This plant is often described as being synonymous with *P. spruceana* (a different species native to Bolivia and Peru) which has rather longer leaves than the rounded ones of *P. involucrata*.

Pilea microphylla (syn. *P. muscosa*) (Tropical America) Artillery Plant. Height and spread to 1 ft. A fresh green plant with tiny leaves that give it a fuzzy, almost ferny, appearance. Tiny red flowers are carried on the plant's succulent stalks and pollen is expelled from them rapidly if the stems are disturbed at flowering time.

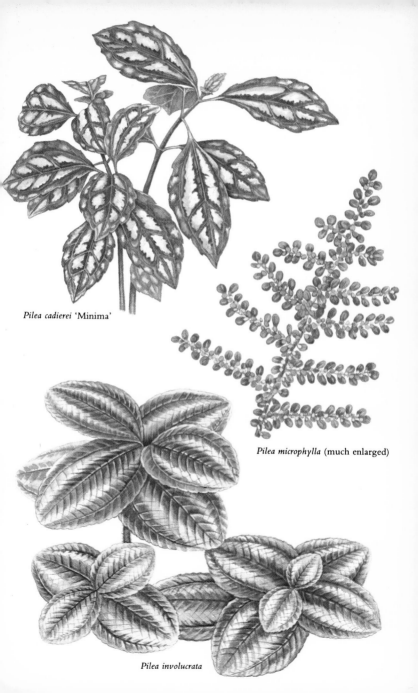

Pilea cadierei 'Minima'

Pilea microphylla (much enlarged)

Pilea involucrata

Pilea (continued)

Pilea **'Moon Valley'** (Often incorrectly described as *P. mollis*). Height 9 in, spread 12 in. Bright green, roughly indented leaves with acute points are veined with deep brown. The colouring is more pronounced at the lower end of each leaf, giving a toned effect and making this an exceptionally handsome plant.

Pilea nummulariifolia (West Indies, South America) Creeping Charlie. This species is different from the others mentioned in that it is a trailer. Its creeping or trailing stems are clad in small, round, green leaves, usually held in groups of three or four, and if planted in a suspended pot or hanging basket it will be seen to good effect. When planted as a trailer in a group arrangement, the stems will root at intervals making propagation easy as it becomes simply a matter of detaching and potting up rooted pieces.

Soleirolia (sol-eye-*roe*-lee-a) Named after Joseph François Soleirol who travelled and collected plants in Corsica in the 19th century.

   Cultivation Soleirolia is one of those plants that grows in spite of the gardener rather than because of him. It is hardy in most parts of Britain and can become a pernicious garden weed that is difficult to eradicate. In the house it is a pleasant plant either for a spot in good but indirect light (bright sun scorches it) or in shade. It prefers to be kept cool (or even cold) and will turn brown in temps. much above 21°C (70°F). Soleirolia looks good planted among other house plants in a group arrangement, but it should be firmly pulled away from any neighbour which it threatens to smother. It is wise to keep the plant out of bottle gardens and terrariums where it will quickly monopolize all available space. Repot in spring into basic soil- or peat-based compost if large plants are required. Feed monthly in summer and keep the compost slightly moist at all times to prevent browning of the foliage. New plants can easily be made by pulling off a few strands and inserting these into 3-in pots of a peat-based compost at any time of year.

THE SPECIES

Soleirolia soleirolii (syn. *Helxine soleirolii*) (Corsica, Sardinia) Baby's Tears, Mind-your-own-business. A dense creeper with tiny round leaves of bright green. Forms with golden leaves or pale green leaves edged with white are also available and are even more attractive than the true species.

Soleirolia soleirolii

Pilea 'Moon Valley'

Pilea nummulariifolia

Passifloraceae Passion Flower Family

Tropical and subtropical trees, shrubs, climbers and herbs. There are 20 genera, of which the most important is undoubtedly *Passiflora*. Most of the plants are cultivated for their ornamental value, though many of them also produce edible fruits which are used in the manufacture of fruit juice. *P. quadrangularis* is the Giant Granadilla and *P. edulis* is the species most widely grown for juice.

Passiflora (pass-ee-*flor*-a) From the Latin: *passio* – passion, and *flos* – a flower; an allusion to the parts of the plant which South American missionaries related to the passion of Christ: the five petals and five sepals represent the apostles (minus Judas Iscariot and either Doubting Thomas or Peter); the frilly blue corona represents the crown of thorns; the five anthers represent the wounds; three stigmas the nails; the hand-shaped leaves are the hands of His persecutors, and the tendrils the whip with which He was scourged.

Cultivation The Passion Flower needs plenty of light and plenty of space if it is to grow well and not look like a rampant weed. A conservatory or sunroom suits it best, but it will also thrive if grown adjacent to large windows. It tolerates a wide range of temperatures and will even survive in unheated rooms during the winter. The plant should be grown in a large pot at least 8 in in diameter and the stems can be trained over a fan-shaped framework of bamboo canes if no larger support system is available. Unwanted stems can be cut out completely at any time of year but will perhaps make more of a nuisance of themselves in spring and summer. Soak the compost in the pot thoroughly whenever it shows signs of drying out, but let it remain drier for longer during the winter. An occasional spray over with tepid water in summer will perk up tired foliage. Feed fortnightly in summer and repot annually in spring using a basic soil-based compost (richer mixes are likely to produce leaf and shoot growth at the expense of flowers). The plant can grow outside during the summer. Propagation is by means of soft shoot tips which can be cut off and rooted in a propagator in spring and summer. Seeds can be sown in a temp. of 18-21°C (65-70°F) in spring or summer.

THE SPECIES

Passiflora caerulea (Brazil) Common or Blue Passion Flower. Height and spread 33 ft or more. An extremely vigorous plant with vine-like stems clad in hand-shaped dark green leaves and equipped with questing tendrils. The flowers may appear at any time through the summer and are white, centred with blue-tinged filaments and purple stigmas. The flowers may be followed by orange egg-shaped fruits which are edible but rather seedy. The plant can be allowed to take over the rear wall of a conservatory and a wire or trellis support system can be constructed against the flat surface to aid its progress.

Passiflora caerulea

Begoniaceae Begonia Family

A family of shrubs and perennial herbs native to the tropics and subtropics. There are only 5 genera in the family, but around 900 species, most of these being in the genus *Begonia*. Nearly all those members of the family that are cultivated are grown for their ornamental value, but one or two are used in native medicine and as vegetables.

Begonia (be-*go*-nee-a) Named after the Frenchman Michel Bégon (1638-1710) a patron of science, especially botany.

Cultivation There are many types of begonia grown as house plants – some for their leaf colour, others for their flowers – but all have the same basic requirements. Make sure they are kept warm (but not excessively hot) all the year round, and position them where the min. winter temp. is unlikely to fall below 13°C (55°F). All appreciate good but indirect light. Bright sunshine will scorch the leaves and flowers. The really tall varieties can be pinched out to encourage bushiness, but older specimens will need the support of a cane or two to prevent them from toppling over. Where a rounded mound of foliage is made, the plant can be encircled with split green canes, and these linked together with soft green twine. Soon the canes and the twine should disappear beneath the foliage. All begonias carry separate male and female flowers; the males are often more spectacular than the females but do not last so long. Water the plants freely when they are dry in summer, but allow them to go a little longer without water in winter.

For specific care of tuberous- and fibrous-rooted flowering begonias, see the details given under the individual descriptions. Feed all begonias fortnightly in summer. Repot in spring when necessary using a standard soil-based compost, though the tuberous-rooted and fibrous-rooted flowering kinds are perfectly happy in a peat-based compost. Propagate the taller-growing varieties by 4-in long stem cuttings in spring. Clump-forming types can be divided in spring or summer, and *Begonia rex, B. masoniana* and the Rieger hybrids can be propagated from leaf cuttings (see page 21). Aphids and red spider mites are the most common pests likely to attack; mildew and botrytis are common diseases. Flower drop can be prevented by standing the plants on a tray of wet gravel and by ensuring that the compost stays evenly moist during the flowering period. Browning of the leaves and flowers may be caused by sun scorch, draughts, lack of water, or too dry an atmosphere.

THE SPECIES

Begonia boweri (Mexico) Eyelash Begonia. Height 6 in, spread 1 ft. The rich green leaves are lopsidedly pointed in typical begonia fashion and edged with purplish brown markings and white hairs – hence the common name. The flowers are about 1 in across, white flushed with pink.

Begonia 'Cleopatra'. Height 9 in, spread 18 in. Here the leaves are deeply lobed, light green and mottled with bronze. The mottling is especially prominent on young leaves and around the margins of older ones. The flowers are pink or white and carried in clusters atop 9-in stems. Looks good in hanging baskets.

Begonia 'Lucerna', (Reputedly a hybrid of *B. corallina*) Spotted Angel-wing Begonia. Height up to 4 ft, spread 2 ft or more. One of the taller varieties with stout stems jointed rather like bamboo. The pointed leaves are green,

Begonia 'Lucerna'

Begonia 'Cleopatra'

Begonia boweri

spotted with silver grey on the upper surface, and a rich wine red on the undersides. They may be as much as 10 in long. The flowers are rich pink and carried in generous-sized pendent clusters, the female blooms last much longer than the males. Mature plants are seldom out of flower.

Begonia maculata (Brazil). Height up to 4 ft, spread up to 3 ft. Another species with green, pointed leaves that are spotted with silver grey on the upper surface. The undersides of the leaves are a rich rosy crimson. The flowers, carried in drooping clusters, may be pale pink or white (this is a variable species) and usually appear in summer. Similar in appearance to *B.* 'Lucerna', but the leaves are not so long – up to 6 in – and the flowers less deeply coloured. The flowering season is also limited.

Begonia masoniana (syn. **B. 'Iron Cross'**) (South East Asia) Iron Cross Begonia. Height up to 1 ft but usually less, spread up to 18 in. The leaves are rough and warty, single pointed and pale green in colour, with a central cross marking (usually with five or six points) of deep brown. This is a bushy plant, rather like *B. rex* in habit, but a little looser. Its thick rhizomes lie on the surface of the compost and so it is often best grown in a fairly wide-rimmed half-pot – say 6 in – which is only half the depth of a normal plant pot. The small flowers are white tinged with green but are often obscured by the leaves. *B. masoniana* prefers a lightly shaded position. Leaf cuttings (made from a single leaf with its stalk, or from postage-stamp-sized pieces of leaf) may take longer to root than those of *B. rex*. Make sure that they are not overwatered or they may rot off.

Begonia metallica (Salvador) Metal Leaf Begonia. Height up to 4 ft, spread up to 3 ft. The pointed leaves can reach 6 in in length and the upper surface is a metallic green. Below the leaves are decorated with red veins and hairs. The flowers are flushed pink and are carried in large clusters in summer and autumn. The female blooms possess red hairs. This begonia is easy to grow provided that it is not subjected to rapid fluctuations in temperature and water content of the compost. If it is shocked in any such way it will suddenly shed all its leaves. Keep the plant warm and evenly moist if this does happen and new leaves should sprout again, though the extreme tips of the shoots may have to be removed.

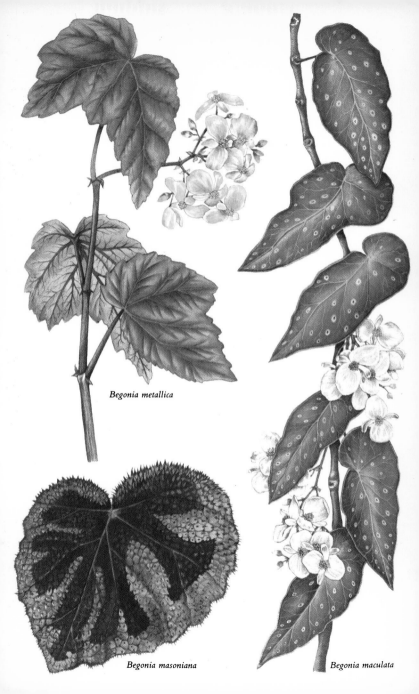

Begonia metallica

Begonia masoniana

Begonia maculata

Begonia pendula (Strictly a name of no specific value, but one which is almost always used to describe these pendulous begonias which are really forms of *B*. x *tuberhybrida)*. Height 6-9 in, spread 1 ft. The green leaves are the usual single-lobed begonia shape, and the flowers (single or double) may be pink, white, red, yellow or orange. The arching, pendent habit of these begonias makes them ideal subjects for hanging baskets, and this is where they are usually grown. The plants are raised and treated in exactly the same manner as *Begonia* x *tuberhybrida*, but planted in groups of 3 or 4 in hanging baskets, rather than singly in pots. Like all plants grown in baskets, pendulous begonias will suffer from drought if the compost is not watered frequently in the summer months. Take the basket outdoors, stand it on the rim of a bucket for support, water it thoroughly and take it back indoors when it has drained.

Begonia rex (syn. **B. rex-cultorum**) (Assam) Fan Begonia, Painted Leaf Begonia, Rex Begonia. Height up to 18 in, spread up to 3 ft. The most beautiful of the begonias grown for foliage. The single-lobed leaves may be marbled and patterned in crimson, purple, pink, brown, green and pure, shining silver. The plants have a tendency to grow rather one sided, but this can be avoided if the pots are turned from time to time. Be prepared for plants to deteriorate after two or three years, for they really grow best under warm greenhouse conditions. However, plenty of leaves are available for propagation purposes, and one mature plant can give rise to a few dozen young ones if treated in the right way (see page 21). Pinkish-white flowers are produced but a dense mound of leaves may obscure these from view.

***Begonia* 'Rieger Hybrids'.** Height and spread 1 ft. This new race of begonias will no doubt become very popular. They can be bought in flower at any time of year and will last for at least 3 months in the home. The most popular flower colour is scarlet, but other shades are available. Kept in reasonable warmth and good, but indirect, light, the plant should perform well. When it is past its best it can be used as a stock plant and youngsters raised from individual leaves whose stalks have been inserted into a rooting medium such as equal parts peat and sand. Keep the cuttings in a warm and humid atmosphere and pot them up when more leaves begin to appear from them. In spite of its appearance this is a fibrous-rooted begonia, not a tuberous-rooted one.

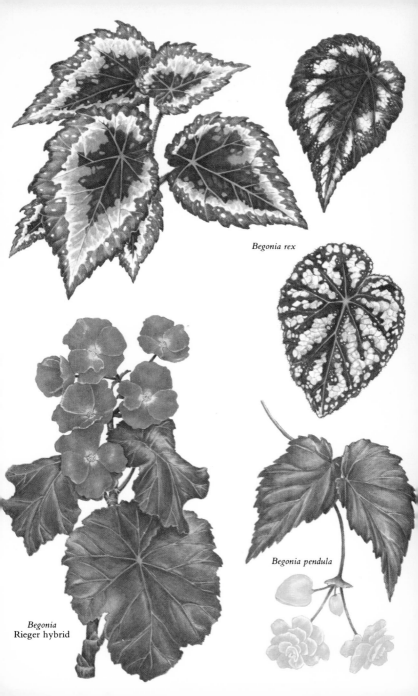

Begonia rex

Begonia
Rieger hybrid

Begonia pendula

Begonia (continued)

Begonia semperflorens (syn. ***B. cucullata hookeri, B. x semperflorens cultorum***) (Brazil) Wax Begonia. Height and spread 6–12 in. The species name indicates that it is always flowering and this is no exaggeration if it is in the right position, for it is possible to have it in bloom all the year round. The leaves may be vivid green or chocolate brown, but always they are bright and glossy and rather succulent – which explains the common name. The flowers may be white, pink or rich red and are centred with a bright yellow tuft of stamens or a stigma. They can be double or single. The plant is frequently grown outdoors as a bedding plant, but it can be potted up before the first frosts of autumn and brought indoors. Placed in full light it will bloom unabated right through the winter. Pinch it regularly to keep it bushy, and propagate it by stem cuttings which can be rooted in water.

Begonia socotrana* 'Gloire de Lorraine'** (syn. ***B. x cheimantha) Lorraine Begonia. Height and spread 1–1½ ft. An elegant, rather difficult plant with rounded green leaves and masses of dainty pink flowers in winter and spring. It is fibrous rooted. This plant is best treated as an annual and raised each spring from cuttings to flower the following winter. Allow the compost in the pot to dry off a little after flowering, then cut the stems back to 2 in and start to water again. Take these shoots as cuttings, later potting them up in a basic soil-based compost. Pinch them to encourage bushiness, and support the stems. The plants should end up in 5-in pots. Place the plants on a tray of wet gravel to keep the atmosphere moist and shade them from direct sunlight. Red spider mite can be a problem.

Begonia x tuberhybrida Tuberous Begonia. Height and spread up to 2 ft. The most spectacular of the flowering begonias, these plants carry double flowers up to 6 in and more across. They may be white, yellow, orange, pink, scarlet or crimson, and some of them have frilly 'fimbriated' edges or petals margined with a contrasting colour. The leaves are usually plain green with the characteristic one-sided lobe.

The tubers are bought dry in spring and are started into growth on seed trays filled with moist peat. Alternatively, individually bed the tubers, hollow side uppermost, into the surface of some peat-based potting compost placed in a 4-in pot. This saves the plants from the shock of a subsequent move in the early stages. Keep the tubers warm, around 15°C (60°F) and in a rather humid atmosphere. As growth progresses the plants should be kept at an even temperature and the compost in the pot should never be allowed to dry out completely or the flower buds may drop. Pot on into 6-in pots using a peat-based compost when the smaller containers are filled with roots. Feed weekly in summer and remove any faded flowers. The female flowers (which are single and backed by a swollen pouch) can be taken off as soon as they appear if the double flowers are preferred on their own. When the plant starts to get leggy and stops producing flowers allow the compost to dry out and the leaves and stems to die down. In winter the tubers can be cleared of their dead stems and leaves and stored in a cool dry place. Start them off again the following spring. Tubers will last for many years if treated in this way.

Begonia socotrana
'Gloire de Lorraine'

Begonia x tuberhybrida

Begonia semperflorens

Ericaceae   Heath Family

A cosmopolitan family of trees and shrubs in 100 or so genera. To the gardener the genera *Erica*, *Calluna* and *Rhododendron* are the most important, and many members of the family are ornamental to some degree. One or two species are of economic value: *Erica arborea* produces the wood for briar pipes, and species of *Vaccinium* yield cranberries and bilberries.

Erica (*e*-rick-a) From the Greek: *ereike*, or Latin: *erice*; the names for the tree heath.

   Cultivation It is the heaths native to South Africa which are cultivated as house plants, not the hardier kinds to be found growing in gardens. Give any of these heaths a spot in bright but indirect light, a north-facing windowsill suits them well, and keep them cool at all times. In warm rooms where temperatures rise higher than 13°C (55°F) they will fade quickly and both the leaves and flowers may be shed. Keep the compost slightly moist at all times and never let it dry out. Use rainwater rather than tapwater as the latter may contain quantities of lime which these plants cannot tolerate. When the flowers fade the plants can be cut down to within 1 in of the surface of the compost and placed outdoors during the summer. Repot them in a lime-free peat-based compost and bring them back indoors in autumn before the first frost. The plants will benefit from being sprayed with rainwater all the year round, and in summer they can be fed fortnightly. Cuttings of shoot tips can be rooted in a warm propagator in summer but they are not the easiest things to establish. Most indoor gardeners either discard their plant after flowering, or cut it down and grow it on again.

THE SPECIES

The following are known as Cape Heaths.

Erica canaliculata (South Africa) Christmas Heather. Height usually up to 3 ft when grown indoors, 6 ft and more in the wild, spread slightly less. This heath is potentially one of the tallest and carries masses of tiny white or pink bells with brownish anthers. The foliage is dark green and needle like.

Erica **'Hyemalis'** (South Africa) French Heath. 1 ft or slightly more, spread 9-12 in. The most widely available of the Cape Heaths and probably the most attractive with its pink and white flowers that look like coconut ice. Each bloom is quite large with a long tube-like mouth. The linear leaves are fresh green and quite soft to the touch. Unlike *E. canaliculata*, this one is a hybrid. Its parentage is unknown.

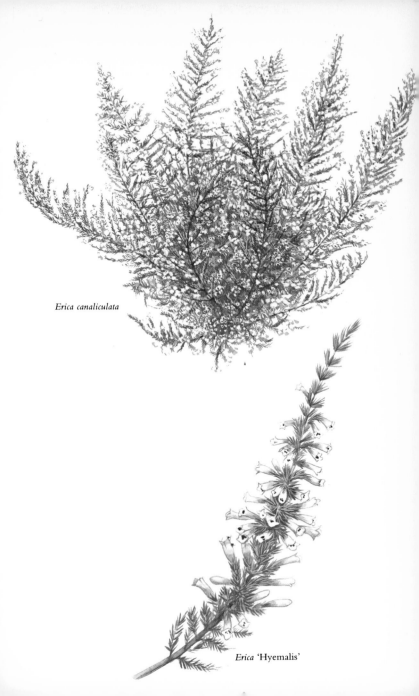

Erica canaliculata

Erica 'Hyemalis'

Rhododendron (roe-doe-*den*-dron) From the greek: *rhodon* – a rose, and *dendron* – a tree; the name was originally applied to the oleander (*Nerium*) and later transferred to this genus.

Cultivation The secret of success with the pot-grown azalea is to give it the two things it most needs: cool temperatures and plenty of water. Stand it in good light but not direct sunshine – this is another good plant for a north-facing window – and choose for it a room which is not very warm. In temps. over 15°C (60°F) it will rapidly fade. Every day the plant should be plunged in a bucket of rainwater for half an hour so that the pot is totally immersed. Remove and drain it afterwards and then return it to its spot in the room. Let the compost get even slightly dry or the air around the plant become too warm and the flower buds will turn brown and drop before they have a chance to open. When you buy a rhododendron in a pot, always choose one which has a few blooms open, but still plenty of buds unfurled. In this state the plant will stand the best chance of succeeding. Make sure that the compost is moist at the time of purchase. An occasional spray with tepid rainwater will keep the plant in good condition. Take off the blooms as they fade.

In spring, when there is no longer any danger of frost, plunge the plant to its pot rim in the garden and keep the compost moist through the summer – spraying the foliage with rainwater whenever you remember. Feed fortnightly and never allow it to dry out and it may produce buds the following autumn. Then bring the plant indoors to decorate your rooms. It is not fully hardy and if left in the garden through the winter it will probably perish. When the plant has outgrown its pot, repot it in spring into a lime-free peat-based compost before plunging it in the garden. Cuttings of firm young shoots taken 3 in long can be rooted in a heated propagator in midsummer.

THE SPECIES

Rhododendron simsii (syn. ***Azalea indica***) (China, Thailand, Burma, Taiwan) Indian Azalea, Florist's Azalea. Height 1½ ft or so, spread up to 3 ft. Evergreen or semi-evergreen dark and glossy leaves carried on a flat-topped bush show off well the spectacular double or single flowers of this plant. The blooms may be red, mauve, pink, orange or white and the coloured shades are sometimes contrastingly edged with white. They open in winter.

Rhododendron simsii

Primulaceae Primula Family

Annual and perennial herbs from temperate, alpine and one or two tropical areas of the world. There are nearly 30 genera. A few have been used in native medicine and for dyestuffs, most are grown for ornament.

Cyclamen (*sick*-la-mun; not *sike*-la-men) From the Greek: *kyklos* – circular; the flower stalks of many species twist into a helix and force their way towards the soil with the seeds.

   Cultivation Grow them in a cool room with a max. temp. of 15°C (60°F) in good light, such as on a north-facing windowsill. Water only when the compost feels dry or as soon as the leaves become a little limp. Where the plant has made a dense rosette, lift the pot up and weigh it in your hand. You should soon be able to judge whether or not it is dry by its relative lightness. If it is dry stand the pot in a bowl of water for half an hour. Feed fortnightly while the plant is growing and flowering. Cyclamen may be discarded after flowering but they can be kept growing by watering carefully all the year round. Alternatively let the compost slowly dry out after flowering, to dry off the corms, and then repot them in fresh standard soil-based compost. The top of the corm should protrude above the surface of the compost. Water carefully at first, then more freely as growth begins. Propagation is by seeds sown in late summer.

THE SPECIES

Cyclamen persicum **cultivars** (Originally Eastern Mediterranean including Greek Islands) Florist's Cyclamen, Sowbread. Height and spread 1 ft. The rounded leathery leaves are often handsomely patterned with dark green and grey; held on reddish stalks they should make a firm dome, over which the reflexed-petalled flowers hover on rosy stems. The blooms may be white, pink, salmon, mauve, crimson or magenta and are sometimes frilled at the edges. The original species was delicately scented but this fragrance has been lost in most of the modern hybrids. Easily killed by excessive heat and water.

Primula (*prim*-yew-la) From the Latin: *primus* – first; the name was originally given to the spring-flowering species.

   Cultivation Give these good indirect light and a temp. of 10–15°C (50–60°F). Water thoroughly when the surface of the compost feels dry, and feed fortnightly when the plants are in flower. Discard the plants after flowering and raise new plants from seed. However, *Primula vulgaris* can be planted in the garden and *P. obconica* can be repotted in a standard soil- or peat-based compost and grown on for another year.

THE SPECIES

Primula x *kewensis* (*P. floribunda* x *P. verticillata*). Height 9-12 in, spread 6 in. The bright yellow flowers are carried in tiers on upright stalks in winter and spring. The leaves are fresh green, often dusted with white farina.
Primula malacoides (Western China) Fairy Primrose. Height 1-1½ ft, spread 9 in. This plant has many tall stalks smothered in tiers of magenta, lilac, pink or white flowers which are sometimes exquisitely scented. The soft green leaves are toothed along the margins.

Cyclamen persicum cv.

Primula x *kewensis*

Primula malacoides

Primula (continued)

Primula obconica (Western China) German or Poison Primrose. Height and spread around 1 ft. Perhaps the most robust of the tender primulas, *P. obconica* makes a dense mound of whiskery-edged leaves with reddish stalks. The large flowers are carried above this mound and may be white, salmon pink, mauve, pale blue or magenta. Unlike other indoor primulas, this plant is reliably perennial and can even be propagated by division of the clump in spring. It will flower all the year round. In nurseries and garden centres the plants are usually of a mixed strain, though one variety, 'Apricot Brandy' (also known as 'Appleblossom') is now becoming very popular. Its flowers are a delicate shade of salmon pink. *P. obconica* in any of its varieties can cause some people to develop an uncomfortable rash. If this does occur the plant should be discarded (or passed on to someone less sensitive).

Primula sinensis (China) Chinese Primrose. Height 9 in, spread 6 in. A delicate plant with downy green leaves and pink, purplish or white flowers carried on stalks above them. Water this plant with especial care as soggy compost can result in rotting of the central crown. Seedsmen are now offering a wider colour range than before with brighter shades of red and orange. Some strains also have attractively fringed petals and these are worth seeking out.

Primula vulgaris (syn. *P. acaulis*) (Europe, Western Asia) Common or English Primrose. Height 4-9 in, spread 6-12 in. It is the hybrids of the common primrose that are offered as house plants. They make stocky pot plants with long, oval leaves that tend to curl gracefully downwards. The flowers may be anything from white through soft to brilliant yellow, orange, bright red, magenta, purple and true blue. Many blooms have a contrasting yellow 'eye'. The stalks may carry single flowers or a dense whorl of blooms at the top. It is especially important that this primula be kept cool and in good light. There are usually plenty of buds on each plant and if these are to open and the plant is not to become drawn and spindly then good growing conditions are essential. When the flowers eventually fade, or the plant looks rather tired, it can be planted out in the garden. Large plants can be divided into several smaller ones and planted 9 in apart.

Primula obconica

Primula sinensis

Primula vulgaris

Myrsinaceae

Tender trees and shrubs from tropical and temperate regions. There are 32 genera, and those which are cultivated are of ornamental rather than economic value, though one or two are still used in native medicine.

Ardisia (ar-*diss*-ee-a) From the Greek: *ardis* – a point; the anthers are pointed.

Cultivation Keep ardisia in a reasonably warm room for best results, though it will tolerate temps. as low as 7°C (45°F) in winter. A spot in good light will suit the plant best, though direct sunshine may scorch the leaves if the plant is kept in a south-facing window in summer. Water the compost thoroughly as soon as the surface begins to feel dry; never let it become parched. Although it is rather slow growing, the plant does benefit from a little cutting back in spring to keep it in trim. Remove the shoot tips as far back as is necessary to produce a balanced shape. When the flowers open the plant can be sprayed daily with tepid water to encourage fruit formation. Feed fortnightly from May to September, and repot only when pot bound in spring using a standard soil- or peat-based compost. Plants can be propagated from cuttings made from the sideshoots and rooted in a propagator (or a pot placed in a polythene bag) in spring or summer; seeds can be sown in the same conditions in spring.

THE SPECIES

Ardisia crispa (syn. ***A. crenulata***) (Malaysia) Spear Flower, Marlberry, Coral Berry. A quaint evergreen up to 3 ft tall and about 18 in across. The oval leaves have crimped edges and the white, fragrant flowers are followed by scarlet berries carried in clusters about halfway up the stem. The flowers open in summer and the berries follow, so the plant is quite colourful in winter.

Ardisia crispa

Pittosporaceae   Parchment-bark Family

Evergreen trees and shrubs native to the Old World Tropics and Australasia. There are 9 genera, mostly grown for ornament.

Pittosporum (pitt-*oss*-por-um) From the Greek: *pitta* – pitch, and *spora* – seed; the seeds are sticky.

Cultivation This needs plenty of light if it is to grow into a healthy bush. It will tolerate a wide range of temperatures but prefers not to be kept too hot and will survive well in unheated rooms. Little or no pruning is needed, but the bush can be trimmed to shape in spring. Water thoroughly in spring and summer whenever the compost feels slightly dry, but keep it a little drier in winter when growth is slower. Feed monthly in summer and stand outdoors. Repot in spring when necessary using a rich soil-based compost. Propagation is by stem cuttings taken with a heel and rooted in a propagator in midsummer or by sowing seeds.

THE SPECIES

Pittosporum tobira (China and Japan). Height 10 ft, spread 6 ft, though considerably less indoors. Stout woody stems support glossy convex evergreen leaves. Well-grown plants will produce scented creamy white flowers in dense clusters between spring and autumn.

Droseraceae   Sundew Family

A widely distributed group of carnivorous herbs which may be annual or perennial. They are found in Australasia, Europe, Asia, North America and the Tropics. The two most important genera of the four contained in this family are *Drosera* and *Dionaea*.

Dionaea (dy-oe-*nee*-a) From one of the Greek names for the goddess Venus.

Cultivation Maintain a min. temp. of 7°C (45°F) in winter, and keep the plant in very good light. It needs very high humidity to grow well and so must really be given a position in a terrarium, or its pot covered with a glass or plastic dome. The plant itself (often dormant when purchased) should be potted in almost pure sphagnum moss with just a little peat mixed into it. The moss should never be allowed to dry out, so stand the pot in a saucer which is always kept topped up with water. The plants can be divided and repotted in spring or summer when they are of a good size with more than one crown. Seeds can be sown and left uncovered in a pot of the recommended compost at the same time. Germinate in a warm propagator or under a plastic dome.

THE SPECIES

Dionaea muscipula (United States) Venus Fly Trap. Height and spread 3–4 in. The fresh green, winged stalks carry clam-like traps tinted pink on the inside and edged with spines. When an insect alights on the sensitive hairs on the trap's surface it snaps shut. The plants normally grow in soil that lacks nitrogen and this fly killing may supplement their diet. White flowers sometimes appear in summer.

Dionaea muscipula

Pittosporum tobira

Crassulaceae   Stonecrop Family

Shrubs and herbs of succulent habit native to tropical and temperate areas
of the world. There are over 30 genera, of which the most important to
gardeners are *Sedum, Sempervivum, Crassula, Echeveria, Kalanchoe, Rochea* and
Aichryson.

Aichryson (ay-*cry*-zon) The name originally given to the related *Aeonium
arboreum* by the Greek physician Dioscorides.

Cultivation Like most succulent plants, aichryson enjoys full sun, though
it will also put up with good indirect light. A min. winter temp. of around
7°C (45°F) will be adequate. Allow the compost to dry out between waterings
in summer; keep it dry right through winter. Feed monthly in summer.
Repot when necessary in spring using 3 parts standard soil-based compost
to 1 part sharp sand or grit. Individual stems may be cut off during spring
and summer and rooted in a sandy compost in warmth.

THE SPECIES

Aichryson x *domesticum* **'Variegatum'** Height and spread 6-12 in. A hybrid
of dubious origin but an attractive and easily-grown pot plant provided it
is not overwatered. The leaves are paddle shaped and carried on curved
stems. Occasionally clusters of bright yellow flowers appear in early summer.

Crassula (*crass*-yew-la) From the Latin: *crassus* – thick; an allusion to the
succulent leaves.

Cultivation Exactly the same as for *Aichryson*. Crassulas can be placed
outdoors during the summer where they may flower.

THE SPECIES

Crassula arborescens (syn. *C. cotyledon*) (South Africa) Jade Plant, Money
Tree. Height and spread up to 3 ft but usually less in the home. A shrubby
succulent with stout, much-branched stems that become quite woody with
age. The leaves are broadly oval, narrow at the base and tinged with crimson
around the tips. The overall appearance is greyish. In the wild, white flowers
appear in summer which turn pink with age, but this plant seldom blooms
in cultivation. *C. arborescens* is often confused with *C. portulacea* (syn. *C.
argentea*) whose leaves are darker green and shiny, and whose pink flowers
are more freely produced in cultivation.

Echeveria (eck-ev-*ee*-ree-a) Named after Athanasio Echeverria Godoy,
a botanical artist who travelled with Sessé on a Spanish-Government-spon-
sored expedition to New Spain (now known as Mexico) from 1787 to 1803.

Cultivation The same as for *Aichryson*, but propagation can be carried
out either by rooting individual leaf scales or by severing and rooting smaller
rosettes. The plants may be stood outdoors in summer.

THE SPECIES

Echeveria secunda **var.** *glauca* (syn. *E. glauca*) (Mexico) Blue Hen and
Chickens. Height 1 in, spread 4 in or more. The rosettes of glaucous-green
pointed leaves are very fleshy and the tips may be tinged with maroon.
Ruddy 1 ft long stems may emerge from between the leaves in summer
carrying red and yellow bell-shaped flowers.

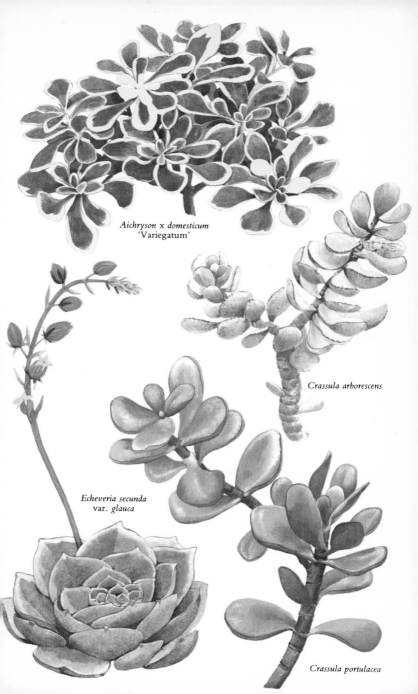

Aichryson x *domesticum*
'Variegatum'

Crassula arborescens

Echeveria secunda
var. *glauca*

Crassula portulacea

Kalanchoe (kal-an-*coe*-ee, and sometimes kal-*an*-coe) Derived from the Chinese name given to a single species of this genus.
    Cultivation Give these succulent plants a spot in full light – even bright sunshine – and maintain a min. temp. of 10°C (50°F) in winter if possible, though 7°C (45°F) will be tolerated. Water the compost freely in summer when it feels dry to the touch, but keep it on the dry side throughout the winter. Feed fortnightly in summer to keep the plants in good condition and encourage flowering of those species grown for their bright blooms. Repot in spring when necessary using 3 parts standard soil-based compost to 1 part sharp sand or grit. Cut back the dying stalks of flowering varieties to a point above a healthy leaf. Propagate by removing and rooting single fleshy leaves in a sandy compost, or by scattering plantlets (when these are produced) on the surface of moist compost. Seeds can be sown in spring.

THE SPECIES

Kalanchoe blossfeldiana (Malagasy) Christmas Kalanchoe. Height 6–12 in, spread 4–9 in. A well-branched plant with rich green glossy leaves that usually have a concave surface and a red edge. Masses of small red flowers are produced on stalks held above the leaves in spring, though by giving the plants 'short days' (that is, by blocking out the light for at least 12 hours a day) the plants can be forced into flower in winter, and indeed at any time of year. Strains are also available with yellow, orange or pink flowers.

Kalanchoe daigremontianum (syn. **Bryophyllum daigremontianum**) (Malagasy) Devil's Backbone, Good-Luck Plant, Mexican Hat. Height 2 ft or more, spread 9 in or more. The usually single stem is clothed in glaucous-green triangular leaves that are shiny above and mottled liver brown on the undersides. The margins of the leaves are toothed and carry a little plantlet at each point. Knock the leaf and the plantlets are dislodged and can be easily rooted. It is better to start with a new plant every year as older ones will become bare at the base. Yellow, green or pink flowers may be carried on pendent stems in winter.

Kalanchoe pinnata (syn. **Bryophyllum pinnatum**) (Tropics and sub-tropics). Height 3 ft or more, spread 1 ft. The lower leaves are simple while the upper ones are pinnate, having three or five leaflets with scalloped edges. Tiny plantlets are carried in the notches on the foliage. Inflated pale green flowers tinged with red are occasionally produced. Best treated like *K. daigremontianum*. (Not illustrated.)

Kalanchoe tomentosa (Malagasy) Panda Plant, Pussy Ears. Height up to 1½ ft, spread 1 ft. The oval, succulent leaves of this plant are coated with white hairs which turn deep chocolate brown around the tips. Flowers are seldom produced in cultivation. The plant resembles *Echeveria leucotricha*, but the leaves of the latter tend to be more pointed.

Kalanchoe tubiflora (syn. **Bryophyllum tubiflorum**) (Malagasy) Chandelier Plant. Height 3 ft or so, spread 1 ft. A single glaucous, blue-grey stem carries tubular leaves of a similar colour which are spotted with liver brown. Plantlets are carried at the leaf tips and these root as easily as those of *K. daigremontianum*. Pendulous orange and pink flowers may be produced in a cluster at the top of the stem in winter.

Kalanchoe tomentosa

Kalanchoe blossfeldiana

Kalanchoe tubiflora

Kalanchoe daigremontianum

Rochea (*roe*-she-a) Named after Daniel de la Roche (1743-1813), a physician native to Switzerland but resident in Paris. He contributed to *Pharmacopaea Genevensis* (1780).

Cultivation Rochea needs excellent light but will tolerate a winter temp. as low as 7°C (45°F) if it is kept almost bone dry at the roots. In summer it will cope with quite high temperatures provided that ventilation is good and it is watered thoroughly when the compost feels dry. Cut back straggly stems quite hard in late winter to keep the plant in good shape. Feed monthly in summer and repot in spring when necessary using 3 parts standard soil-based compost to 1 part sharp sand. Root 3-in long cuttings in sandy compost.

THE SPECIES

Rochea coccinea (syn. **Crassula coccinea**) (South Africa). Height 12 in, spread 9 in. The neat green succulent leaves are arranged symmetrically up the stem which is topped in summer with clusters of rich reddish-pink flowers. These are strongly scented. Future flowering is encouraged if the plants are stood outdoors in late summer to ripen their shoots and given one or two feeds of a liquid rose or tomato fertilizer.

Sedum (*see*-dum) From the Latin: *sedo* – to sit; some species grow 'sitting' on walls.

Cultivation Most sedums are easy plants to grow in the home, but one or two can be a little difficult. All need very good light. A winter temp. as low as 7°C (45°F) is tolerated by all species except *S. morganianum* which will prefer 13°C (55°F). The species which make very long or very tall growths can be cut back in late winter to encourage bushiness. Water freely in summer but keep the plants almost completely dry in winter. Feed monthly in summer and repot in spring if necessary using 3 parts standard soil-based compost to 1 part sharp sand. Give *S. morganianum* a very sandy compost (half standard soil-based compost, half sharp sand) and cover the surface of the compost with gravel. Alternatively, carefully tease the roots from the compost in which the plant is growing, wrap them in wads of moist sphagnum moss and attach these to a piece of cork bark (see *Platycerium*, page 38). The plant grows well supported like this. Immerse in water whenever the moss feels dry. Propagation of most sedums is by lightly bedding plump leaves into the surface of some sandy compost in a propagator or in a pot under a polythene bag. The less fleshy varieties can be propagated by stem cuttings rooted in a similar fashion. Clump-forming species can be divided.

THE SPECIES

Sedum lineare 'Variegatum' (Originally China and Japan) Carpet Sedum. An easy trailer with slender rosy stems that are clad in narrow pale green leaves edged with creamy white. These stems may attain a length of 1 ft or so, but the rarely-produced flowering stems are more upright, growing to 6 in and carrying clusters of yellow blooms. Suspend in pots or grow in troughs where the stems can dangle freely.

Sedum morganianum (Mexico) Burro's Tail, Donkey's Tail. The trailing stems are closely covered with glaucous-green leaves, so fat and packed together that each stem looks like a thick rope. The pinkish-purple flower clusters appear at the ends of the 1-2 ft stems in spring.

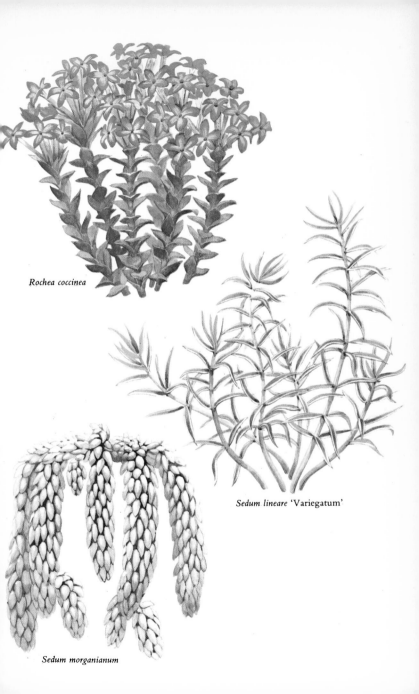

Rochea coccinea

Sedum lineare 'Variegatum'

Sedum morganianum

Sedum (continued)

Sedum x rubrotinctum, Christmas Cheer. Height and spread 1 ft. The upright stems carry close-packed, inflated, glossy green leaves that are flushed with rosy red. The flushing is more pronounced in bright light. The flowers are bright yellow and carried in clusters. A handsome and easily grown succulent that will propagate easily either from single plump leaves or from stem cuttings (the stems often produce thin aerial roots).

***Sedum sieboldii* 'Medio-variegatum'** (Japan) October Plant. Height 3-4 in, spread up to 1 ft or more. A pretty trailer with rounded grey-green leaves carried in threes. The centre of each leaf is broadly striped with cream and the rim is lined with crimson. Clusters of pink flowers may be carried in autumn. An excellent plant for troughs or suspended pots where its stems will cascade freely over the edge of the container.

Sempervivum (sem-per-*vy*-vum) From the Latin: *semper* – always, and *vivum* – living; the rosettes are evergreen.

Cultivation Although sempervivums are hardy in countries like Britain they are frequently grown as house plants. They demand a spot in full light – a sunny windowsill suits them well – and will tolerate a wide range of temperatures, so unheated or centrally-heated rooms will grow equally good plants. During the summer, give the compost a good soak whenever it feels dry (or, if the plant totally covers the surface of the compost, weigh the pot in your hand and water when it feels light). Through the winter keep the compost much drier at all times, giving water only when the leaves show signs of shrivelling. Feed monthly in summer. Repot when the existing container has become overcrowded with rosettes – spring is the best time to move the plants and they should be repotted in a basic soil-based compost plus half its bulk of sharp sand. The plants can be divided at the same time and single rosettes potted up individually. Should a plant flower, the rosette which carried the blooms will die off as the blooms fade, but others will spring up to replace it.

THE SPECIES

Sempervivum arachnoideum (Pyrenees to Carpathians) Cobweb Houseleek. Height 1 in, spread 1 ft or more. The small green rosettes, often flushed with maroon, are covered in a spider's web of silky white hairs. Masses of tiny rosettes can be grown in a small pot. The rosy crimson flowers are starry and carried on 4-in stalks in summer.

Sempervivum tectorum (syn. ***S. triste***) (Pyrenees to Balkan Peninsula) Common Houseleek, Roof Houseleek, Old Man and Woman. Height 1–2 in, spread 1 ft or more. There are many varieties with rosettes tinged with deep crimson, or coloured a bright, fresh green. The pinkish-red flowers are carried on stalks up to 1 ft long in summer. *Sempervivum tectorum* was originally planted in pads of clay soil on rooftops in the belief that it guarded against damage from lightning.

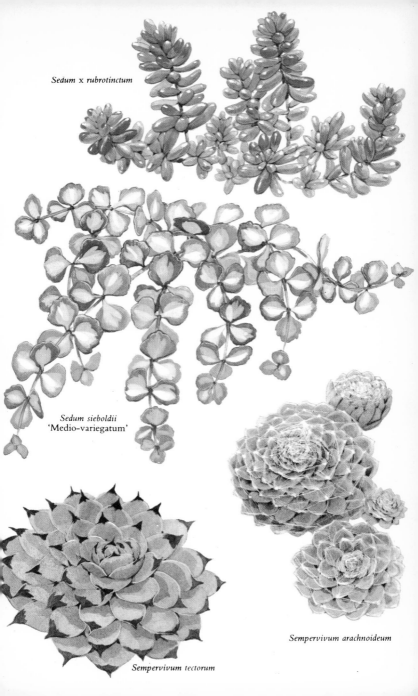

Sedum x *rubrotinctum*

Sedum sieboldii
'Medio-variegatum'

Sempervivum arachnoideum

Sempervivum tectorum

Saxifragaceae   Saxifrage Family

Shrubs, herbaceous perennials and a few annuals and trees of almost world-wide distribution, but mostly established in temperate regions. There are 80 genera including currants and gooseberries, and *Hydrangea*, *Escallonia*, *Saxifraga*, *Astilbe*, *Philadelphus*, *Deutzia* and *Tolmiea*.

Saxifraga (sax-ee-*frar*-ga) From the Latin: *saxum* – a rock, and *frango* – to break; the plant, reputedly, can break the rocks in which it grows.

Cultivation Most saxifrages are grown as hardy garden plants, but the slightly tender one grown as a house plant should be given a spot in good light in a room which is not too hot. It will tolerate a winter temp. of 7°C (45°F). Water thoroughly whenever the compost feels dry but keep it drier in the winter. Feed fortnightly in summer, and repot in spring and summer when necessary in a standard soil-based compost. Use a basic soil-based compost for the young plantlets which can be removed and potted up individually at any time as long as they are kept warm and moist for a week or two. Greenfly can be a problem. If the plantlet-bearing runners become brown and dry, then the plant is either being kept short of water, or the atmosphere is too dry, in which case spray daily with tepid water.

THE SPECIES

Saxifraga stolonifera (syn. ***S. sarmentosa***) (China and Japan) Mother of Thousands, Strawberry Geranium. Height 4 in, spread 9 in or more. The rounded leaves of this saxifrage are mauve on the undersides and dark green above with greyish veins. Tiny plantlets are produced on thin runners. The white flowers open in late summer and have two petals noticeably longer than the others. Best grown in a suspended pot or on a shelf so that the 2-ft runners can hang down.

***Saxifraga stolonifera* 'Tricolor'**. Similar to the true species but with leaves irregularly margined with white and flushed with pink.

Tolmiea (*tol*-me-a) Named after Dr William Fraser Tolmie (1830-1886), surgeon to the Hudson Bay Company who botanized in North America.

Cultivation Although hardy in British gardens, this plant can be grown indoors in cool rooms with an average summer temp. of 18°C (65°F). In winter tolmiea will survive in unheated rooms. Give it good light at all times. Water well during the growing season whenever the compost feels dry but keep it drier during the winter. Feed fortnightly in summer. Repot annually in spring using a standard soil- or peat-based compost, and divide mature plants at the same time to increase your stock. The young plantlets which grow from the older leaves can be removed complete with their parent leaf and bedded into a basic soil- or peat-based compost. Greenfly can be a problem.

THE SPECIES

Tolmiea menziesii (syn. ***Tiarella menziesii***) (North West America) Baby on its Mother's Knee, Pick-a-back Plant, Youth on Age. Height 6 in or more, spread 1 ft or more. The downy green sycamore-shaped leaves produce new young plants – a feature which accounts for the many common names. In spring greenish flowers may be produced. Stand outdoors in summer and any large specimens can be planted out permanently.

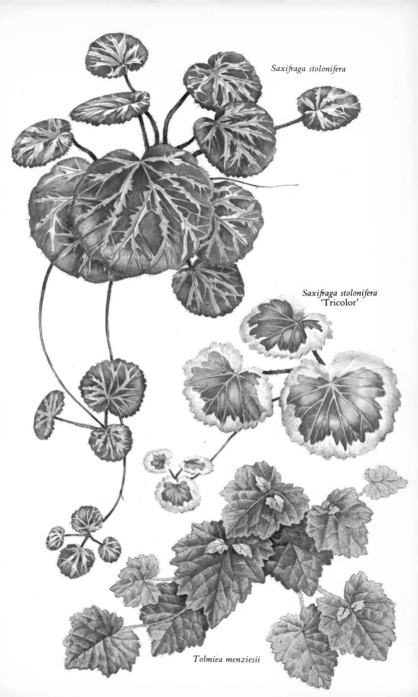

Saxifraga stolonifera

Saxifraga stolonifera
'Tricolor'

Tolmiea menziesii

Leguminosae Pea Family

A large and cosmopolitan family of trees, shrubs and herbs which include xerophytes and aquatics. There are 700 genera, many of which are of ornamental value. Others are of economic importance, producing soya, peanuts, beans and peas, as well as animal foodstuffs, timber, dyes and medicines.

Cytisus (sy-*tiss*-uss) From the Greek: *kytisos* – a name given originally to several woody members of the family.
   Cultivation The broom commonly sold as a house plant needs good indirect light and cool conditions with a winter min. temp. around 5°C (40°F). The flowers will fade very quickly if a room is too warm. Cut back sideshoots to within 2 in of the main stem after flowering to promote new growth. Stand the plant outdoors in summer in a sheltered spot. Water thoroughly whenever the compost shows signs of becoming dry in summer, but keep it just damp in winter. Stand the plant on a tray of moist gravel indoors, or spray it every day with tepid water. Repot every other year after flowering using a standard soil- or peat-based compost. Take cuttings of firm sideshoots with a short heel in summer (pages 20–1).

THE SPECIES

Cytisus x *spachianus* (*C. stenopetalus* x *C. canariensis*) (Also sold as *C. racemosus, C. canariensis* and *Genista fragrans*) (Tenerife) Broom, Florist's Genista. Height up to 16 ft, but usually around 2 ft in the home, with a spread of 2-3 ft. A tender evergreen with three-lobed leaves clothed on the undersides with silvery silky hairs. Long sprays of fragrant yellow pea-shaped flowers are produced in winter and spring.

Lythraceae Henna Family

A family comprising 22 genera of tropical and temperate trees, shrubs and herbs. Many are ornamental; others produce dyes including henna, derived from *Lawsonia inermis*.

Cuphea (*kew*-fee-a) From the Greek: *kyphos* – curved; an allusion to the shape of the seedpods.
   Cultivation Give cuphea good light and a min. winter temp. of 7°C (45°F). Water well as soon as the compost starts to feel dry in summer, but keep drier in winter. Feed fortnightly in summer. Repot in a standard soil-based compost in spring, cutting back the stems by half at the same time to encourage new growth and a bushy habit. Alternatively, sow seeds or root cuttings in spring.

THE SPECIES

Cuphea ignea (syn. *C. platycentra*) (Mexico) Cigar Flower, Cigar Plant. Height 1 ft, spread 9 in. Pointed green leaves and a profusion of red tubular flowers tipped with black and grey appear between spring and autumn.

Cytisus x *spachianus*

Cuphea ignea

Punicaceae Pomegranate Family

Shrubs and trees from South-east Europe, the Himalaya and Socotra. There is one genus, *Punica*, which is valued for its fruit.

Punica (*pew*-nick-a) Derived from the old Latin name of the plant.
   Cultivation This will survive in a winter temp. as low as 4°C (40°F) provided the light is good and the compost kept rather dry. In summer water more freely whenever the compost shows signs of drying out. Lightly pinch back any spindly shoots to encourage bushiness. Feed the plants fortnightly from spring until autumn. Repot in spring if the plant has outgrown its existing container using a standard soil-based compost. Propagate in spring by taking stem cuttings or sowing seeds.

THE SPECIES

Punica granatum **var. *nana*** (South-east Europe to Himalaya) Dwarf Pomegranate. Height 3 ft, spread 2 ft. A woody shrub with small oval leaves. The rosy red flowers are produced from late summer onwards and may give rise to small fruits. The leaves may fall in winter, but appear again the following spring. Large plants may be planted out in a sheltered sunny spot at the foot of a wall where they may survive mild winters.

Onagraceae Fuchsia Family

A cosmopolitan family of herbs, shrubs and aquatic plants in 18 genera; the best known ornamentals are *Clarkia, Oenothera* and *Fuchsia*.

Fuchsia (*few*-shee-a) Named in honour of Leonhart Fuchs, a 16th century German herbalist and physician.
   Cultivation Fuchsias need plenty of light to stop the shoots from becoming spindly, and a min. winter temp. of 7°C (45°F). Avoid high temperatures in summer. Pinch out the tips of growing stems to encourage bushiness. Young plants should be pinched back while they are still quite small. Feed them weekly from spring to autumn. Water freely in the growing season, but keep the compost drier in winter when the leaves will probably fall (unless the plant is kept warm). Cut the stems down to within 2 in of the compost in spring and repot into a standard soil-based compost to encourage new growth. Avoid moving plants once they are in flower or the blooms may drop. Stem cuttings can be rooted in spring and summer. Grow pendulous varieties in hanging baskets or pots. Vigorous cultivars can be grown as standards: pinch out all the sideshoots and support the single stem. When it reaches 18 in or more, pinch out the tip to encourage a bushy head. Whitefly and red spider mite are common pests.

THE SPECIES

Fuchsia **cultivars.** These vary greatly in height. Their flowers may be single coloured or combinations of white, pink, scarlet or purple. Some cultivars have variegated or colourfully-veined leaves. Choose plants from a nursery or garden centre while they are in flower, or make your selection from a catalogue. Those fuchsias offered as house or greenhouse plants are not reliably hardy outdoors in Britain.

Fuchsia cvs.

Punica granatum var. *nana*

Proteaceae   Protea Family

Trees and shrubs from South America, Asia, southern Africa and Australasia. There are over 60 genera, the most important being *Protea*, *Banksia*, *Embothrium*, *Grevillea* and *Telopea*. Most are of ornamental value, though some are of economic importance, yielding timber and edible seeds.

Grevillea (grev-*ill*-ee-a) Named after Charles Francis Greville (1749–1809) who was a founder of the Royal Horticultural Society.

Cultivation Choose a spot in excellent light where temperatures will not rise too high. It is well suited to a cool room with a winter min. of 7°C (45°F). Plants tend to grow with a single stem but if you would prefer a bushy specimen then pinch out the centre of the growing shoot so that branching is encouraged. Water well from late spring to autumn but allow the compost to remain a little drier in winter. Feed fortnightly in summer. Repot each spring using a standard soil-based compost. New plants can easily be raised from seeds sown in spring. Old plants are best discarded after 2 or 3 years. Older leaves should be pulled off when they turn brown, a condition which is sometimes brought about by dryness at the roots.

THE SPECIES

Grevillea robusta (Australia) Silk Oak, Silk Bark Oak. Height 160 ft, spread 20 ft or more, though considerably less in the home. An elegant and graceful plant with green ferny leaves that are bronze when they first emerge. The plant is hardy outdoors in summer and is sometimes used in bedding displays.

Celastraceae   Spindle Tree Family

Trees, shrubs and climbers native to tropical and some temperate areas. There are over 50 genera including *Euonymus* and *Celastrus*; many are ornamental, others are grown for timber, dye and oil, and a few are used in native medicine.

Euonymus (yew-*on*-ee-muss) From the Greek meaning 'of good name'.

Cultivation The species of euonymus grown as a pot plant is really quite hardy, so it will tolerate very cold rooms and prefers good light. In high temps. it will shed its leaves. Pinch out the shoot tips regularly to encourage bushiness, and spray the plant daily with tepid water in summer. Water freely in summer, more carefully in winter. Feed monthly from early summer to autumn. Repot in spring only when the plant has outgrown its existing container. Stem cuttings can be rooted in spring. Mature plants that have become too large for the home can be planted out in the garden in spring. Cut out any plain green shoots as soon as they are noticed. Red spider mite can be a problem.

THE SPECIES

Euonymus japonicus 'Aureus' (China, Japan) Japanese Spindle Tree. Height and spread 6 ft or more, rather less in the home. An evergreen shrub with dark green glossy leaves with a central butter-yellow blotch.

Grevillea robusta

Euonymus japonicus 'Aureus'

Euphorbiaceae Spurge Family

An enormous family of trees, shrubs and herbs native to tropical and temperate areas of the world. Of the 300 or so genera, many are valued as ornamentals while others are of great economic importance producing rubber, oils, dyes and timbers. Many species exude latex. To the house-plant grower the genera *Acalypha*, *Codiaeum* and *Euphorbia* are of prime importance.

Acalypha (a-*cal*-ee-fa) The ancient Greek name for the nettle was *akalephe*, but it was given to this genus by Linnaeus who considered its foliage to be nettle like.

Cultivation Acalyphas like hot and humid conditions. They cannot cope with temps. lower than 16°C (60°F) and prefer to be kept at around 21°C (70°F). For a bright or shady corner in a centrally-heated room they are ideal provided they can be given a little extra humidity, so stand them on a moist gravel tray. Cut the plants back by half in spring to encourage the production of new shoots and to keep them within bounds. Keep the compost just moist at all times, but not too soggy in winter. A daily spray over with tepid water will help to prevent leaf fall (a problem in a dry atmosphere) as well as keeping red spider mite at bay. Feed monthly in summer and repot in a rich soil- or peat-based compost in spring when necessary. Cuttings of young shoot tips can be rooted in a heated propagator in spring.

THE SPECIES

Acalypha hispida (New Guinea) Red-hot Cat's Tail, Chenille Plant. Height and spread up to 10 ft but can be kept to 3 ft by yearly pruning. The oval leaves are nothing remarkable, but when the 1-ft long red flowers appear the plant is transformed. The blooms last for many weeks and are produced over a long period. *A. hispida* likes light shade.

Acalypha wilkesiana (syn. *A. tricolor*) (Pacific Islands) Copperleaf. Height and spread 6 ft, but can be kept to 2-3 ft by yearly pruning. In contrast to *A. hispida*, this species is bright in leaf and dull in flower. The foliage is a patchwork quilt of red, orange, copper and bronze, while the fluffy flower tassels are short and dingy. Keep this species in good light or the leaves will lose a lot of their colouring. Best replaced annually from cuttings for it is rather more difficult to grow than *A. hispida*. Overwatering is a common cause of death, as is too dry an atmosphere.

Acalypha wilkesiana **'Godseffiana'** (syn. *A. godseffiana*) Height 1-3 ft, spread 1-2 ft. In this variety the leaves are green margined with cream. The flowers are insignificant.

Acalypha wilkesiana

Acalypha wilkesiana
'Godseffiana'

Acalypha hispida

Codiaeum (*coe*-dee-um is the commonest method of pronunciation, but coo-dee-*ay*-um is, strictly speaking, correct) Derived from *kodiho* – the name given to the plant by the natives of Ternate, an island in East Indonesia.

Cultivation This is one of the most popular house plants but one which often proves difficult to grow well. Give the plant what it needs and it will thrive. Maintain a min. temp. of 16°C (60°F) and try to prevent too much fluctuation. Position the plant in good but indirect light, not in shade. The compost should be kept just moist at all times, never keep it soggy but similarly never let it dry out completely, even in winter. Codiaeum needs a humid atmosphere if its lower leaves are to be prevented from falling off, so stand it on a tray of moist gravel or peat which is kept constantly damp. Warmth, humidity and good light are the basic needs, but take care too that the plant is not positioned in a draught or the leaves will fall. Feed codiaeum fortnightly from spring to autumn (starvation is yet another cause of failure) and repot in spring every other year in a standard soil- or peat-based compost. Stem cuttings can be rooted in a heated propagator in spring and summer. The plants get rather tall with age but pinching out the growing point will encourage sideshoots to form, so making a bushier specimen. Tall plants can be reduced in size by air layering in spring (see page 22).

THE SPECIES

***Codiaeum variegatum* cultivars** (syn. *C. variegatum pictum*) (Originally Pacific Islands and Malaysia) Croton, Joseph's Coat. Height 3 ft or more, spread 12-18 in. A beautiful house plant when it is in peak condition, the croton is available in many forms. The leaves may be narrow or broadly oval and are often indented like the body of a violin. Whatever their shape they are almost always spectacularly veined, blotched or margined with red, orange or yellow on top of their basic shiny green. The flowers are insignificant.

Codiaeum variegatum cvs.

Euphorbia (yew-*for*-bee-a) The name from the Greek meaning 'good fodder', but usually said to have been given to the plant by Dioscorides (first-century Greek physician and herbalist) in honour of Euphorbus, Physician to King Juba of Mauretania.

Cultivation See below, under species.

THE SPECIES

Euphorbia fulgens (syn. ***E. jacquinaeflora***) (Mexico) Scarlet Plume. height 2-3 ft, spread 2 ft. The long green leaves are carried thickly on the arching stems and are interlaced in autumn and winter with orange-red flowers. Try to avoid winter temps. below 16°C (60°F). In summer the plant can tolerate much higher temperatures provided that the atmosphere is kept humid by spraying the foliage daily with tepid water. Place in good light, even full sun. Cut back as required after flowering, keeping the milky sap away from your mouth and eyes. Water freely in summer, but keep it slightly drier and cooler in winter and spring immediately after flowering. Feed monthly in summer and repot when necessary in spring using a standard soil-based compost. Cuttings of young shoot tips can be rooted in spring.

Euphorbia milii **var. *splendens*** (syn. ***E. splendens***) (Malagasy) Crown of Thorns. Height 1 ft, spread 3 ft. The greyish, mainly horizontal branches are thickly set with very sharp thorns. There are relatively few leaves, but the plant is seldom out of flower. The rosy-red long-stemmed blooms shoot from the stem tips. An easy plant to cultivate, this needs a min. winter temp. of 7°C (45°F) and plenty of bright light. Water the compost thoroughly when it dries out in summer but keep it drier in winter, dampening the compost perhaps once a month. In spring cut out any unwanted stems (keep the sap away from your eyes and mouth) and repot when necessary in a standard soil-based compost mixed with a little sharp sand. Feed monthly in summer. Propagate from stem cuttings allowed to dry for a day and then rooted in heat in summer.

Euphorbia pulcherrima (syn. ***Poinsettia pulcherrima***) (Mexico) Poinsettia. Height 1-4 ft, spread 2-3 ft when treated with growth retardant but considerably larger in the wild. The true flowers are small and display yellow anthers when they are open. The coloured leaves (bracts) that surround them may be scarlet, pink or creamy white.

Maintain a min. winter temp. of around 13°C (55°F) or slightly higher if possible. Keep the plant in good light and out of draughts. Water thoroughly when the compost feels dry and then let it dry out on the surface before watering again. Spray the plant occasionally with tepid water or stand it on a tray of moist gravel. When the bracts fade in spring the plant can be cut back to within 4 in of the compost. Then repot in a standard soil- or peat-based compost. Feed fortnightly in summer. The bracts will not colour up unless they have long dark nights, unbroken by electric light. To achieve this, place the plant in a completely dark cupboard at 6 p.m. each evening, and remove it the following morning at 8 a.m. Do this *every night* for 8 weeks, starting in early autumn. The plant should be in full colour after about 12 weeks. It will also be noticeable that the poinsettia will grow taller as the effect of the growth retardant wears off. New plants can be propagated from stem cuttings taken in spring. Dip the bases of the cuttings in crushed charcoal to stop them bleeding (keep the sap away from your mouth and eyes).

Euphorbia pulcherrima

Euphorbia milii var.
splendens

Euphorbia fulgens

Vitaceae Grape Vine Family

Climbers and a few shrubs native to tropical and subtropical areas of the world but widely cultivated in warmer temperate areas. There are 12 genera, the most important of which are *Vitis, Parthenocissus* and *Cissus*. Many species are grown for their ornamental value, but the grape industry – producing wine and dried fruits such as currants, sultanas and raisins – is the family's greatest claim to fame.

Cissus (*siss*-uss) From the Greek: *kissos* – ivy; the plants have a climbing habit.

Cultivation The two species described here need rather different growing conditions. *Cissus antarctica* is relatively easy to grow in good but indirect light in a room which is cool. Maintain a min. winter temp. of 7°C (45°F) and train the stems around a support. Cut back the stems severely in spring if the plant becomes overgrown. In summer water well as soon as the surface of the compost feels dry, but in winter let it remain dry for longer. Feed fortnightly in spring and summer. Repot in spring when necessary using a standard soil- or peat-based compost. Spray occasionally with tepid water. Propagate from stem cuttings in spring or summer or sow seeds in spring. *Cissus discolor* is rather more difficult and prefers to grow in light shade with a min. temp. of around 16°C (60°F). Stand the plant on a tray of moist gravel or peat to increase humidity, and otherwise train and cultivate as *C. antarctica*.

THE SPECIES

Cissus antarctica (syn. *Vitis antarctica*) (Australia) Kangaroo Vine. Height 3 ft or more, spread 2 ft or more. A fine scrambling foliage plant with glossy green scalloped-edged leaves. A good choice for a cool room which is well lit.

Cissus discolor (Java, Kampuchea) Begonia Vine. Height to 6 ft, spread to 3 ft or so. The leaves are more heart shaped and succulent and marked with grey on their deep reddish green base colour. The undersides are maroon and the leaf stalks are red. Difficult to grow unless conditions are ideal.

Rhoicissus (roy-*siss*-uss) Presumably derived from the Latin: *rhoicus* – the name for the sumach (*Rhus*), and the Greek: *kissos* – the name for ivy; due to the plants supposed similarity to these genera.

Cultivation Cultivation is the same as for *Cissus antarctica*, but rhoicissus is more tolerant of shade and seems to survive (if not flourish) in dark corners. It is one of the most vigorous house plants available and can be trained on a light framework over walls and around arches.

THE SPECIES

Rhoicissus rhomboidea (South Africa) Grape Ivy, Natal Vine. Height and spread considerable. The dark green leaflets are carried in threes and are attractively scalloped. The rampant stems are rather wiry and coated in bronzy hairs. The young leaves as they unfurl are rich bronze and decorated with silky hairs.

Rhoicissus rhomboidea 'Ellen Danica' (syn. *R. ellendanica*) Similar in most respects to the species, but the leaves are quite deeply cut instead of scalloped giving a more decorative effect.

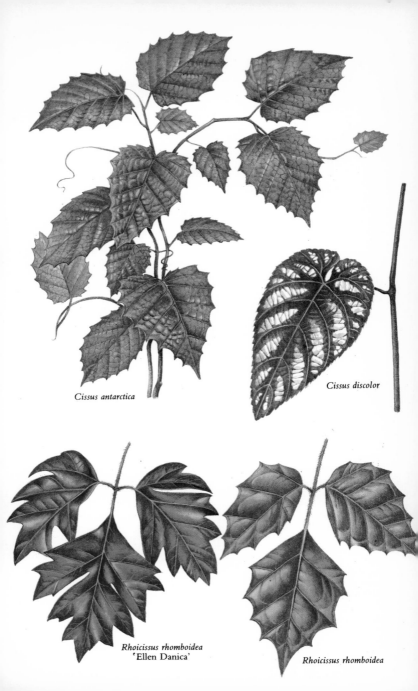

Cissus antarctica

Cissus discolor

Rhoicissus rhomboidea
'Ellen Danica'

Rhoicissus rhomboidea

Rutaceae Citrus Family

Shrubs and herbs from tropical and warm temperate areas of the world. There are around 150 genera, and while many of them are of ornamental value, those which produce oranges, lemons, limes and grapefruits are the most important economically. Others yield essential oils used in medicine and perfume manufacture.

x *Citrofortunella* (sit-ro-for-tew-*nell*-a) A bigeneric hybrid between *Citrus* and *Fortunella*.

Cultivation Try to ensure a min. winter temp. of 7°C (45°F) and keep the plant in good light (preferably direct sun) at all times. During the summer it will benefit from being stood outdoors in a sunny, sheltered spot for 2 or 3 months. Not only does this improve the plant but it also ripens the wood and encourages flowering and fruiting. Water the plant very freely in summer whenever the compost starts to feel dry on the surface. Never let it dry out completely or the leaves will fall. Be a little more circumspect in winter and keep the compost only just moist. Pinch out lengthy shoots to encourage bushiness, and cut away completely after flowering any stems which spoil the shape of the plant. Regular pruning is not necessary. Feed fortnightly from spring to autumn and bring the plant indoors before the first frosts. Repot in spring when necessary using standard soil-based compost. Propagate by seeds sown in a temp. of 18°C (65°F) in spring, and by rooting stem cuttings in a propagator in mid- to late summer. Scale insects can be a problem, as can little green caterpillars which eat the leaves.

THE SPECIES

x *Citrofortunella mitis* (syn. ***Citrus mitis, C. microcarpa***) (Philippines) Cal-amondin Orange. Height and spread 3 ft. A marvellous house plant if you can give it the light and airy position it likes. The leaves are evergreen and a good, fresh colour all the year round. The heavily scented white flowers open in summer and the oranges, 1 in across, grow slowly afterwards. The fruits are bitter but are fine when candied and they make excellent marmalade. Even small plants fruit well (unlike other citrus plants which usually take many years to come into bearing). Any pips that you find in the fruits are worth sowing; in spite of their hybrid origin they seem to come true.

Citrus (*sit*-russ) The Latin name for the citron (*Citrus medica*) but used by Linnaeus for the entire genus.

Cultivation Exactly the same as for x *Citrofortunella*.

THE SPECIES

Citrus sinensis (syn. ***C. aurantium sinense***) (Originally Vietnam and Southern China) Common or Sweet Orange. Height and spread 6 ft, considerably larger in the wild. The oval green leaves are produced on long stems equipped with vicious (and often partially hidden) thorns. It may be ten years before a plant sown from a pip comes into flower, and even then there is no guarantee that it will carry fruits of any consequence.

x *Citrofortunella mitis*

Citrus sinensis

Geraniaceae Geranium Family

A family of herbs and small shrubs native to temperate and subtropical areas. There are 11 genera, the most important to gardeners being *Geranium*, *Pelargonium* and *Erodium*.

Pelargonium (pel-a-*go*-nee-um) From the Greek: *pelargos* – a stork; the seed capsule is shaped like a stork's beak.

Cultivation Pelargoniums need full sunlight. Their leaves yellow and their stalks become spindly in the slightest shade. They like an airy room and will tolerate temperatures only slightly above freezing point provided they are not too wet around the roots. Water, throughout the year, when the compost in the pot is quite dry to the touch. Stand plants outdoors in summer and pinch out the shoot tips to encourage bushiness, otherwise they will grow tall and lanky. Remove all dead leaves and flower stalks. Feed monthly in spring and summer and repot in spring using a standard soil-based compost or a mixture of this and a peat-based compost. Propagate by taking 4-in long stem cuttings in spring and summer and rooting these around the edges of pots of sandy compost in a well-lit spot. The new F_1 hybrids can be propagated from seeds sown in a temperature of 21°C (70°F) in late winter, but these will not flower until late summer.

Old plants can be cut down in autumn and overwintered by keeping them cool and very dry at the roots. They are best discarded after one or two years and replaced with plants grown afresh from cuttings. The plants can spend their first year in 4½-in plastic pots, but larger specimens should be potted on into 6- to 10-in pots. Botrytis (blackleg) may affect cuttings (see page 24), and rust disease may attack mature plants (yellow blotches appear on the upper surface of the leaf beneath which are circles of brown spores). Destroy any affected plants. Any plants distorted and mottled with virus diseases should also be destroyed.

THE SPECIES

Most of the pelargoniums we grow are hybrids; the result of much cross-breeding. They are grouped as follows:

Regal pelargoniums These are larger than the zonals (page 126) but only flower in summer. The fresh green leaves are whiskered at the edges; the flowers are large and beautifully marked. Sometimes listed as varieties of *P. x domesticum*.

'Carisbrooke' – rose pink blotched with maroon.

'Grand Slam' – rose red and crimson.

Ivy-leaved pelargoniums Trailing and scrambling varieties, these are the best in hanging baskets and troughs. Some have interestingly marked leaves. Often described as varieties of *P. peltatum*.

'L'Elegante' – leaves edged with pinkish white; flowers white striped with deep pink.

'Mexicanerin' (also known as 'Mexicana' or 'Rouletta') – green leaves; spectacular flowers are white broadly edged cerise-red.

Regal Pelargonium

Ivy-leaved Pelargonium

Zonal pelargoniums These are the aromatic-leaved plants grown in greenhouses and for summer bedding in Britain. They are frequently referred to as 'geraniums' and are often described as cultivars or varieties of *P.* x *hortorum* or *P. zonale*. They are called zonal pelargoniums because of the distinct horseshoe marking, often coloured, on the leaves of many varieties. They are available with double or single flowers in shades of red, orange, magenta, pink, white and mauve.

Singles and doubles

'Kingswood' – single scarlet with white eye.

'New Life' (also known as 'Peppermint Stick') – single red and white striped and occasionally pink.

'Highfields Attracta' – pink and white double, like coconut ice.

'Orangesonne' – bright orange double.

Rosebud or Noisette Varieties

'Apple Blossom Rosebud' – fully double white blooms edged with pink.

'Red Rambler' – rich red fully double blooms.

The singles may bloom all the year round if supplied with a little water. The doubles are less likely to flower through the winter.

Coloured-leaved Varieties (The leaf colour may vary slightly depending on the light available and the age of the leaf.)

'Distinction' (also known as 'One in a Ring') – green leaves with dark purple ring; single rosy red flowers.

'Frank Headley' – green leaves edged with white; single pink flowers.

'Freak of Nature' – cream leaves edged with green; single vermilion flowers.

'Golden Crest' – acid yellow leaves; single pink flowers.

'Mrs Henry Cox' (or 'Mr Henry Cox') – green, cream, red and dark brown leaves; single salmon pink flowers.

'Ravensbeck' – red, yellow and green leaves; single pink flowers.

Scented-leaved pelargoniums Some of these are true species, others are hybrids. All have fragrant foliage which may also be pleasantly variegated. The flowers are relatively inconspicuous.

'Attar of Roses' – strong scent which is a combination of mint and roses.

'Graveolens' – downy green fingered leaves; lemon scent.

'Lady Plymouth' – fingered leaves variegated cream and pale green; peppermint scent.

'Apple Blossom Rosebud'

'Golden Crest'

Zonal Pelargoniums

'New Life'

'Ravensbeck'

'Mrs Henry Cox'

'Freak of Nature'

'Distinction'

'Lady Plymouth'

'Frank Headley'

Balsaminaceae Balsam Family

Annual or perennial herbs with rather succulent stems. The 4 genera are native to tropical and temperate areas of the world and are grown for their ornamental value. One or two species of *Impatiens* are rampant weeds.

Impatiens (im-*pat*-ee-ens) From the Latin word for impatient; the seeds explode from the capsules as soon as they are ripe.

Cultivation Impatiens is one of those plants which can grow exceptionally well if it has the conditions it likes, and rather badly if it is not suited. The fleshy stems and leaves are a clue to the fact that the plant needs a reasonably high min. winter temp. of around 13°C (55°F). During summer it will put up with higher temperatures but should never be kept too hot or it may dehydrate. It will also curl up if it is put in brilliant sunshine on a window-ledge which faces south. Place it instead on a windowsill which faces north, east, or west, so that it has good light but direct sunshine for only part of the day. Remove it from the windowsill on winter evenings or it may be frosted. In spring pinch out the shoot tips of young plants to encourage bushiness and, above all, be generous with food and water. The compost should never be allowed to dry out completely between waterings, even in winter (though at that time it will need far less). Feed the plant fortnightly from spring to autumn, and repot it every spring in a standard soil- or peat-based compost. Cut back the stems by half at this time if the plant is growing out of bounds.

Propagation is by means of seeds sown in gentle heat in spring, or by stem cuttings which root readily in a jam jar of water at any time of year. Pot up these cuttings when the roots are 2 in long, and keep them lightly shaded for a few days until they establish themselves. Greenfly and whitefly can be a problem.

THE SPECIES

Impatiens wallerana (also referred to as *I. sultanii* and *I. holstii*) (Mozambique, Tanzania) Balsam, Busy Lizzie, Patience Plant. Height and spread up to 2 ft. The leaves are a fresh green and the stems fleshy and almost transparent. The flowers may be red, orange, magenta, pink or white. Varieties are available with leaves that are variegated with white, and with flowers that are bicoloured. 'Harlequin' is a popular variety with orange and white blooms. The 'New Guinea Hybrids' have foliage with a central orange splash, and the variety usually sold as 'Petersiana' has deep maroon leaves prominently veined with red. The flowers are scarlet.

Impatiens wallerana

Araliaceae   Ivy Family

Trees, shrubs and herbs from tropical and temperate countries. There are over 50 genera, including *Hedera* (ivy), *Fatsia*, *Aralia* and *Dizygotheca*. *Panax quinquefolia* produces ginseng.

Cussonia (cuss-*oe*-nee-a) Named in honour of Peter Cusson (1727-1785) Professor of Botany at the University of Montpelier.

Cultivation Give cussonia good indirect light and a min. winter temp. no lower than 13°C (55°F). The brittle stem benefits from being supported. It enjoys warmth for most of the year and so is well suited to centrally-heated rooms. Water freely in summer whenever the surface of the compost feels dry, but keep the compost only just moist in winter. Feed fortnightly in summer and repot every spring in a standard soil-based compost. Propagate by sowing seeds. A daily spray over with tepid water will benefit the plants.

THE SPECIES

Cussonia spicata (South Africa) Cabbage Tree. Height up to 20 ft, spread 3 ft or more. A fast-growing evergreen plant usually with a single stem. The leaves are composed of between five and nine leaflets which are coarsely indented, glossy and very attractive. A good plant for a warm, well-lit house where there is plenty of vertical space to spare. The plant can be cut back to just above a leaf and encouraged to branch if it gets too tall.

Dizygotheca (dizz-ee-goth-*ee*-ca) From the Greek: *dis* – twice; *zygos* – a yoke, and *theke* – a case; the anthers are double-lobed.

Cultivation Grow dizygotheca in a warm room with a min. winter temp. of 16°C (60°F). It prefers light shade but will suffer in very dingy corners. Water carefully at all times. If the compost is kept too wet the plant will die; if it is kept too dry the leaves will shrivel and fall. Try to keep the compost slightly moist right through the spring and summer, and barely damp in winter. Stand the plant on a tray of damp peat or gravel to increase atmospheric humidity. Feed monthly with a weak solution of liquid fertilizer in summer, and repot in a peat-based compost every other spring. The plant can be cut back to just above one of its lower leaves in spring if it grows too big (the foliage of older plants is less attractive than that carried by young ones). Propagate by sowing seeds in a warm propagator in spring. Stem cuttings can also be rooted in a warm propagator in spring and summer but they are not easy to strike. Thickish sections of root can be removed from the plant in spring and bedded into the medium within the propagator where they may form shoots.

THE SPECIES

Dizygotheca elegantissima (syn. *Aralia elegantissima*) (New Hebrides) False, Finger or Spider Aralia. Height to 6 ft in the home, spread 2 ft or more. A delicate plant with a graceful habit. The fingered leaves are coarsely toothed and a dark bronze-green in colour. The central stem is slender at first, thickening with age. Flowers are seldom carried when the plant is container grown. If you have plenty of patience and the right conditions this plant will do well, but be prepared to accept that it may have a short life.

Cussonia spicata

Dizygotheca elegantissima

x *Fatshedera* (fats-*hed*-er-a, and sometimes fats-*hee*-der-a) This plant is a bigeneric hybrid; a cross between *Fatsia japonica* 'Moseri' and *Hedera helix* 'Hibernica'. It was raised in 1910 by the French nursery firm of Messrs Lizé Frères at Nantes.

Cultivation A cool and reasonably well lit room is really all that fatshedera needs. It can even be grown outdoors in most parts of Britain, so it is unlikely that temperatures within the house will fall low enough to do it any harm. However, the plant might suffer if the air becomes too hot, so try to keep it in a well-ventilated room where temps. are unlikely to rise above 24°C (75°F). Although the plant prefers to grow in good light (though not brilliant sunshine) it will put up with light shade, but growth will be slower and rather more spindly as a result. Train the stems upwards around a central bamboo cane or a moss-covered stick, or let them hang over the edge of the pot from a shelf or window-ledge. Pinch out the tips of the stems if you want to encourage them to branch from lower down. Water the plant whenever the compost feels dry, but allow rather longer between waterings in winter – fatshedera does not like a waterlogged compost. Repot each spring in a standard soil- or peat-based compost, and feed monthly in summer. Propagation is by cuttings.

THE SPECIES

x *Fatshedera lizei*, Ivy Tree, Fat-headed Lizzie. Height and spread up to 10 ft, though usually considerably smaller when grown as a house plant. The flexible stems sport hand-shaped leaves with five pointed lobes. They are evergreen, glossy and very attractive if kept clean. Starry pale green flowers are sometimes produced in autumn. Repeated pinching out of the growing points on young plants will produce bushy specimens that can more easily hold themselves upright.

x *Fatshedera lizei* **'Variegata'**. The variegated form has leaves irregularly margined with creamy white. It is slightly more difficult than the species and certainly needs quite bright light if its variegation is to be maintained.

Fatsia (*fat*-see-a) Latin version of *Fatsi* – a name supposedly given to this plant by the Japanese.

Cultivation This is exactly the same as that for *Fatshedera* except that the plant does not need staking. Cool conditions and good light are its prime requirements, but a little shade will be tolerated. It can be propagated from seed and cuttings in a warm propagator.

THE SPECIES

Fatsia japonica (syn. *Aralia japonica, A. sieboldii*) (Korea, Taiwan, Japan) False Castor|Oil|Palm, Figleaf|Palm, Japanese Aralia, Japanese Fatsia. Height and spread 3-5 ft in the home. A handsome plant with massive hand-shaped leaves that are glossy green. The plant is very shapely, forming a rounded bush, and it is very easy to care for provided that the leaves are not scorched by sun and that the compost is not kept too soggy or too dry. Mist the leaves with water occasionally in summer, and keep them free of dust. When too large for your rooms, the plant can be transferred to the garden. Even before it outgrows its space indoors it will appreciate a summer break in the open air.

Fatsia japonica **'Variegata'**. The leaves are marbled with creamy white and relatively bright conditions will produce the best variegations.

x *Fatshedera lizei*
'Variegata'

Fatsia japonica
'Variegata'

x *Fatshedera lizei*

Fatsia japonica

Hedera (*hed*-er-a) The Latin name for the plant which was sacred to Bacchus, the god of wine, and associated with his orgies.

Cultivation Ivies are easy to grow if they are kept cool, but in stuffy centrally-heated rooms they often suffer. Position them in good light (especially important for the variegated varieties) but out of direct sun and where temperatures do not rise above 18°C (65°F); unheated rooms are ideal. Ivies can be trained over a framework of canes or some trellis. The aerial roots may cling to the surface of walls, but this makes decorating rather difficult. Smaller-leaved ivies are often grown as trailing plants in suspended pots or on shelves. Trim off unwanted shoots at any time, and pinch out shoot tips in spring to encourage bushiness. Feed monthly in summer and repot in spring when necessary using a standard soil-based compost; ivies prefer their roots to be rather restricted. Water freely in summer when the compost feels dry. In winter water less, but never let it dry out completely or the leaves will shrivel and fall. Spray daily with water. Propagate from stem cuttings. The aerial roots make ivy cuttings easy to strike. In hot, dry rooms, red spider mite can be a serious pest, and greenfly may colonize the shoot tips.

THE SPECIES

Hedera canariensis **'Gloire de Marengo'** (syn. *H.c.* **'Variegata'**, *H.c.* **'Souvenir de Marengo'**) (Originally Africa, Canaries, Madeira, Azores) Algerian Ivy, Canary Island Ivy. Height and spread unpredictable. The large and only slightly-lobed leaves are dark green in the centre, becoming marbled with grey-green and turning white, even yellowish towards the margins. The youngest leaves bear the most striking variegations, and the young stems are a burgundy colour, as are the leaf stalks. Grow up a cane tripod.

Hedera helix (Europe, including Britain) Common or English Ivy. Height and spread unpredictable. There are many different foliage variations and variegations in the common ivy. These are some of the best and most popular varieties for indoor pot, trough and hanging basket culture:

'Chicago' – Leaves three lobed, fresh green; stems and leaves stalks pinkish.

'Cockle Shell' – Leaves a mixture of light and dark green, usually without lobes, and quite concave with a shell-like appearance; stems and leaf stalks purplish.

'Eva' – Leaves three lobed, grey-green in the centre, margined with creamy white; stems and leaf stalks tinged purple.

'Fluffy Ruffles' – Leaves fresh green and deeply frilled like rosettes; stems and leaf stalks brownish green.

'Glacier' – Leaves have three to five lobes, are dark green in centre merging to grey green and then white just around the margin; leaf stalks and stems purplish.

'Gold Child' – The five-lobed leaves are slightly dished, greyish-green in the centre, margined with yellow. The stems and stalks are purplish. Difficult to grow well.

'Little Diamond' – Leaves three lobed, arranged in a diamond shape with a dull green centre and a whitish margin; stems and leaf stalks green.

'Luzii' – Leaves with five lobes, fresh green, mottled and marbled with yellow green; leaf stalks and stems purplish brown.

'Parsley Crested' – Unlobed rich green leaves which are irregularly crimped and crested at the edges; leaf stalks and stems purplish.

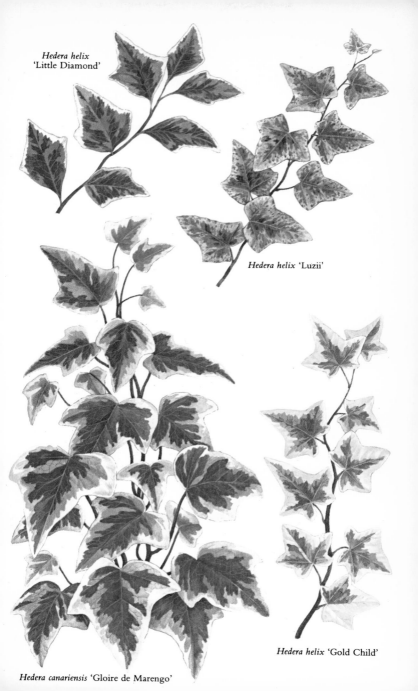

Hedera helix
'Little Diamond'

Hedera helix 'Luzii'

Hedera canariensis 'Gloire de Marengo'

Hedera helix 'Gold Child'

Polyscias (pol-*iss*-ee-ass) From the Greek: *polys* – many, and *skias* – canopy; the flowers are composed of many umbrella-like umbels.

Cultivation A good plant for centrally-heated rooms, polyscias likes a fairly constant temp. around 18°C (65°F), but will tolerate 13°C (55°F) in an emergency. Give it a spot in good but indirect light or slight shade. The best shaped plants are produced if the shoot tips are nipped out of young plants regularly to encourage branching lower down. Continue to pinch even when the plant is older. Water the compost when it begins to feel dry but allow longer between waterings in winter. Never let it dry out completely. Spray the leaves occasionally with tepid water. Feed once a month in summer. Repot every other year in spring using a rich soil- or peat-based compost in a clay plant pot – the weight of the latter will help to keep large plants upright. Propagate by stem cuttings rooted in a heated propagator, or by thick sections of root bedded into the propagating medium. Cuttings are not easy to strike, and root sections may be more successful.

THE SPECIES

Polyscias balfouriana (syn. ***Panax balfourii***) (New Caledonia) Balfour Aralia, Dinner Plate Aralia. Height 3 ft or more when grown in pots, spread 2 ft. An evergreen shrub with rounded, coarsely toothed leaflets held in threes. The leaves are darkish green margined with white.
***Polyscias balfouriana* 'Marginata'.** Even more attractive with its highly coloured leaves which show tinges of fresh green and cream. (Not illustrated.)
Polyscias fruticosa (India to Polynesia) Ming Aralia. Height 3-6 ft but usually less in the home, spread to 3 ft. The pinnate leaves are much finer than those of *P. balfouriana* and give a fern-like effect.

All three are still relatively uncommon as house plants but deserve a greater popularity.

Polyscias balfouriana

Polyscias fruticosa

Schefflera (*shef*-ler-a) Named after the 19th-century German botanist J. C. Scheffler of Danzig (now Gdańsk) in Poland.

Cultivation Splendidly statuesque plants for a room which is heated and likely to have a winter min. of 13–16°C (55–60°F). Scheffleras will just tolerate a slighty shaded position, but they do much better if given bright but indirect light and grow more quickly and evenly. Little pruning is necessary, for the plants form a single stem and look better when kept like that rather than pinched to encourage bushiness. However, if they look like hitting the ceiling their tops can be removed and some branching expected just below the cut – they seldom seem to shoot right from the base. Water thoroughly when the surface of the compost feels dry in summer, but keep it only just moist in winter and avoid waterlogging. A daily spray with tepid water will keep the plant fresh, and it looks its best if its leaves are cleaned regularly. Feed once a month in summer and repot every other year in spring using a rich soil- or peat-based compost. Propagate by sowing seeds in a heated propagator in spring, or by trying to root cuttings made from severed shoot tips. These will need a heated propagator and are not easy to strike.

THE SPECIES

Schefflera actinophylla (syn. **Brassaia actinophylla**) (Queensland) Australian or Queensland Umbrella Tree. Height up to 10 ft in pots, more in the wild, spread 3–5 ft. One of the most stately specimen pot plants. The glossy evergreen leaflets are oval and held in hand-shaped clusters of six or more, rather like a tropical horse chestnut. The long leaf stalks support the leaves in tiers. Position the plant where it will have room to spread itself both sideways and upwards without being knocked.

Schefflera arboricola (syn. **Heptapleurum arboricola**) (South East Asia) Green Rays, Heptapleurum, Parasol Plant, Umbrella Tree. Height 10 ft, spread 2 ft. Smaller in leaf and general stature than *S. actinophylla*, this is becoming a popular house plant due to its ease of cultivation and the fact that it takes up little lateral space. The 8 or more leaflets are curled under at the tips and are shiny when young but become dull with age. There is a variegated form which needs good light to retain its colouring; I have seen one specimen revert entirely to green.

Schefflera actinophylla

Schefflera arboricola
variegated form

Schefflera arboricola

Gentianaceae Gentian Family

A family of around 80 annual and perennial herbs and several shrubs of cosmopolitan distribution; the majority of which are ornamental.

Exacum (*ex*-a-cum) From the Latin: *ex* – out, and *ago* – to arrive; a reference to the plant's supposed expulsive properties.
    Cultivation Exacum likes to be kept relatively warm with a winter min. temp. of around 10-13°C (50-55°F). It needs bright sunshine and the compost should never be allowed to dry out completely. Feed fortnightly in summer. Although it is a perennial plant, exacum often dies back partially or wholly after flowering, and new plants are best raised from seeds sown in spring (though stem cuttings can be taken from the plant while it is in good health and rooted in a pot or propagator). If the plant is allowed to dry out too often then it may die prematurely. Pinch off the flowers as they fade.

THE SPECIES

Exacum affine (Socotra) Persian Violet. Height 9 in, spread 6 in. An upright little grower with glossy bright green leaves. The lilac-blue flowers centred with bright yellow stamens appear in summer and autumn. It grows best in a small pot, about 4 in. in diameter, or can be planted in mixed arrangements in troughs or bowls, in which case care will have to be taken when watering to prevent the compost from becoming waterlogged.

Apocynaceae Periwinkle Family

Tropical and temperate trees, shrubs and climbers in nearly 200 genera. *Allamanda*, *Vinca*, *Plumeria* and *Nerium* are the most widely known ornamentals. Some of the plants are highly poisonous.

Allamanda (al-a-*man*-da) Named after Dr Frederik Allamand of Leyden, Switzerland (1713–1787) who collected seeds of the plant in Surinam.
    Cultivation Allamanda is really happiest in a conservatory where it has room to explore with its questing stems. It likes good light but some shade from brilliant sunshine in summer. Maintain a winter temp. of 13°C (55°F). If given the opportunity it will take over your sunroom so prune the side branches back to two buds in late winter to keep it in trim. Water the compost in the soil bed or large pot whenever it starts to dry out, but keep it rather drier in winter. Repot (or re-tub) in a standard soil-based compost every other year in spring, and feed fortnightly in summer. Propagate by taking firm stem cuttings in spring and rooting these in a heated propagator. The plant can either be trained over a wire framework or a large tripod of canes if it grows in a pot. Plants that are established in soil borders in a sunroom or conservatory can be trained on wires attached to the walls and roof.

THE SPECIES

Allamanda cathartica (Brazil). Height and spread 10 ft. A vigorous but exceptionally beautiful climber with oval green leaves carried on long stems. The glorious bright butter-yellow flowers are produced in early summer over a period of many weeks. Each flower has five overlapping petals and a deep tube in the centre. The blooms of the cultivar 'Grandiflora' may be up to 4 in across, while those of the true species are rather smaller.

Exacum affine

Allamanda cathartica

Nerium (*nee*-ree-um) The ancient Greek name for the plant.

Cultivation Like many pot plants, neriums are not difficult provided they are given the conditions they like: plenty of light and an airy room which does not get colder than 7°C (45°F) in winter; do not keep them in shade. Eventually the plants will grow too large for most rooms, but they can be kept within bounds for a few years by cutting back some of the stems completely in autumn. Water freely in summer whenever the compost feels dry, but keep it rather drier in winter. The plant can be stood outdoors through the summer and will enjoy fortnightly liquid feeds. It can be repotted into a rich soil-based compost each spring until its container is too large to be accommodated in the house, when it is best transferred to a tub in a conservatory. Propagation is by means of stem cuttings which can be rooted in a propagator or pots of cutting compost kept at a temp. of 18-21°C (65-70°F). Mealy bug and scale insects can be a problem on neriums.

THE SPECIES

Nerium oleander cultivars (Mediterranean region) Oleander, Rose Bay. Height 20 ft, spread 10 ft but considerably less in the home. Oleanders have leathery willow-shaped leaves carried on stout stems. Between summer and autumn clusters of spectacular single or double flowers are produced which may be white, red, pink, mauve, cream or purple.

Plumeria (ploo-*meer*-ee-a) Named after Charles Plumier (1646-1704), a French monk who travelled widely in search of plants making descriptions and 'rather crude drawings . . . not of much interest artistically', *Wilfrid Blunt*. He is reputed to have revived the custom of naming plants after people.

Cultivation Plumeria likes warmth even in winter when it should be assured of a min. temp. around the 18°C (65°F) mark. Position the plant in good light but out of scorching sun and give it plenty of water as soon as the compost feels dry during the summer. Keep it just a little drier in winter. Cut back any over-long shoots as soon as the flowers have faded, and feed the plant fortnightly in summer. Spray the foliage with tepid water daily in warm weather. Repot in spring when necessary into a standard soil-based compost. Propagation is by means of firm young shoots rooted in a warm propagator (or a pot covered with polythene) in summer.

THE SPECIES

Plumeria rubra (Tropical America) Frangipani, West Indian Jasmine. Height 20 ft, spread 10 ft but less in the home. A vigorous shrub with very thick stems and large oval leaves. The large clusters of strongly fragrant flowers are produced from early to late summer and the blooms may be white, yellow, pink or mauve. The plant may be rather ugly when out of flower but transforms itself into a highly desirable pot plant when it blooms. Move it to a conservatory or greenhouse when it outgrows its space.

Nerium oleander cv.

Plumeria rubra

Asclepiadaceae   Wax Plant Family

Tropical and subtropical trees, shrubs, climbers and herbs. Most have milky sap. There are many genera, of which the most important are *Asclepias*, *Ceropegia*, *Hoya*, *Stapelia* and *Stephanotis*. The plants are mainly grown for ornament, though some have been used in native medicine.

Ceropegia (ser-o-*pee*-jee-a) From the Greek: *keros* – wax, and *pege* – a fountain. The waxy flowers are carried in arching clusters.

Cultivation Temps. as low as 4°C (40°F) are tolerated in winter, but 7-10°C (45-50°F) is a more desirable minimum. Good light is essential for healthy growth. Water well when the compost feels dry, then let it dry again before re-watering. Keep the compost on the dry side in winter. Feed once a month from spring to autumn. Repot in spring only when the plant is potbound using a basic soil-based compost. Cuttings of young shoots are easy to root in a propagator in spring and summer, or the stems can be layered into small pots of cutting compost and severed from the parent when they have rooted.

THE SPECIES

Ceropegia woodii (Natal) Hearts Entangled, Rosary Vine. The thread-like trailing stems may be 6 ft or more long and carry succulent heart-shaped leaves that are mauve on the undersides and marbled grey and green above. Spherical tubers appear on the stems at intervals like beads on a string, hence the common name of rosary vine. The plant does best when grown in a hanging basket or a suspended pot. It is curious rather than beautiful.

Hoya (*hoy*-a) Named after Thomas Hoy, head gardener to the Duke of Northumberland at Syon House, Middlesex in the 18th century.

Cultivation Prevent temps. falling below 13°C (55°F) in winter and position the plants where they will receive direct sunshine for at least part of the day; an east- or west-facing windowsill suits them well. *Hoya bella* prefers more indirect light. Water the compost thoroughly whenever the surface feels dry, but keep it drier in winter. The climbing species should be trained around wire hoops, over tripods of canes or up trelliswork. Old and overcrowding stems can be cut out in spring if the plant grows out of bounds. Spray daily with tepid water, except when the flowers are open. Feed fortnightly from spring to late summer, and in spring repot into a standard soil-based compost only when the plant is potbound. Cuttings of one-year-old shoots can be rooted in a heated propagator in spring, or younger shoots can be layered into pots of cutting compost during summer. Cut them from the parent plant and grow them on as soon as they are rooted. Mealy bug and scale insects are common pests of hoyas.

THE SPECIES

Hoya bella (India) Miniature Wax Plant. Height 1 ft, spread 2 ft. A neat, arching, semi-pendulous plant with light green, oval, waxy leaves that are thickly packed on the stems. The waxy star-shaped flowers are white and carried in rounded clusters intermittently from spring to autumn. This plant grows exceptionally well in a hanging basket.

Hoya bella

Ceropegia woodii

Hoya (continued)

Hoya carnosa (Australia) Wax Plant, Wax Flower. Height and spread unpredictable as the plant is a vigorous climber in the right situation. It grows best when planted in conservatory borders but often flowers better in pots. The vigorous questing stems are naked at first, the thick, waxy, glossy leaves appearing later. The clusters of pinkish-white, crimson-centred waxy flowers may be produced at any time between spring and autumn. Taste the sweet drops of nectar which appear at the centre of each flower. Do not cut off old flower stalks – they will produce more blooms. There is a variety *H.c.* 'Variegata' with leaves attractively splashed creamy white. It is slower growing and more reluctant to flower than the true species but is a handsome foliage plant.

Stephanotis (stef-a-*no*-tiss) From the Greek: *stephanos* – a crown, and *otis* – an ear; an allusion to the shape of the crown of stamens.

Cultivation Aim for a min. temp. of 13°C (55°F) and position the plant in good but indirect light where the temp. is unlikely to fluctuate wildly. Water thoroughly as soon as the compost feels dry, and spray with tepid water every few days. Keep the compost on the dry side in winter. Do not move the plant when it is in flower or the blooms may drop. Feed fortnightly from spring to late summer. Repot in spring every other year using a standard soil- or peat-based compost. Train the stems of the plant around a wire hoop or over trellis and cut out one or two old stems after flowering. Cuttings of firm shoot tips will root in a heated propagator in summer. Mealy bug and scale insects are frequently a problem.

THE SPECIES

Stephanotis floribunda (Malagasy) Clustered Wax Flower, Madagascar Jasmine, Madagascar Chaplet Flower. Height and spread variable but to around 10 ft. The dark green, glossy leaves are carried on twining stems and the clusters of white, waxy flowers are powerfully scented. They may be produced at any time from late spring to autumn.

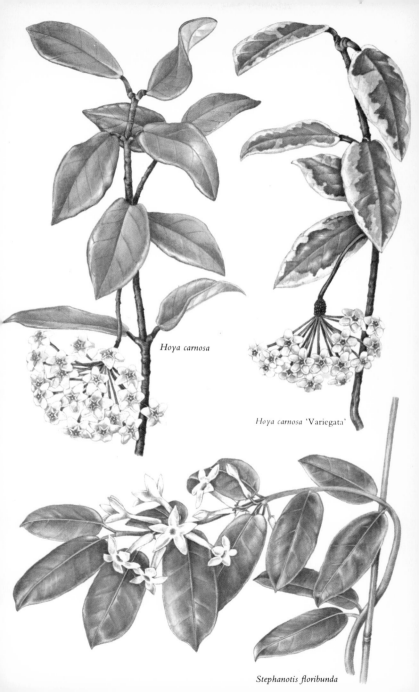

Hoya carnosa

Hoya carnosa 'Variegata'

Stephanotis floribunda

Oleaceae Olive Family

Trees and shrubs from tropical and temperate areas. There are almost 30 genera, many of which are ornamental, but one of which, the olive (*Olea europaea*), is of great economic importance. The most important genera for the gardener are *Fraxinus* (ash), *Syringa* (lilac), *Ligustrum* (privet) and *Jasminum* (jasmine).

Jasminum (jazz-*my*-num) Latinized form of the Persian name for these shrubs – *yasmin*.

Cultivation The jasmines are plants for cool, well-lit rooms; they resent being kept in dull corners and enjoy a little direct sunshine for at least part of the day. In winter they can tolerate a min. of 7°C (45°F), but will suffer if temps. rise above 24°C (75°F) for long in summer, so give them plenty of ventilation at that time. The long, wiry stems need some kind of support – train them round a wire hoop or on a small piece of trelliswork. Thin out the stems after flowering and cut back some of them by half so that the production of next year's flowering stems is encouraged. Try to keep the compost moist (but not waterlogged) at all times, and spray the foliage with tepid water every day if possible. The plants will enjoy being stood outdoors in summer when there is no danger of frost. Feed monthly in summer and autumn, and repot in a standard soil-based compost in spring when necessary. Propagate by rooting stem cuttings in a heated propagator in spring.

THE SPECIES

Jasminum mesnyi (syn. *J. primulinum*) (China) Japanese or Primrose Jasmine. Height 10 ft or more but usually much smaller in pots, spread dependent upon support system. An evergreen scrambler with trifoliate leaves. The bright primrose-yellow flowers are semi-double and appear in spring and summer. A fine plant for a sunroom or conservatory where it can be planted in a border and trained up a trellis-covered wall.

Jasminum polyanthum (China) White or Pink Jasmine. Height 20 ft but much less in containers, spread dependent on support system. The pinnate leaves are dark green and usually carried all the year round. The dainty white flowers are pink in bud and possess a delightful scent. The blooms appear in thick clusters in winter – a time of year at which they are greatly appreciated. Like *J. mesnyi* this species can be trained to cover a wall in a conservatory or sunroom.

Jasminum polyanthum

Jasminum mesnyi

Solanaceae Potato Family

A large family of shrubs, trees and herbs with fairly cosmopolitan distribution. There are 90 genera, a number of which are grown for food: *Lycopersicon esculentum* (tomato), *Solanum tuberosum* (potato), *Solanum melongena* (aubergine), and *Capsicum* species (peppers); others are used in medicine and *Nicotiana tabacum* yields tobacco. *Browallia*, *Brunfelsia*, *Cestrum*, *Schizanthus*, *Solanum* and *Streptosolen* are of ornamental importance.

Browallia (bro-*wal*-ee-a) Named in honour of the Swedish botanist Johan Browall (1707-1755), Bishop of Abo, who, in his *Examen epicriseos* defended the sexual system of classification devised by his fellow countryman Linnaeus.

Cultivation This will take as much light as you can give it and needs good ventilation with temp. around 16°C (60°F). The blooms will fade faster in higher temperatures, but the plant is susceptible to frost. The dwarf varieties bush out naturally on their own; taller varieties can be nipped back when they are young. Water well when the surface of the compost feels dry. Feed fortnightly in summer. The plant is best discarded after flowering and new stock raised from seeds. Greenfly and whitefly are sometimes a nuisance.

THE SPECIES

Browallia speciosa (Colombia) Bush Violet, Sapphire Flower. Height and spread 9 in-3 ft. The deeply veined, pointed green leaves set off the lavender-blue five-petalled flowers that can smother this plant at any time of year. Sow in autumn for spring flowers; in summer for winter flowers, and in early spring for summer flowers. The dwarf cultivars such as 'Blue Troll' grow to around 9 in and are best for windowsills. There are also white-flowered cultivars.

Brunfelsia (brun-*fel*-see-a) Named after Otto Brunfels (1489-1534), a German botanist and Carthusian monk whose *Herbarum Vivae Eicones* (1530), with woodcuts after drawings by Hans Weiditz, reached new standards in botanical illustration.

Cultivation Grow brunfelsia in bright light but not direct sun which will scorch the flowers. It likes warmth but not stuffiness and tolerates a winter temp. of 10°C (50°F). Avoid draughts and rapid temperature fluctuations. Lightly cut back any straggly stems in spring. Water thoroughly when the compost shows signs of drying out in summer, but keep it barely moist in winter. Stand the plant on a tray of moist gravel or peat to increase atmospheric humidity, or spray it over daily with tepid water. Repot when necessary in spring using a standard soil- or peat-based compost. Feed monthly from spring to autumn. Propagate by taking cuttings of firm young shoots in summer.

THE SPECIES

Brunfelsia pauciflora (syn. *B. calycina*) (Brazil, Peru) Yesterday, Today and Tomorrow, Winter to Summer. Height and spread up to 3 ft. The common names have arisen as a result of the fragrant flowers changing colour as they age. They open lavender purple and age through pale blue to white over three days or so. The leathery leaves are oval and light green in colour and are carried all the year round. A good conservatory or sunroom plant.

Browallia speciosa

Brunfelsia pauciflora

Capsicum (*cap*-see-cum) From the Greek: *kapto* – to bite; many peppers are hot to the tongue.

Cultivation Needs plenty of light and temps. between 10–16°C (50–60°F). Keep compost slightly moist at all times and spray foliage daily with tepid water. Feed fortnightly in summer. Discard this annual after fruiting. Propagate by seed. Plants will fruit best in 4-in pots. Greenfly and red spider mites can be a problem.

THE SPECIES

Capsicum annuum (Tropics) Cherry or Christmas Pepper. Height 1 ft, spread 6 in. The leaves are small and oval. White flowers with yellow centres appear in summer and are followed by pointed berries which range in colour from cream through pale yellow, purple and orange to fiery red.

Schizanthus (sky-*zan*-thuss) From the Greek, *schizo* – to divide, and *anthos* – a flower; the blooms are deeply cut.

Cultivation Stand the plants where there is plenty of light, but keep them cool. They will tolerate 7°C (45°F) but suffer in high temperatures. The stems need support. Feed monthly during the growing period and pick off faded flowers. Discard after flowering. Easy to grow from seeds sown in autumn for spring flowers or in spring for a summer display.

THE SPECIES

Schizanthus* x *wisetonensis (*S. pinnatus* x *S. retusus grahamii*) (Sometimes described as cultivars of *S. pinnatus*) (Originally from Chile) Butterfly Flower, Poor Man's Orchid. Height 9 in-3 ft. Light green feathery foliage and abundant flowers intricately marked in shades of pink, mauve, magenta, purple-red and white. Dwarf cultivars can be left unstaked and allowed to trail. Tall cultivars should be potted on before they become rootbound or they will bloom before they reach their maximum size.

Solanum (sol-*ay*-num) From the Latin name given to one species, later used by Linnaeus for the entire group.

Cultivation Bright light and cool temps. 13°C (55°F) are essential for good growth and fruit production. Spray daily with tepid water when the plant is in flower to ensure good fruiting. Keep the compost just moist. A monthly watering of 1 tsp Epsom salts dissolved in 1 pt water will prevent the leaves turning yellow. As the berries begin to shrivel, cut back the stems by half and use the tips as cuttings. Plants can also be raised from seed. Repot the old plant in a standard soil-based compost after pruning and stand outdoors in summer, feeding fortnightly. Bring indoors before the frosts. Whitefly is a problem.

THE SPECIES

Solanum capsicastrum (Brazil) Winter or False Jerusalem Cherry. Height 1-1½ ft, spread 1 ft. The dull green oval leaves set off the orange poisonous 'cherries' that appear in winter. White flowers precede the fruits.

Capsicum annuum

Solanum capsicastrum

Schizanthus x wisetonensis

Streptosolen (strep-toe-*so*-len) From the Greek: *streptos* – twisted, and *solen* – tube; the corolla tube of the flower is twisted.

Cultivation Streptosolen is a sun lover, so give it plenty of light at all times. It can tolerate being put outdoors in summer, and through the winter will survive indoors in a temp. as low as 4°C (40°F). It is a rather woody plant and can be grown either as a shrub, as a standard (on a long, clean stem) or as a climber up a supporting framework, when all its stems should be tied in. Pinch out the shoot tips to encourage bushiness and remove one or two old stems completely each winter. Water thoroughly when dry. Feed fortnightly in summer. Repot in a standard soil-based compost in spring when necessary, and take stem cuttings in spring to replace old plants. Root the shoots in a pot of cutting compost or a propagator. Whitefly may be a problem.

THE SPECIES

Streptosolen jamesonii (syn. ***Browallia jamesonii***) (Colombia) Firebush. Height 6 ft, spread 2 ft, though the plant can be kept much smaller by pruning. The woody stems are clad in oval light green leaves and in summer orange trumpet-shaped flowers are carried in profusion.

Verbenaceae Verbena Family

A vast family of trees, shrubs, herbs and climbers native mainly to tropical and subtropical areas, though a few are found in temperate zones. There are around 75 genera, among which are to be found *Tectona* (teak), *Verbena*, *Lantana*, *Vitex*, *Callicarpa*, *Clerodendrum* and *Caryopteris*. Many members of the family are ornamental, but a good proportion are of economic value, being grown for timber, fruit, gums, essential oils, tannins, medicines and teas.

Lantana (lan-*tar*-na) A name formerly applied to *Viburnum* but now used for this genus.

Cultivation Keep in a brightly lit spot and maintain a min. winter temp. of 7°C (45°F). Cut back the stems quite severely in spring to encourage a bushy habit, and pinch out the shoot tips as they extend until a good framework of stems has been formed. The plant can also be grown as a standard on a long, bare stem. Water freely when the compost feels dry, but keep it on the dry side in winter. Feed fortnightly in summer, and repot into a standard soil-based compost in spring when necessary (probably every year). Plants tend to become woody and straggly after 2 or 3 years so replace them by taking stem cuttings in spring and summer and rooting these in warmth. Seeds can also be sown in spring. Whitefly seem to prefer lantana to any other plant (except *Pachystachys*!).

THE SPECIES

Lantana camara (Tropical America) Jamaican Mountain Sage, Shrubby Verbena, Yellow Sage. Height 4 ft or more, spread 4 ft; it can be kept within bounds by pruning. Rough green leaves and prickly stems should not deter you from growing this shrubby plant which carries plenty of rounded flower clusters from summer to autumn. The flowers change from yellow to fiery red as they age. Other colour variations are sometimes noticed.

Streptosolen jamesonii

Lantana camara

Labiatae Mint Family

A vast cosmopolitan family of herbaceous plants and a few shrubs. There are around 200 genera. Some of economic value, producing essential oils and flavourings (e.g. lavender, mint, sage, thyme and marjoram). *Coleus* and *Plectranthus* are the most important genera to the house-plant grower.

Coleus (*coe*-lee-uss) From the Greek: *koleos* – a sheath; the stamens are united at the base and so sheathe the style.

Cultivation They need the brightest light possible to keep their leaf colour brilliant and their habit shapely. Temps. as low as 10°C (50°F) will be tolerated, but those a little higher are preferred. Pinch out the shoot tips regularly to encourage bushiness. Remove any flower spikes that form to encourage leaf production. If the plant looks a mess in winter, discard it, although it can be cut back within 3 in of the compost in spring. New shoots will grow and can be pinched at the tips to make a new framework of stems. Water the compost thoroughly whenever it feels dry on the surface in summer, but keep it drier in winter (watch for the plant to wilt a little before watering). Feed the plant fortnightly from spring to autumn, and repot older plants in a standard soil- or peat-based compost when they have been cut back in spring. Stem cuttings root easily in compost or water. Sow seed in spring.

THE SPECIES

Coleus blumei (Java) Flame Nettle, Painted Nettle, The Foliage Plant. Height and spread 1-2 ft. The brightest of foliage plants, the oval pointed leaves are toothed and may be mottled, margined and veined in bright green, acid yellow, fiery orange, fluorescent pink, crimson, caramel and plum purple. The blue flower spikes should be removed to encourage leaf production. Named cultivars are available in mixed colours and varying leaf shapes.

Glechoma (gleck-*oe*-ma) From the Greek name for a type of mint.

Cultivation This hardy ground-cover plant is useful for planting in hanging baskets indoors so long as it is kept cool and given plenty of light. Alternatively it will thrive for a year or so in a suspended pot until it runs out of root space and nourishment. Water the compost well in summer whenever it shows signs of drying out, but keep it rather drier in winter. Repot in spring when necessary using a peat-based compost for lightness, and feed monthly from spring to autumn. Cut out any old straggly growth. Cut back hard in spring to encourage the production of new stems. Propagate by stem cuttings and division of old plants in spring.

THE SPECIES

Glechoma hederacea **'Variegata'** (syn. *Nepeta hederacea* **'Variegata',** *N. glechoma* **'Variegata')** (Europe, Asia) Variegated Ground Ivy. A trailing plant which can cascade for 3 ft or more from a suspended container. The plentiful leaves are carried like little parasols on the thin stems; they are circular, with crimped edges margined with white on a background of greyish green. An easy fast-growing plant for a cool bright place such as a sunroom or conservatory.

Coleus blumei

Glechoma hederacea 'Variegata'

Plectranthus (pleck-*tran*-thuss) From the Greek: *plectron* – a spur, and *anthos* – a flower; the flowers are spurred.

Cultivation These are excellent plant for centrally-heated rooms, even where the light intensity is rather low. They need a winter min. of 10°C (50°F) and will thrive in either good indirect light or slight shade. Water thoroughly when the compost starts to feel dry in summer, but in winter let it remain on the dry side for rather longer as the plants do not like waterlogged compost. An occasional mist over with a hand spray will cheer the plants up, and they can be fed once a month from spring to autumn. Repot every spring and divide or take stem cuttings at the same time to make new plants. Root them in a polythene-covered pot or in a heated propagator. Plectranthus thrives equally well in a standard soil- or peat-based compost. Cut out unwanted stems at any time of year and pinch out shoot tips regularly to encourage bushiness. Wait until spring before severely cutting back older plants, although it is best to raise new plants from cuttings every two years.

THE SPECIES

Plectranthus australis (Australia) Swedish Ivy (the plant is popular in that country). Height 9 in but trailing for up to 2 ft or more. It is the glossy, bright green, serrated leaves of this plant that make it popular, allied to its trailing habit and facility for coping with shade. The purplish flowers rarely appear. Grow it in a trough, suspended pot or hanging basket to see it to best effect. It really is very easy to cultivate provided it is not overwatered.

Plectranthus coleoides 'Marginatus' (India) Candle Plant. Height and spread around 1 ft when grown in pots. A picturesque beauty that lacks the gloss of *P. australis* but which is lifted out of the ordinary by its clear white leaf margins. Purplish-white flowers are sometimes produced.

Plectranthus oertendahlii (South Africa) Brazilian Coleus. A trailer with stems that may be up to 2 ft long. The rounded green leaves have greenish-white veins and in summer slender spikes of hooded, pale lavender flowers are produced.

Plectranthus australis

Plectranthus coleoides
'Marginatus'

Plectranthus oertendahlii

Scrophulariaceae   Foxglove Family

An enormous family of herbs and shrubs of cosmopolitan distribution but concentrated in the northern temperate areas of the world. There are over 200 genera, and while most, such as *Antirrhinum, Calceolaria, Mimulus, Penstemon, Veronica, Hebe, Verbascum* and *Nemesia* are grown for garden ornament, the foxglove (*Digitalis*) is important in the production of the drugs digoxin and digitalin. One or two members of the family are noxious weeds and a few are parasitic.

Calceolaria (cal-see-oe-*lair*-ee-a) From the Latin: *calceolus* – a slipper; the flower is pouch- or slipper-shaped.

Cultivation Keep the calceolaria cool if you want it to last as long as possible. Temps. between 10 and 16°C (50 and 60°F) suit it best, and it will put up with a min. of 7°C (45°F). It needs bright light to flourish but may wilt in direct sunshine, so find it a spot in good but indirect light. Try to keep the compost just moist at all times. If it is either too wet or too dry the leaves may wilt and turn brown. Stand the plant on a tray of moist peat or gravel to maintain the atmospheric humidity it likes, and keep it out of draughts. Feed it fortnightly as soon as it comes into bud. The plant should be discarded once the flowers fade, but new plants can be raised from seed although this is not very easy as the seeds are very fine. Sow them in early summer on the surface of a potful of peat-based seed compost and do not cover them except with a sheet of glass covered with paper. Germinate them in a temp. of 16°C (60°F). Prick out the seedlings as soon as they are easy to handle and later pot them up individually in 3½-in pots of peat-based compost. In autumn move the plants to 5-in pots of the same mixture and grow them on to flower. Keep them outdoors during the summer in a warm, sheltered spot. Greenfly should be sprayed with a specific aphicide as soon as an attack is noticed.

THE SPECIES

Calceolaria **x** *herbeohybrida* (Hybrids of dubious origin numbering the Chilean species *C. crenatiflora* and *C. corymbosa* among their parents) Pouch Flower, Slipper Flower, Slipperwort. Height and spread 1 ft or slightly more. Most people either love or loathe calceolarias. The leaves are unremarkable enough, being broadly oval and dull green, but the flowers are in a class of their own. They are formed like pouches and may be red, yellow, white or orange with contrasting dark spotting. Keep the plant cool and it will remain spectacular for several weeks. The flowering time is spring or summer, depending on the date of seed sowing, but the earlier the plants flower the more they are appreciated. Seedsmen offer many different strains.

Calceolaria integrifolia (syn. *C. rugosa)* (Chile) Slipperwort. Height 1 to 1½ ft, spread 1 ft. Here the leaves are rather more wrinkled and downy. The flowers are smaller, like little golden bubbles, but carried in large clusters on long stalks in summer and autumn. This species may be propagated from cuttings taken in spring and summer and rooted in a warm propagator.

Calceolaria x *herbeohybrida*

Calceolaria integrifolia

Gesneriaceae African Violet Family

Tropical, and occasionally temperate, shrubs and herbs in over 220 genera. *Achimenes, Aeschynanthus, Columnea, Episcia, Hypocyrta, Saintpaulia, Sinningia, Smithiantha* and *Streptocarpus* are of value to pot plant growers.

Achimenes (ack-im-*ee*-neez) The name may be derived from *chemaino* – to dislike cold; the plants being natives of warm countries. They were also often started into growth by being plunged in hot water.

Cultivation These plants need a min. temp. of around 13°C (55°F). They enjoy good light but should not be placed in brilliant sunshine all day. Achimenes are grown from small rhizomes which are potted on their sides, ½-in deep, in peat-based compost in late winter and spring (5 to a 4-in pot). Start them into growth by keeping the compost slightly moist and a temp. of at least 16°C (60°F). Pinch out the tips of any shoots when they reach 3 in to encourage bushiness and flower production. Feed fortnightly as soon as flower buds are visible, stop feeding when flowers fade. Support taller varieties. After flowering, stop watering. When the compost is quite dry pull off the shrivelled growths. Take out the rhizomes, store them in dry sand or peat in a temp. of 13°C (55°F) until spring. Propagate also from stem or leaf cuttings, or sow seeds in spring.

THE SPECIES

Achimenes **cultivars** (syn. *A.* **x** *hybridus*) (Originally Mexico) Cupid's Bower, Hot Water Plant, Magic Flower. Height 9-12 in, spread 6-9 in. The trumpet flowers are in shades of pink, magenta, mauve, purple, yellow and white and may be produced in large numbers right through summer into autumn. The leaves are small, dark, pointed and softly hairy.

Aeschynanthus (ess-kin-*an*-thuss) From the Greek: *aischune* – shame, and *anthos* – flower; the scarlet blooms are apparently blushing!

Cultivation Like many gesneriads this one needs to be kept relatively warm all the year round with a min. temp. of 13°C (55°F) and a position in good indirect light. Keep the compost slightly moist throughout summer, but rather drier in winter. Cut out unwanted stems in spring. Spray the foliage daily with tepid water to give the plant some humidity. Feed monthly in spring and summer. Repot only when necessary in a peat-based compost. Take stem cuttings in late spring.

THE SPECIES

Both these species are grown to trail from a hanging basket, although they can be encouraged to scramble over a supporting framework.

Aeschynanthus radicans (syn. *A. lobbianus*) (Java) Lipstick Plant, Lipstick Vine. Trailing to 2 ft or so. The leaves are a greyish-green, rather fleshy, and carried opposite in pairs so that they look like wings. The scarlet blooms have a yellow throat and appear during early summer.

Aeschynanthus speciosus (syn. *A. splendens, Trichospermum splendens*) (Borneo, Malaya, Java). Trailing to 2 ft. The pale green leaves are often arranged in rosette-like clusters (whorls). The flowers are orange with a yellow throat and open in summer.

Achimenes cv.

Aeschynanthus speciosus

Aeschynanthus radicans

Columnea (col-*um*-nee-a) Named in honour of the Neopolitan Fabio Colonna (Latinized to Fabius Columna) (1567-1640). A lawyer by profession, Colonna was nevertheless a keen amateur botanist and in 1592 published *Phytobasanos* which illustrated and described the plants that Dioscorides and other classical authors had listed. He appears to have prepared the drawings and the finely crafted engravings himself, and a high degree of botanical accuracy is plainly evident.

Cultivation Fine for hanging basket plants in centrally-heated rooms, the columneas like a position in good but indirect light where temps. are unlikely to fall below 13°C (55°F). Water well in summer whenever the surface of the compost shows signs of drying out, but keep it only just damp in winter when growth is slower. Feed fortnightly in summer and replant during spring in a basket of fresh compost only when the plant is showing signs of starvation (probably every other year). Use a peat-based compost for lightness. Smaller plants can be grown in suspended pots. Spray the plants daily if possible to maintain a humid atmosphere. Shorten any straggling stems after flowering. Propagate by taking stem cuttings in spring and summer and rooting these in a heated propagator.

THE SPECIES

Columnea x *banksii* (*C. oerstediana* x *C. schiediana*). Goldfish Plant. Trailing to 2 ft or more. The leaves are oval and glossy and thickly packed on the stems. The hooded scarlet flowers spurt like fierce dragons from the stems in winter and spring. The easiest columnea to grow.

Columnea gloriosa (Costa Rica). Goldfish Plant. Trailing stems to 3 ft or more. Here the leaves are felted with brown hairs and are slightly smaller than those of *C.* x *banksii*. The hooded orange-red flowers are very wide mouthed, yellow in the throat and extremely spectacular. They open at any time between autumn and spring.

Columnea microphylla (Costa Rica) Goldfish Plant. Trailing to 2 ft or slightly more. The leaves are very small, only $\frac{1}{4}$ in or so long, and thickly set with dark hairs. The flowers are red with a yellow throat and are produced in spring.

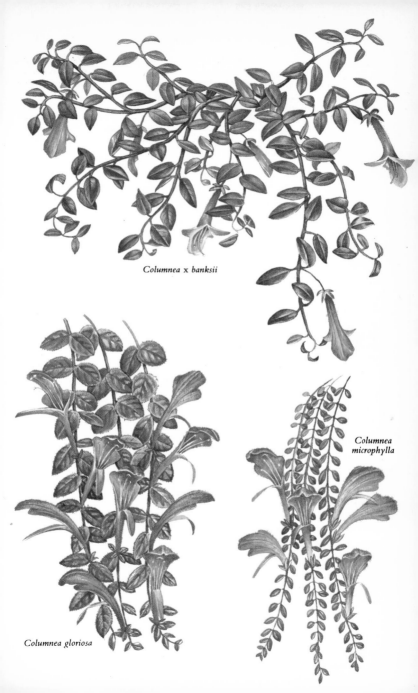

Columnea x banksii

Columnea microphylla

Columnea gloriosa

Episcia (ep-*isk*-ee-a) From the Greek: *episkios* – shady; the plants appreciate shade.

Cultivation Do not be misled by the origin of the name of this plant, for although it likes a little shade it will not thrive in a really dark corner where the light intensity is even lower than in a tropical jungle. It will enjoy a position in good light, but never in direct sunshine. Suitable for a centrally-heated room which never falls below 16°C (60°F). The atmosphere must be kept humid, so stand the pot on a tray or bowl of peat or gravel which can be kept constantly moist. Water the compost whenever it shows signs of drying out in summer – try to keep it slightly moist at all times. In winter the compost should be just damp. Feed monthly in summer and repot each spring in a peat-based compost. All episcias are excellent in group plantings or in troughs where they will appreciate the extra humidity generated by a large amount of compost. Propagate by removing the sections of plant carried on long stems or runners.

THE SPECIES

Episcia cupreata (Colombia) Flame Violet. Height to 6 in, spread 1 ft or more. The coarse-textured leaves are broadly oval and bronzy-green in colour, veined with grey green. The trumpet-shaped flowers are a rich red and produced quite freely in spring and summer and occasionally through the rest of the year. These plants look good in hanging baskets or suspended pots.

Episcia dianthiflora (Mexico) Lace Flower Vine. Height 4 in, spread 1 ft or more. Here the leaves are less spectacular, being mid-green in colour, covered with a soft down and carried on purple-tinged stalks. The fringed, white flowers will appear in succession during the summer. The habit of the plant makes it well suited to hanging basket and suspended pot culture as the plantlet-carrying runners will fall over the edge of the container.

Hypocyrta (hy-poe-*ser*-ta) From the Greek: *hypo* – under, and *kyrtos* – swelling; the lower side of the flower is swollen.

Cultivation Grow in bright but indirect light and a temp. that never falls below 16°C (60°F). Centrally-heated rooms are ideal provided that the plant can be given extra humidity in the form of a daily spray over with tepid water, or a tray of moist gravel or peat on which to stand. Long stems can be shortened after flowering. Try to keep the compost evenly moist throughout the summer but allow it to remain just a little on the dry side during the winter. Feed monthly in summer and repot in spring when necessary using a peat-based compost. Propagate by stem cuttings in spring and summer.

THE SPECIES

Hypocyrta glabra (South America) Clog Plant, Pouch Flower. Height and spread 1 ft or more. The oval, glossy and rather fleshy leaves of this plant are attractive enough on their own, but they also provide a foil to the inflated orange flowers that give the plant its common names. The blooms appear along the length of the stems in spring and summer and last for many weeks. Planted in a hanging basket or suspended pot the plant will look delightful as its stems arch downwards.

Episcia cupreata

Episcia dianthiflora

Hypocyrta glabra

Saintpaulia (sent-*por*-lee-a) Named after Baron Walter von Saint Paul-Illaire (1860-1910), a German who discovered the African violet (*Saintpaulia ionantha*) in East Africa in the late 19th century.

Cultivation The saintpaulia's ease of culture has made it a widely popular house plant. It likes no place better than a bright windowsill where it will receive direct sun for part of the day – in shade it will not do well but in constant burning sunshine it may scorch – so stand it on a windowsill which faces north, east or west. Bring the plant inside the curtains at night. It is surprisingly tolerant of fairly low temp. in emergencies, but should be assured of at least 16°C (60°F) for preference. It hates draughts. Remove any faded flowers and leaves as soon as they are noticed or rot may spread to healthy parts of the plant. Damaged leaves should be snapped or cut off as close to the main stem of the rosette as possible. Remove any additional rosettes which form or the symmetry of the plant will be spoiled.

The tightly packed leaves usually make watering from above rather difficult, so get used to weighing the plant in your hand and predicting by its lightness or heaviness if it needs watering. When it does it should be stood in a bowl of water for half an hour, by which time it will have taken up all it needs. It can then be returned to its windowsill, preferably standing on a saucer of moist gravel which will increase the humidity around it. Let the compost dry out a little between waterings. Feed fortnightly in spring and summer with diluted tomato fertilizer to encourage flowering. Use at the dilution recommended for tomatoes to force older plants into bloom, but make up a half strength solution for younger ones. Repot every other spring using a peat-based compost. Propagate from leaf cuttings with stalks, inserting these in a warm propagator or a pot kept in a warm place. The leaves can also be rooted in jam jars of water and potted up as soon as the roots are 1 in long. Replace older plants every few years when they show signs of being worn out. Seeds can be sown in warmth in spring.

THE SPECIES

Saintpaulia ionantha **cultivars** (Originally from the Tanzanian coast) African Violet, Usambara Violet. Height up to 4 in, spread to around 1 ft. The saintpaulia forms a neat and symmetrical rosette of rounded, hairy leaves which are held on fleshy stalks 4 in or so long. The flowers are produced mainly in the lighter months of the year but can open even in winter if the plant is stood under fluorescent lights. The blooms may be single or double and cultivars are available with white, pink, mauve, purple, magenta and violet blooms. Some of the cultivars have crimped-edged flowers, while on others the flowers may be star shaped, crested in the centre or bicoloured. The leaves vary too. Some are plain (in which case they are referred to as 'boys'), others have a pale mark where the leaf blade meets the stalk (girls), some are variegated with creamy white and others have turned up leaf edges and are known as 'spoons'. The variegated types tend to be rather more difficult to grow than the plain-leaved kinds. Saintpaulias are frequently planted in mixed bowl arrangements, but their performance is usually poor compared with pot-grown specimens which have a restricted root run and are therefore likely to flower better.

Saintpaulia cv.

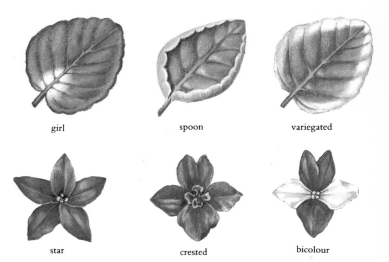

girl   spoon   variegated

star   crested   bicolour

Sinningia (sin-*in*-gee-a) Named after Wilhelm Sinning (1794-1874).

Cultivation Place in a bright draught-free spot out of direct sunlight with
a min. temp. of 16°C (60°F). Let the compost dry out on the surface between
watering, then give it a really good soak. Stand the plant on a tray of moist
gravel or peat to increase humidity and feed fortnightly while it is in bud or
flower. After the flowers have faded allow the compost to dry out between
waterings. When the leaves turn yellow, stop watering. Once the foliage has
died down remove the tuber and store it in dry peat or sand. In spring bed
it, right side up (look for the dormant buds and a slightly concave surface),
in a 5-in pot of moist peat-based compost. Water carefully at first, keeping
the plant warm, and it will soon come into growth. Propagate from young
shoot cuttings, each with a piece of tuber attached, in late spring or early
summer. Large tubers can be cut into sections (each with a bud), dusted with
a fungicide and potted up individually in a peat-based compost. Sow seeds
in a temp. of 21°C (70°F) in a peat-based seed compost.

THE SPECIES

Sinningia speciosa **cultivars** (syn. *Gloxinia speciosa*) (Originally from Brazil) Gloxinia. Height and spread up to 1 ft. Large downy leaves and huge
flared trumpet-like flowers of bright red, purple, pink, lavender or white;
the deeper shades often margined with white.

Smithiantha (smith-ee-*an*-tha) Named in honour of Matilda Smith
(1854-1926), a botanical artist at The Royal Botanic Gardens, Kew.

Cultivation As for *Achimenes* (see page 162). Start the rhizomes into
growth at a temp. of 18°C (65°F). Do not pinch out the shoot tips.

THE SPECIES

Smithiantha zebrina (syn. *Naegelia zebrina*) Gesneria, Temple Bells. Height
and spread up to 1½ ft. Downy green leaves with purplish veining grow
symmetrically from a fleshy stalk and are topped with scarlet tubular flowers
marked with yellow in their throats. They need warmth and humidity.

Streptocarpus (strep-toe-*car*-puss) From the Greek: *streptos* – twisted, and
karpos – a fruit; the seed capsules are twisted.

Cultivation Place in good light but not direct sunshine. It likes warmth
but will tolerate a min. temp. of 13°C (55°F). Stand the pot on a tray of
moist gravel to increase humidity around the plant. Water well as soon as
the compost feels dry, then allow it to dry out a little before watering again.
Feed fortnightly in summer and repot in a half pot filled with peat-based
compost each spring. Dust the brittle leaves carefully with a dry brush when
they are dirty. Propagate from leaf cuttings early in summer. Older plants
can be divided in spring and seeds sown in heat at the same time.

THE SPECIES

All are known as Cape Primroses and originate from Africa and Malagasy.
Steptocarpus **x** *hybridus* **'Constant Nymph'** (*S.* x *hybridus* 'Merton Blue'
x *S. johannis*). Height 1 ft, spread up to 1½ ft. The shapely lavender-blue
flowers are held on slender stems. The leaves are long, deeply veined and
rather brittle. Flowers will be produced at any time from spring to autumn.
Streptocarpus **x** *hybridus* **cultivars**. Height and spread 1 ft. The larger-
flowered hybrids are of mixed parentage. The flowers are extremely showy.
Most cultivars have girls' names.

Streptocarpus x *hybridus* cv.

Streptocarpus x *hybridus*
'Constant Nymph'

Sinningia cv.

Smithiantha
zebrina

Acanthaceae Acanthus Family

Tropical and temperate shrubs, trees, herbaceous plants, aquatics and climbers. There are over 200 genera. Most members of the family are of ornamental value, though a few are used medicinally.

Aphelandra (a-fel-*an*-dra) From the Greek: *apheles* – simple, and *aner* – male; an allusion to the one-celled anthers.
   Cultivation A min. temp. of 13°C (55°F) and a position in good but indirect light will help the plant to retain all its leaves. Spray the foliage daily with tepid water from spring to autumn and keep the compost moist at all times. Cut off all faded blooms just above a good pair of leaves. Repot in a standard soil-based compost each spring and propagate by taking stem cuttings in early summer (page 20).

THE SPECIES

Aphelandra squarrosa (Brazil) Zebra Plant. Height and spread 1 ft. A spectacular plant with lustrous dark green leaves contrastingly striped with creamy yellow around the veins. The flowers are carried in yellow cockades at the tips of the stems in summer. There are several cultivars, the most popular being 'Louisae', but 'Brockfeld' and 'Dania' are more recent introductions that are more compact and, in some situations, less temperamental.

Beloperone (bel-o-per-*o*-nee) From the Greek: *belos* – an arrow, and *perone* – a rivet; the anthers are joined to the filament like arrowheads.
   Cultivation Choose a position in good light. It will tolerate a temp. as low as 7°C (45°F). Keep the compost moist from spring to autumn and a little drier in winter. Feed fortnightly from spring to autumn. Cut back the stems to within 3 in of the compost in spring, and repot into a standard soil- or peat-based compost at the same time. Cuttings of shoot tips will root in a propagator in spring and summer (page 20).

THE SPECIES

Beloperone guttata (syn. *Drejerella guttata*) (Mexico) Shrimp Plant. Height and spread 2-3 ft. An arching bush with angular stems clad in soft green leaves. The white, maroon-spotted, hooded flowers are hidden among the dusky pink arching bracts that give the plant its common name. It is seldom out of flower.

Crossandra (cross-*an*-dra) From the Greek: *krossos* – a fringe, and *aner* – male; an allusion to the fringed anthers.
   Cultivation Place in indirect light with a min. winter temp. of 13°C (55°F). Keep compost moist at all times in summer but drier in winter, and stand the plant in a tray of moist peat or gravel. Feed fortnightly in summer; repot in a peat-based compost in spring when necessary, cutting back the stems by half at the same time. Take cuttings of firm young shoots in spring or sow seeds.

THE SPECIES

Crossandra infundibuliformis (syn. *C. undulifolia*) (India, Sri Lanka) Firecracker Flower. Height 1-3 ft, spread 1-1½ ft. Shiny, rich green leaves are topped with bunches of orange-yellow, fan-shaped flowers at any time between spring and autumn.

Crossandra
funbibuliformis

Beloperone
guttata

Aphelandra
squarrosa

Fittonia (fit-*oe*-nee-a) Named in honour of the sisters Sarah Mary and Elizabeth Fitton who together wrote *Conversations on Botany* (1817). The book had 21 hand-coloured plates by Sowerby and went into 7 editions up to 1831. Little information is available on the ladies, other than that Sarah Mary was born in Dublin and died in 1866. The two wrote another book, *Four Seasons*, which was published in 1865.

Cultivation Fittonias like to be kept warm, shaded from bright sun and provided with a humid atmosphere. Position them in a room where the min. temp. is unlikely to fall below 16°C (60°F), and give them a spot in light shade as sunlight will scorch their leaves. Dry air is fatal, so bed the pot into a bowl or tray of moist peat or gravel which is never allowed to dry out. Alternatively, plant the fittonia in a bottle garden or terrarium. Try to keep the compost moist right through the summer, never letting it dry out completely, but never allowing it to become waterlogged. Keep it barely moist in winter when too much moisture will cause stem rot. Feed monthly in summer and repot each spring in a peat-based compost. The plant will grow well in a half pot. Separate and pot up any rooted offshoots in spring, or take stem cuttings at the same time and root them in a heated propagator. Cut off any wayward shoots in spring to tidy up the plant and use these as propagating material. At all stages of its life fittonia should be kept out of draughts and away from cold corners.

THE SPECIES

Fittonia verschaffeltii (Peru) Mosaic Leaf, Painted Net Leaf. Height 6 in, spread 1 ft. The broadly oval bronzy-green leaves are veined in rich carmine pink and achieve an effect seen in few house plants. Occasionally short spikes of yellow flowers may be produced. A plant with a semi-trailing habit which adds sparkle to any terrarium.

Fittonia verschaffeltii* var. *argyroneura (syn. *F. argyroneura*) (Peru) Nerve Plant, Silver Net Leaf. Height 6 in, spread 1 ft. Here the deep green leaves are heavily veined with creamy white, and the effect, while being less colourful, is still extremely attractive.

***Fittonia verschaffeltii* var. *argyroneura* 'Nana'** (syn. *F. a.* 'Nana') Nerve Plant, Snake Skin Plant. Height 1 in, spread 6 in or more. Here is the fittonia for the gardener who cannot provide a constantly humid atmosphere. It will tolerate drier air and is generally easier to manage than its relations. The leaves are much smaller – less than 1 in long – while those of the other two are up to 3 in long. A superb plant for group arrangements or for bottle garden planting.

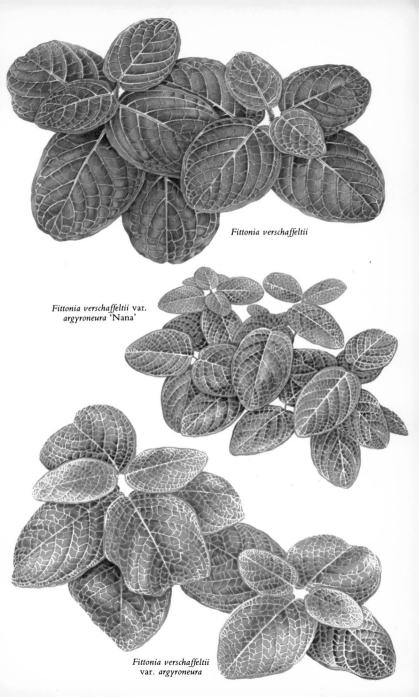

Fittonia verschaffeltii

Fittonia verschaffeltii var.
argyroneura 'Nana'

Fittonia verschaffeltii
var. *argyroneura*

Hypoestes (hy-poe-*ess*-teez) From the Greek: *hypo* – under, and *estia* – house; the flowers are partially housed in bracts.

   Cultivation An easy plant for a sunny windowsill where the temp. is unlikely to fall below 13° (55°F). Good light brings out the colour in the plant and prevents it getting leggy, but regular pinching out of the shoot tips is advisable. Water freely in summer when the surface of the compost dries out, but keep the compost drier in winter. Spray over occasionally with tepid water. Feed monthly in summer. Plants are best treated as annuals and raised from seed each spring. Cuttings can also be rooted in a propagator in spring and summer (page 20).

THE SPECIES

Hypoestes phyllostachya (Often sold as **H. sanguinolenta**) (Malagasy) Freckle Face, Polka-dot Plant. Height and spread 1 ft – more if the tips are not pinched out regularly. Although it carries purplish-white flowers occasionally in summer, it is the dark green, pink-spotted leaves which make this plant so popular. In poor light they will lose much of their brightness.

Justicia (juss-*tiss*-ee-a) Named after the Scottish gardener James Justice (1698-1763) who wrote *The Scots Gardiners Director* (1754) and who introduced the pineapple to Scotland.

   Cultivation Justicia needs a min. temp. of 13°C (55°F) or a little higher if possible. Keep the plant in good but indirect light and water well when the compost is dry in summer, rather more sparingly in winter. Spray daily with tepid water in summer. Cut back each stem by half to just above a leaf when the flowers fade. Feed fortnightly in summer and repot in spring in a soil- or peat-based compost. Discard old plants after 2 or 3 years and replace with young ones raised from stem cuttings rooted in a heated propagator in spring. Pinch out the shoot tips in the early stages to encourage a bushy habit. Whitefly can be a serious problem.

THE SPECIES

Justicia carnea (syn. **Jacobinia carnea**) (Brazil) Brazilian Plume, King's Crown. Height 2-3 ft or more, spread around 2 ft. Although the summer flower display may be brief, the rich pink plume-like blooms that rise from the tops of the stems are well worth waiting for. The rather ordinary green foliage shows off the blooms to good effect. Keep the plant in a sunroom or conservatory when not in flower.

Pachystachys (pack-ee-*stack*-iss) From the Greek: *pachys* – thick, and *stachys* – spike; the flower spike is very densely packed with bracts and flowers.

   Cultivation As for *Justicia*, but cut the plant back in spring rather than immediately after its long flowering season in autumn. Whitefly is a real problem.

THE SPECIES

Pachystachys lutea (Peru) Lollipop Plant. Height 1-1½ ft, spread 1 ft. Oval, prominently veined leaves form a dense green dome over which the erect flower spikes tower from spring to autumn. The flowers themselves are like white dragon's heads, but it is the bright yellow bracts from which they spurt that provide the lasting spectacle. A fine and shapely plant for a bright spot.

Hypoestes phyllostachya

Justicia carnea

Pachystachys lutea

Campanulaceae Bellflower Family

A family of herbs and a few shrubs native mainly to north temperate areas of the world. There are 35 genera which are almost entirely grown for ornament; the most important to gardeners are *Campanula, Phyteuma, Jasione, Codonopsis* and *Edraianthus*. Nearly all are hardy garden plants in Britain.

Campanula (cam-*pan*-yew-la) From the Latin: *campana* – a bell; an allusion to the shape of the flower.

Cultivation There is just one campanula which is grown with any frequency as a house plant. It is not reliably hardy outdoors but will often come through relatively mild winters in Britain. Stand the plant on a bright windowsill where it has the maximum light possible. It will tolerate temperatures as low as they are likely to fall, but excessive heat will cause the flowers to fade quickly and the foliage to become unduly sappy and prone to fungal attack. Cut out at any time shoots which are straggly and unsightly, and shorten the plant by cutting off all its stems at compost level in winter. This will encourage the formation of fresh young growth which will flower in summer. Water freely in summer when the compost is dry, but rather more sparingly in winter. Divide plants in spring immediately after cutting back and pot them up in a basic soil- or peat-based compost. Feed fortnightly in summer. Cuttings can be rooted in pots of compost on a widowsill as well as in a propagator in spring. Greenfly is the only pest likely to be troublesome.

THE SPECIES

Campanula isophylla (Italy) Italian Bellflower, Star of Bethlehem. A trailing plant growing to $1\frac{1}{2}$ ft or so. The grey-green, downy leaves set off to perfection the starry blue flowers that stud the plant right through summer and into autumn. A real beauty for a suspended pot or hanging basket.

Campanula isophylla **'Alba'** Star of Bethlehem. The white-flowered form has identical measurements to its blue-flowered parent, but the foliage is fresh green and lacks the greyish down. The blooms are pure white. The easiest of the three to grow.

Campanula isophylla **'Mayi'**. Here the downy leaves are variegated with whitish cream and the flowers are mauve-blue. Perhaps the most difficult of the three.

Campanula isophylla
'Alba'

Campanula isophylla

Campanula isophylla
'Mayi'

Rubiaceae   Coffee Family

A massive family of trees, shrubs and herbs native mainly to tropical and subtropical areas of the world. There are 500 genera, many of which are of economic value producing coffee (*Coffea*), quinine (*Cinchona*), ipecacuanha (*Cephaelis*) and various other drugs and dyes.

Coffea (*coff*-ee-a) Derived from the Arabic name for the drink – *kahwah*.

Cultivation Coffee will tolerate a winter temp. as low as 10°C (50°F) and likes a spot in good but indirect light; constant bright sunshine will scorch the leaves. Pinch out the shoot tips regularly to encourage a bushy habit (old stems can be cut back in spring), and feed the plant monthly in summer. Water freely when the surface of the compost feels dry, never let it dry out completely but keep it barely damp in winter. Keep away from radiators and out of draughts, both of which will cause leaf browning. Repot in a standard soil- or peat-based compost every other spring. Propagate by rooting stem cuttings in a heated propagator in spring. Sow seeds in a temp. of 21°C (70°F) in spring. Buy seeds specially for the purpose, do not try to germinate roasted coffee beans. Mealy bug and scale insects may be a problem.

THE SPECIES

Coffea arabica (Originally Ethiopia) Arabian Coffee. Height and spread 4 ft or more. The dark green oval leaves are evergreen and prominently veined, and it is for these that the plant should be grown rather than for the white flowers or red 'cherries' that yield the beans (two to a berry). In the home the flowers and fruits are seldom produced, though they may appear if the plant is grown in a sunroom or conservatory.

Gardenia (gar-*dee*-nee-a) Named after the Scot, Alexander Garden (1730-1791), a physician and correspondent of Linnaeus.

Cultivation Give this pride of place in a room where the temp. never falls below 13°C (55°F). It needs bright light but definitely not scorching sun. Spray daily with tepid water to produce slightly humid conditions. Never allow the compost to dry out completely but keep it slightly moist at all times and barely damp in winter; use rainwater if possible as hard tap water causes the leaves to turn yellow. Keep away from radiators and out of draughts. Feed monthly in summer and repot in spring but only when the existing container is full of roots, using a lime-free ericaceous compost or a peat-based equivalent. Pinch out the shoot tips of young plants to make them bushy, and cut back any old and untidy stems by half after flowering. Water with diluted iron sequestrene if the foliage looks pale and yellow. Propagate by rooting stem cuttings in a heated propagator in summer. Scale insects can be a problem.

THE SPECIES

Gardenia jasminoides (syn. ***G. florida***) (China, Japan) Cape Jasmine, Common Gardenia. Height and spread up to 3 ft in the home. A shapely shrub (if pinched in the early stages) with rich green oval leaves and large thick-petalled double white flowers, exquisitely scented. The flowers may appear in summer and autumn and even into winter if the early ones are nipped out while still in bud.

Coffea arabica

Gardenia jasminoides

Ixora (ix-*or*-a) Named after the Indian god to whom the flowers were once offered.

Cultivation This is a plant for a warm room where temperatures are unlikely to fluctuate too much. Try to maintain 18°C (65°F) during the day, with a night min. of 16°C (60°F). This may sound rather precise, but in cool rooms the plant will quickly shed its leaves. It likes a position in good but indirect light. Try to keep the compost evenly moist at all times, but let it become a little drier between waterings in winter. Feed monthly in summer. Stand the plant on a tray of moist gravel or peat to keep up humidity. Long stems can be cut back quite severely in late winter, and the plant repotted in spring when it outgrows its existing container. Use a peat-based potting compost. Propagate by taking stem cuttings in summer and rooting these in a heated propagator as they can be difficult to strike.

THE SPECIES

The plants normally offered for sale as house plants are:
***Ixora* cultivars** (Originally India and China) Flame of the Woods. Height 2 ft in the home, spread 1 ft or more. Shrubby house plants with glossy oval leaves that have a leathery texture. The large flower clusters are carried at the stem tips at any time between spring and autumn and the blooms may be rosy red, pink, yellow or white. Avoid moving the plant when it is in bloom or the flowers may be shed.

Nertera (*ner*-ter-a) From the Greek: *nerteros* – lowly; the plants creep along the ground.

Cultivation A good plant for a bright and airy north-facing windowsill where it can tolerate temps. as low as 5°C (40°F). Direct sunshine may cause desiccation. Water freely during summer whenever the pot feels light (never let it dry out completely), but keep it barely damp in winter when growth is slower. During the summer the plant will benefit from being put outdoors in a sheltered spot where it will not be scorched by strong sun. Large plants (and even quite small ones) can be divided and repotted in spring. Use a standard soil- or a peat-based compost. Seeds, when available, can be sown in spring in a temp. of 16°C (60°F).

THE SPECIES

Nertera granadensis (syn. ***N. depressa*** of gardens) (South American, Mexico) Coral Bead Plant, Fruiting Duckweed. A creeping plant with dense mats of tiny green leaves that look rather like Mind-your-own-business (see *Soleirolia*, page 74). The tiny green flowers are followed in autumn by bright orange berries, about $\frac{1}{4}$ in. in diameter, which last for many weeks.

Ixora cvs.

Ixora 'Super King'

Nertera granadensis

Compositae Daisy Family

One of the largest plant families consisting of over 1,000 genera of shrubs and herbs. A cosmopolitan group of plants many of which are grown for food. Sunflowers (*Helianthus*) are an important source of edible oil, and other genera are used in medicine. Among the ornamental plants are *Chrysanthemum*, *Dahlia* and *Aster*. A diagnostic feature of the family is the disc of florets. These florets are often arranged in the form of the familiar daisy-like flower.

Chrysanthemum (kriss-*an*-thee-mum) From the Greek: *chrysos* – gold, and *anthos* – a flower.

Cultivation These need to be kept cool, around 13-16°C (55-60°F), with a min. of 7°C (45°F), and in a brightly-lit, but not sun-soaked, position. In very warm rooms the blooms will fade quickly. Soak the compost thoroughly when it shows signs of drying out in summer, but keep it just moist in winter. Feed the plants fortnightly when they are in bud or in flower. The dwarf pot chrysanthemums are best discarded after flowering, though they can be planted in the garden.

Charm varieties can be raised from seeds sown in spring. Pinch out any tall shoots and stand the plants outdoors throughout the summer, potting them on into large containers of a standard soil- or peat-based compost as necessary. They may need canes for support. Bring indoors in late summer. Discard after flowering or cut down and propagate in spring from stem cuttings (page 20).

Marguerites are frequently sold as standard plants on a long stem. They can be cut back to leave just an inch or two of the upper stems and all of the standard stem after flowering, and kept on the dry side through winter. Pinch out the shoot tips regularly until late spring to encourage a thick, bushy habit. The plants can be stood outdoors during the summer. Leaf miner and greenflies are common pests.

THE SPECIES

Chrysanthemum frutescens (Canary Islands) Marguerite, Paris Daisy. Height up to 3 ft or slightly more, spread 2 ft. The pretty single daisy flowers of yellow and white or plain yellow cover this plant for weeks on end in summer. Keep the plant in good indirect light at all times or it will become lop-sided and drawn.

Chrysanthemum x *morifolium*. The pot-grown dwarf chrysanthemum of the florist is of hybrid origin and is treated with a dwarfing compound so that it grows no more than 9 in or so high. Several rooted cuttings will be found in each pot. The blooms may be red, yellow, orange, mahogany, white, mauve, pink or yellow and plants are best purchased with some open blooms as well as a good show of buds. Plants bought in tight bud may fail to bloom satisfactorily in the home. Thanks to daylength control (which delays or hastens flowering), the pot chrysanthemum can be had in bloom at any time of year, but if planted in the garden it will revert to flowering in autumn, its natural season, and will become a tall plant as the effect of the retardant wears off.

Chrysanthemum x *morifolium* 'Charm' Charm Chrysanthemum. Height and spread up to 2½ ft or so. The plant makes a dome of growth and the starry flowers may be pink, yellow, orange, white or mauve. Worth raising plants from seed.

Chrysanthemum frutescens

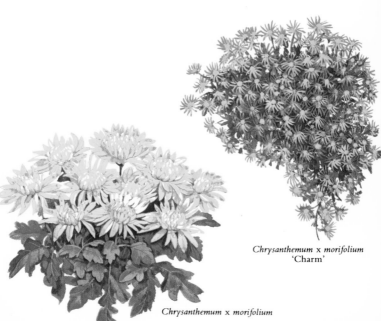

Chrysanthemum x *morifolium*
'Charm'

Chrysanthemum x *morifolium*

Gynura (gy-*new*-ra) From the Greek: *gyne* –female, and *oura* – tail; the stigma is very long.

Cultivation This plant needs a brightly lit spot where a winter min. temp. of 10°C (50°F) can be maintained; it is also tolerant of quite high temperatures. Water well when the compost feels dry in summer, but keep it barely damp in winter. Feed monthly in summer. Cut out any straggly stems in spring. Repot in a peat-based compost every spring or grow as an annual, replacing old plants with rooted stem cuttings taken in spring and summer. Pinch out the shoot tips early on to encourage a branching habit. Whitefly can be a problem.

THE SPECIES

Gynura aurantiaca (Java) Devil's Ivy, Purple Passion Plant, Velvet Plant. Height 9 in, spread 18 in or more. The coarsely cut, dark green leaves are felted with violet hairs so that the overall colour from a distance is purple, provided that the plant receives plenty of light. Allow the pendent stems to trail. Pick off the flower buds as soon as you see them – the orange 'dandelions' stink!

Senecio (sen-*ee*-see-oe) From the Latin: *senex* – an old man; the seeds are usually equipped with white hairs.

Cultivation The cineraria is one of the most difficult house plants to grow, it needs good but indirect light and, above all, a cool room – 7°C (45°F) will be tolerated but at over 16°C (60°F) the plant will suffer. Keep it away from radiators and out of draughts. Overwater and the plant will wilt never to recover; too little moisture and it will still suffer. So watch the plant carefully and as soon as the surface of the compost looks dry and the leaves begin to feel just a little floppy, water well then leave it alone until the same symptoms are noticed once more. Stand the plant on a tray of moist peat or gravel to prolong its life and prevent the foliage from browning. Feed fortnightly while in bud or bloom and discard after flowering. New plants can be raised from seed, although this is best achieved in a greenhouse. Leaf miner and greenfly can attack cinerarias.

The Cape Ivy prefers warm rooms with min. winter temp. of 10°C (50°F) and good light. Water freely when dry in summer, but more sparingly in winter. Spray the leaves occasionally with tepid water. Repot in spring using a peat-based compost and give support to climbing specimens. Propagate by stem cuttings in spring and summer. Young plants should have their shoot tips pinched out to promote branching.

THE SPECIES

Senecio cruentus cultivars Cineraria. Height up to 1½ ft, spread 1 ft. The lobed leaves are felted with grey underneath and carried in a dome, topped by the daisy flowers. These may be blue, magenta, purple, red, pink or white and often have a white 'eye'.

Senecio x hybridus Stellata Group (Offspring of *S. cruentus* x *S. heritieri*) Cineraria. This is daintier and smaller than the above, with plain coloured, finer petalled flowers, more starry in appearance.

Senecio macroglossus 'Variegatus' (Originally South Africa) Cape Ivy. Height and spread 3 ft or more. The waxy green leaves are marbled with creamy yellow and resemble those of ivy. A good trailer or climber; yellow daisy flowers may be produced in winter.

Senecio x *hybridus* Stellata cv.

Senecio cruentus cv.

Gynura aurantiaca

Senecio macroglossus 'Variegatus

Commelinaceae Spiderwort Family

A family of annual and perennial herbs of succulent habit. There are 38 genera distributed in tropical, subtropical and warm temperate areas, and while one or two are used in medicine the majority are grown as ornamental plants.

Rhoeo (roe-ee-oe) Derivation unknown.

Cultivation The best rhoeos are grown in relatively warm rooms where there is a reasonable level of humidity. They prefer bright but indirect light or slight shade. Maintain a min. winter temp. of 13°C (55°F) and spray the plant with tepid water daily, or stand the pot on moist gravel. Overcrowding sideshoots are best cut away to give a single-stemmed plant. Try to keep the compost evenly moist at all times, but slightly drier in winter. Rhoeo dislikes draughts and fluctuating temperatures, both of which will cause leaf-tip browning. Feed monthly in winter and repot every other spring in a standard soil- or peat-based compost. Peel off any leaves which turn brown. Use sideshoots as cuttings in spring or divide multi-crowned plants at the same time. Seeds can be sown in spring in a temp. of 18°C (65°F).

THE SPECIES

Rhoeo spathacea (syn. *R. discolor, Tradescantia discolor*) (West Indies, Mexico, Guatemala) Boat Lily, Moses-in-a-boat, Moses-in-the-cradle. Height usually around 1 ft, spread around 1½ ft. From a stout stem emerges a tuft of 10-in long leathery leaves, green on the upper surface and maroon below. The white flowers are carried in little pink cups among the leaf bases and account for the common names. Each tiny bloom has three petals (Three-men-in-a-boat is another popular name). Rhoeo can also be planted in hanging baskets, when its sideshoots are allowed to develop.
Rhoeo spathacea **'Variegata'**. Of roughly the same stature as the true species, but even more beautifully marked. The leaves are longitudinally striped with creamy yellow.

Setcreasea (set-cree-see-a) Derivation of the name unknown.

Cultivation Give this trailer a position in bright light – even direct sunshine. It will tolerate a wide range of temp. and a min. of 10°C (50°F). Water freely when the compost feels dry in summer, but keep it barely damp in winter. Pinch out the shoot tips occasionally to encourage bushiness. Feed monthly in summer and repot annually in spring using a basic soil- or peat-based compost. Propagation is easy – root stem cuttings individually in small pots of peat-based compost or jars of water. Greenfly may be a problem.

THE SPECIES

Setcreasea pallida **'Purple Heart'** (syn. *S. purpurea*) (Originally Mexico) Purple Heart. Height 9 in, but trailing to 1½ ft or so. The long, oval leaves are a vibrant shade of iridescent purple and each one is wrapped around the stem at its base. The plant produces pretty three-petalled blooms of pink and white in summer. Attractive in hanging baskets and pots, especially against pale backgrounds.

Rhoeo spathacea

Rhoeo spathacea 'Variegata'

Setcreasea pallida 'Purple Heart'

Tradescantia (trad-ess-*can*-tee-a) Named in honour of John Tradescant the younger (1608-1662). Born in Kent, Tradescant succeeded his father as Keeper of His Majesty's (King Charles I's) Gardens at Oatlands in 1638 with a salary of £100 per annum. He travelled to Virginia in the U.S.A. on several occasions. Father and son introduced many plants to Britain, and their collections of other artefacts formed the basis of the Ashmolean Museum at Oxford.

Cultivation Almost all the tradescantias need bright light if they are to give of their best and not look pale and drawn. A bright windowsill suits their pendulous habit and they will tolerate a min. winter temp. of 7°C (45°F). Central heating does not worry them a bit, but if positioned in a hot, dry spot many of the leaves may turn brown and crisp; cut all the stems back to compost level and fresh shoots will grow. Cut out any very straggly or tatty shoots at any time of year, and pinch the shoot tips out of young plants to encourage the production of plenty of sideshoots. An occasional spray over with tepid water will be appreciated but is by no means essential. Water freely in summer whenever the compost looks like drying out, but keep it just slightly moist in winter. Feed monthly in summer. Repot each spring in peat-based compost, or, better still, discard old plants and insert three 4-in long shoot tips around the edge of a 4-in pot filled with moist compost. Kept moist and lightly shaded at first the shoots will soon root and grow away. Cuttings can also be rooted in jars of water and will be ready for potting up in about one week. Greenfly are likely to be the only problem as far as pests are concerned, though red spider mite occasionally rears its ugly head if the atmosphere is too dry. All the species grow well in hanging baskets and suspended pots.

THE SPECIES

Tradescantia blossfeldiana (Argentina) Flowering Inch Plant, Wandering Sailor. Trailing to 2 ft or more. The oval pointed leaves are olive green above and maroon beneath.
***Tradescantia blossfeldiana* 'Variegata'.** Here the leaves are broadly but irregularly striped white and delicately flushed with pink. The stems are tinged with purple.
***Tradescantia fluminensis* 'Quicksilver'** (Originally South America) Wandering Jew. Trailing to 1½ ft. A strong grower, but not so lengthy in the stem as the true species. The leaves are striped white and green and are iridescent.
***Tradescantia fluminensis* 'Tricolor'** Wandering Jew. Rather like *T.f.* 'Quicksilver' except that the leaves are slightly narrower and flushed with pink at the margins.
Tradescantia sillamontana (syn. ***T. pexata, T. velutina*** of gardens, ***Cyanotis sillamontana, C. veldthoutiana*** of gardens) (Mexico) White Gossamer, White Velvet. Height 9 in, spread 1 ft or more. More erect than the other species and less pendent. The firm leaves are prominently wrapped around the stems and coated in white silky wool. Deep pink flowers are produced in summer and autumn. The most difficult to cultivate of the species described here. Keep the compost very much on the dry side in winter and keep the plant cool at the same time.

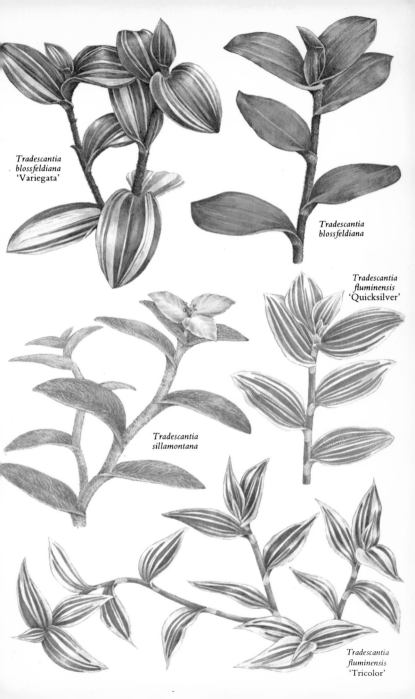

Tradescantia
blossfeldiana
'Variegata'

Tradescantia
blossfeldiana

Tradescantia
fluminensis
'Quicksilver'

Tradescantia
sillamontana

Tradescantia
fluminensis
'Tricolor'

Zebrina (zeb-*rye*-na) From the Portuguese: *zebra* – the leaves of the plant are striped.

   Cultivation Place zebrina in a spot that receives plenty of light. In a dull corner it will grow weak and spindly and the startling colour of its leaves will pale. It will tolerate winter temps. as low as 7°C (45°F) and can put up with quite high temperatures if necessary. The leaves may, however, turn brown and crisp if the plant is permanently situated over a radiator or in brilliant scorching sunshine. Replace such plants from cuttings and position them more carefully, or else cut the old plant back to pot level and force new shoots to grow. Do not let the compost become too dry in summer or leaf scorch will again result, try to keep it moist at all times. In winter the compost should be kept just damp. Give the plant a spray over with tepid water every day or so in summer, and feed monthly from spring to autumn. Repot every year if you want to grow a really big plant, or root several shoot tips in a jar of water each spring and pot these up to replace the ageing parent. Like *Tradescantia*, zebrina needs room to trail, and nowhere does it do this better than in a hanging basket or a suspended pot. Alternatively, position it in an ordinary plant pot on a shelf or window-ledge where it has room to hang down. Greenfly may attack the succulent shoots.

THE SPECIES

Zebrina pendula (syn. ***Tradescantia zebrina***, ***T. viridis***, ***T. vittata***) (Mexico) Inch Plant, Wandering Sailor. Height 9 in, spread 1 ft or more; trails for 1½ ft or so. The broadly oval pointed leaves look as if they have been painted by a brush dipped in green, maroon and silver paint. The stripes run from leaf tip to base on the upper surface of the leaves – below they are a uniform maroon. The three-petalled purplish flowers may appear in summer.
Zebrina pendula* 'Quadricolor'** (syn. ***Tradescantia quadricolor). Here the leaves are spectacularly striped with green, white and red.
Zebrina pendula* 'Purpusii'** (syn. ***Z. purpusii). The leaves are a dull olive green flushed with maroon on the upper surface, and below they are pure maroon. The flowers have a bluish tinge.

Zebrina pendula

Zebrina pendula
'Quadricolor'

Zebrina pendula
'Purpusii'

Gramineae   Grass Family

A massive family of great importance all over the world for cereals, grazing and, not least, for recreational surfaces. There are over 600 genera and around 9,000 species in the grass family. A number of grasses are grown as hardy or tender ornamentals.

Oplismenus (op-liz-*mee*-nuss) From the Greek: *hoplismos* – weapon; the flowers, or spikelets, of the grass have bristle-like projections called awns.

Cultivation An easy plant for a position in good light in a room that does not get colder than 7°C (45°F) in winter. Continuous bright sunshine may scorch the leaves so indirect light is best. Snip off any very long or wayward stems, and any which have lost a lot of leaves (browning is hastened by high temp. and a dry atmosphere). Water well whenever the compost feels dry and spray the leaves with tepid water in warm weather. Feed once a month in summer. Divide and repot in spring into a basic soil-based compost, or, better still, take stem cuttings at that time to act as replacements for worn-out old plants. They will root easily in warmth.

THE SPECIES

Oplismenus hirtellus **'Variegatus'** (syn. *Panicum variegatum*) (West Indies) Basket Grass. A rampant trailing plant with oval leaves most attractively striped cream, green and pink. Good in hanging baskets, troughs and suspended pots, but plant it with care in mixed arrangements or it may swamp less vigorous house plants.

Cyperaceae   Reed and Sedge Family

A family of cosmopolitan distribution and consisting of nearly 100 genera. Many are of considerable economic importance, being used in the manufacture of basketwork and paper as well as for fodder, and some are used in native medicine. A number are grown for their ornamental value.

Carex (*car*-ex) The ancient Latin name of the plant.

Cultivation This is one of the most tolerant house plants which can survive in heated or unheated rooms and in bright sun or shade. It also suits indoor gardeners who frequently overwater their plants for it prefers a compost which is kept moist at all times; it can even be stood in a *shallow* bowl which is kept topped up with water. Feed once a month in summer by applying diluted liquid fertilizer to the compost rather than the bowl. The plant can be repotted into a standard soil-based compost in spring, and divided up into smaller sections at the same time to make more plants. Peat-based composts do not seem to produce such sturdy plants as the soil-based mixtures.

THE SPECIES

Carex morrowii **'Variegata'** (Japan) Japanese or Variegated Sedge. Height and spread 1 ft. A handsome sedge with slender green and white striped leaves that arch gracefully. It makes a pleasing contrast to bold-leaved plants when arranged in a group planting.

Oplismenus hirtellus 'Variegatus'

Carex morrowii 'Variegata'

Cyperus (*sy*-per-uss) The Greek word for the sedge. This genus was used to produce papyrus – the earliest form of writing paper.

Cultivation Just the plant for the indoor gardener who is too handy with the watering can; cyperus is impossible to overwater. The compost should be kept very moist at all times and the plant will be happiest if a shallow bowl is placed beneath the pot and kept filled with water as cyperus is a native of boggy ground. It will perform well either in good but indirect light or in very light shade, and it will survive temps. as low as 10°C (50°F) in winter. An occasional spray over with water will improve it, and a monthly feed in summer will keep it in good condition; pour the feed on to the compost and not into the bowl of water where it may become foul smelling. Cut out at compost level any stems whose leaves turn yellow or brown and if the entire plant becomes straggly do not be afraid to shear off all the stems at pot level and repot the plant in fresh standard soil-based compost. Pruned plants will soon send up new shoots. After a few years certain parts of the rootstock will die off and these can be pulled away and discarded. Do this when repotting, which is best carried out annually in spring. Propagate by division at the same time. If the plant is kept too near a heat source, or in scorching sun, the leaf tips will turn brown. The same will happen if the compost is allowed to dry out, so keep it moist even in winter.

THE SPECIES

Cyperus albostriatus (syn. *C. diffusus, C. laxus*) (Tropics). Height and spread up to 3 ft but usually less – often around 1-1½ ft. Fresh, green, pithy stems produce umbrella-spoke leaves at the top and these may be wreathed in brownish grass-like flowers in summer. The leaves are rather coarser to the touch than those of the next species.

Cyperus alternifolius (Malagasy, Mauritius) Umbrella grass. Height up to 4 ft, spread 2 ft or more. Taller and more robust than *C. albostriatus*. The leaves are narrower and tougher; the flowers are similar and also appear in summer. An excellent specimen plant when grown well.

Scirpus (*sker*-puss) The Latin name for the rush.

Cultivation Exactly as for cyperus, though division of the clump is preferable to cutting off all the shoots at pot level.

THE SPECIES

Scirpus cernuus (syn. *Isolepis gracilis*) (Europe and North Africa) Club Rush. Height 6 in, spread up to 1 ft or so. A fine, tufted, grass-like rush which carries small greenish-white flower heads at the tips of its blades in summer. Good where space is limited and where gardening time is in short supply.

Scirpus cernuus

*Cyperus
alternifolius*

*Cyperus
albostriatus*

Bromeliaceae   Pineapple Family

Mainly rosette-forming herbs native to tropical and warm temperate areas of southern U.S.A. and South America. One species, *Pitcairnea feliciana*, is native to West Africa. The plants are collectively known as bromeliads; all are adapted to growing in dry conditions and many of them are epiphytes. There are around 50 genera, and while some are grown for economic reasons (pineapples for fruit and other species for fibres) most are cultivated as ornamentals. For the house-plant grower *Aechmea*, *Ananus* (pineapple), *Billbergia*, *Cryptanthus*, *Guzmania*, *Neoregelia*, *Nidularium*, *Tillandsia* and *Vriesea* are of importance.

Aechmea (*eek*-mee-a) From the Greek: *aichme* – a point; a reference to the spiky flower parts.

Cultivation Although aechmea is native to tropical areas and enjoys reasonable warmth, it will tolerate a temp. as low as 10°C (50°F). Position it in good but indirect light. Keep the 'vase' in the centre of the rosette topped up with water at all times, but keep the compost in the pot just moist, not soggy (the water from the vase will give the plant the moisture it needs). Keep the air around the plant as humid as possible, either spray the rosette daily with tepid water, or stand the plant on a tray of moist peat or gravel. Feeding is not really necessary but some gardeners give a dilute foliar feed once a month in summer.

For such a large plant the root system is quite small, so a clay pot 5 in in diameter is usually suitable for a mature rosette. If small specimens are acquired and repotting is necessary use a peat-based compost and a pot barely large enough to hold the roots. After flowering the large central rosette will die and one or more offsets should emerge to take over. Repot these individually in spring, cutting off and discarding the old rosette. Take care not to keep the compost around the young roots too wet at this stage or they may rot off.

THE SPECIES

Aechmea fasciata (syn. **A. rhodocyanea, Billbergia rhodocyanea**) (Brazil) Urn Plant, Silver Vase. Height and spread 1½ ft. The massive rosette of green leaves is covered in a white farina that rubs off easily on the fingers, and the edges of the leaves are clad in short spines. The 'urn' or 'vase' is quite pronounced, and from it a spiky head of pink bracts and lavender-blue flowers will emerge in summer if the plant is grown in a sufficiently high temp. around 24°C (75°F). The flower head will last for several months but can be cut off once it has turned brown, then the rosette will fade too.

Aechmea fulgens **var. discolor** (Brazil) Coral Berry. Height 1½ ft, spread 1 ft. Not so robust in appearance as *A. fasciata*, this species has narrower leaves that arch but remain more upright. They are green on the upper surface and flushed maroon below. The purple flowers are carried in summer on a tall, loosely branched spike and are followed by long-lasting scarlet berries.

Aechmea fasciata

Aechmea fulgens
var. *discolor*

Ananas (an-*an*-ass) From the name given to the plant by South American Indians of the Tupi tribe.

Cultivation The pineapple is a sun lover, so give it a position in full light near a window. It also needs heat but will tolerate a modest 13°C (55°F) in winter. Keep the compost moist all the year round – never soggy, but never bone dry – and the plant will respond well. Spray the foliage daily with tepid water if you have the time, or stand the plant on a tray of gravel or peat that is kept constantly moist. Feeding is not really necessary if the plant is grown in a good peat-based compost or a standard soil-based compost mixed in equal parts with peat. Repot in spring only when the plant is obviously top heavy. When the plant comes into fruit keep it very much on the dry side and use the sideshoots that are formed at this time as cuttings, rooting them in a warm and humid propagator. The tops of shop-bought pineapples can also be rooted to form house plants. Cut off the tufted top of the fruit with just a little of the flesh and bed this into a pot containing equal parts of peat and sand. Keep the compost moist and place the pot in a heated propagator. The shoot will soon take root and grow away. Remember that the central rosette always dies after fruiting.

THE SPECIES

***Ananas bracteatus* 'Striatus'** (Brazil, Paraguay) Red Pineapple, Wild Pineapple. Height and spread 2-3 ft. The real stunner of the pineapple family. The long leaves are furnished with painfully sharp spines, so stand the plant where it will not be able to catch on clothes or skin. The leaves are boldly striped with butter yellow at the margins and, as the fruit begins to develop, they become suffused with rich pink, especially towards the centre of the rosette. The fruit itself is no bigger than a tennis ball and is rosy red and preceded by lavender-blue flowers. The whole display lasts for several months.

Ananas comosus (syn. *A. sativus*) (Brazil) Pineapple. Height and spread 1-1½ ft. The leaves of the ordinary pineapple are a rather dull grey-green, but there is the added thrill of waiting for the long-stalked fruit to appear from the rosette. Give the plant plenty of sun and warmth and there is no reason why, after a couple of years, the pineapple should not emerge, but do not expect it to be anything like as large (or as tasty) as the one from which the plant was grown.

***Ananas comosus* 'Variegatus'**. Here the leaves are margined with creamy white and take on a pinkish tinge at fruiting time. More spectacular than the true species.

Ananas bracteatus
'Striatus'

Ananas comosus

Ananas comosus
'Variegatus'

Billbergia (bill-*ber*-jee-a) Named after J.G. Billberg (1772-1844), a Swedish botanist.

Cultivation This is the easiest of the bromeliads to cultivate and one of the longest lasting. It is tolerant of surprisingly low temps. having repeatedly survived 5°C (40°F) in my greenhouse when the heating has failed. It prefers to be kept a little warmer for comfort, but provided that its other wants are met it is very tolerant. Stand it where it receives good light, or else in very light shade, and water the compost only when it feels quite dry. The pot will quickly become filled with shoots so it is advisable to get used to weighing it in your hand to judge whether it is wet or dry. An occasional feed is beneficial in summer, and the plant will enjoy being sprayed with tepid water in warmer weather. Repot only when the plant has filled its existing container with shoots and is beginning to look starved (the leaf tips will start to turn yellow and eventually brown, but do not wait until the plant looks a mess). Repot in a peat-based compost in spring or summer when the plant is not in flower. Take the opportunity of dividing it at the same time if you wish, simply slicing it into smaller sections with a sharp knife. Do not overpot the divisions – give them containers just large enough to hold their roots. They can be potted on again when necessary. Keep them warm and shaded for a few days after potting.

THE SPECIES

Billbergia nutans (Brazil) Queen's Tears. Height and spread 1-1½ ft. The erect grey-green leaves of billbergia are nothing to look at, but when the flower spikes emerge in late winter the plant is transformed. Each arching spike is swathed in luminous pink bracts and these open out at the end to reveal pendent flowers contrastingly painted in shades of green, yellow and pink, edged with blue. The flowers will last for just a few weeks but the wait is well worthwhile. Pull them out of the rosettes when they have faded. A good plant for hanging baskets as well as pots.

Billbergia x windii (*B. decora* x *B. nutans*). Here the leaves are broader and, like the flower stems, more arching than those of *B. nutans*. The flowers may appear at any time during the winter and have broader pink bracts. Also good in hanging baskets, but not quite so tough as *B. nutans*. (Not illustrated.)

Billbergia nutans

Cryptanthus (krip-*tan*-thuss) From the Greek: *krypto* – to hide, and *anthos* – a flower; the bracts conceal the flowers.

Cultivation Easily accommodated bromeliads due to their modest size, these have, nevertheless, some of the most spectacularly marked foliage. They do well in warm rooms where a winter min. of 13°C (55°F) can be assured, and prefer a position in brilliant or indirect light to one in shade. Only in the middle of summer might bright sunshine necessitate their being moved to a spot in more indirect light. Keep the compost around the roots only just moist, never soggy or the roots may rot; spray the foliage daily with tepid water and subsequent watering may not be necessary. Feeding is seldom necessary if the plants are grown in a good peat-based compost. Repot them in a peat-based compost only when absolutely necessary for they make very little root. Spring is the best time to move them. As an alternative to being grown in pots, the plants can be attached to a 'bromeliad tree'. A stout dead tree branch is anchored in a large clay plant pot or tub which is weighted for stability. The plants are knocked out of their pots, the roots wrapped in moist sphagnum moss and then tied to the tree branches with plastic-covered wire. The roots and leaves will need a daily spray with tepid water but the plants should soon become established in what to them is a more natural environment. The smaller species can also do well in bottle gardens and terrariums if not kept too wet. Propagation is by the removal and potting up of offsets in spring and summer. These are only produced slowly so new plants may have to be bought in if you wish to increase your collection rapidly.

THE SPECIES

All the lower-growing species are referred to as Earth Stars or Starfish Plants. They are valued for their foliage effect rather than their insignificant flowers.
Cryptanthus acaulis (Brazil). Height 2-3 in, spread up to 6 in. Neat green rosettes that are finely toothed at the leaf margins and whitish on the undersides. The leaves are rather wavy, which gives them an added attraction, and white three-petalled flowers may be produced from the centre of the rosette.
***Cryptanthus acaulis* 'Roseus'**. Of the same dimensions as the true species, but here the leaves are longitudinally banded with various shades of dusky pink and horizontally banded in cream. Very eye catching.
Cryptanthus bivittatus (Brazil). Height 6 in or so, spread around 1 ft. A spreading rosette with rich green leaves, each having two creamy stripes.
***Cryptanthus bromelioides* 'Tricolor'**, Pink Cryptanthus, Rainbow Star. Height 6 in or more, spread 1 ft or more. One of the most spectacular of the group. The leaves are green in the centre, creamy yellow on either side of this and ruddy pink at the margins.
Cryptanthus fosterianus (Brazil). Height around 6 in, spread 1 ft. A species for the lover of muted contrasts; the leaves are striped with white farina on a bronze background.
Cryptanthus zonatus (Brazil) Zebra Plant. Height 5 in, spread 10 in. Similar to *C. fosterianus* except that the base colour of the leaves is deep green lightly tinged with bronze.

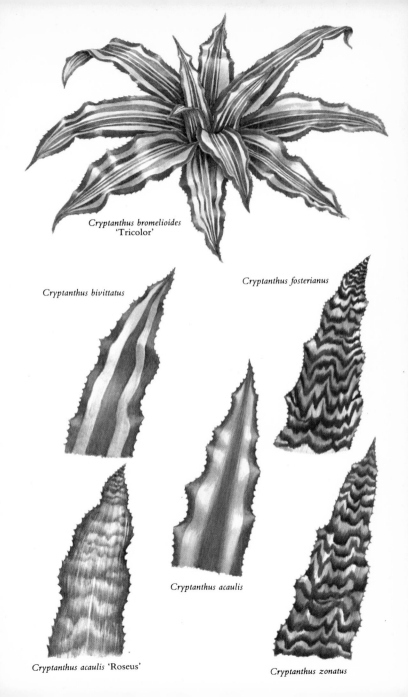

Cryptanthus bromelioides
'Tricolor'

Cryptanthus bivittatus

Cryptanthus fosterianus

Cryptanthus acaulis

Cryptanthus acaulis 'Roseus'

Cryptanthus zonatus

Guzmania (guzz-*man*-ee-a) Named after Anastasio Guzman, an 18th-century Spanish naturalist.

Cultivation The species mentioned here enjoys similar conditions to the *Cryptanthus* species (see page 204) except that it prefers a slightly higher min. temp. of around 16-18°C (60-65°F) and a position in indirect light rather than bright sun.

THE SPECIES

Guzmania lingulata var. minor (Tropical America, West Indies) Orange Star. Height up to 6 in, spread up to 1 ft. The leaves are glossy and bright green and from their centre appears a bright red flower spike with glossy bracts. The flowers are hidden among the bracts. This plant is a dwarf form of *G. lingulata* which is rather larger in all its parts and not suitable for growing on a bromeliad tree – a situation enjoyed by this modest-sized variety.

Neoregelia (nee-o-reg-*ee*-lee-a) Named after E. Albert von Regel (1815-1792), a German who became Director of the Imperial Botanic Gardens at St Petersburg (now Leningrad), and a noted Russian botanist. The genus was formerly known as *Aregelia*.

Cultivation Grow according to the instructions given for *Aechmea* (see page 198). When the central rosette has flowered it will die. The offshoots which then appear can either be removed and potted up separately, or allowed to grow on in the same pot where they will make a large cluster of attractive leaves. Empty the vase of water in winter unless the plant can be kept at temps. above 16°C (60°F).

THE SPECIES

Neoregelia carolinae (Many synonyms including: **N. marechalii**) (Brazil). Height 9 in or so, spread 1½ ft or more. The outer leaves of the large rosette are glossy green and the inner ones a bright red, especially at their bases. The leaves are quite broad and a spike of violet flowers sheathed in red bracts will eventually appear from the centre of the rosette in summer.

Neoregelia carolinae 'Tricolor'. The dimensions are roughly the same as the true species but the leaves are heavily striped with rich yellow. When the flower spike starts to emerge from the centre of the rosette in summer, the leaves around it turn a vivid red. Very spectacular and very beautiful if it can be positioned where its leaves will not be damaged, as the spines tend to catch on clothing.

Neoregelia spectabilis (Brazil) Painted Fingernail Plant. Height and spread slightly less than *N. carolinae*. The leaves of this species are uniformly rich, glossy green, but they are tipped with bright red – hence the common name. The inner leaves show a purple striping, and the flowers that emerge in summer are blue.

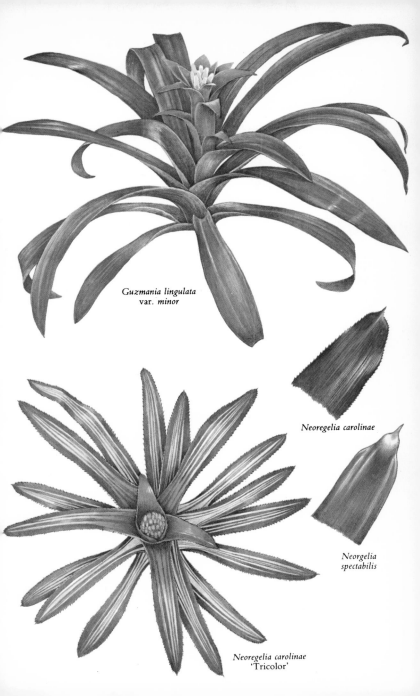

Guzmania lingulata
var. *minor*

Neoregelia carolinae

Neorgelia spectabilis

Neoregelia carolinae
'Tricolor'

Nidularium (nid-yew-*lair*-ee-um) From the Latin: *nidus* – a nest; the flowers sit like nestling birds in the rosette of leaves.

Cultivation This is the same as for *Aechmea* (see page 198) but try to keep nidulariums slightly warmer in winter, with a min. temp. of 16°C (60°F).

THE SPECIES

Nidularium fulgens (syn. **N. picta, Guzmania picta**) (Brazil) Blushing Bromeliad). Height 1 ft, spread 1 ft or more. The leaves are mottled with different shades of green and possess small spines along their margins. The purple and white flowers push out from the centre and the small leaves surrounding them are bright red.

Nidularium innocentii (Brazil) Birdsnest Bromeliad. Height 9-12 in, spread 1 ft or more. A statuesque and rather upright bromeliad with broad leaves that are purplish on the undersides and green flushed-purple on the upper surface. The inner leaves are reddish when the white flowers emerge.

Tillandsia (till-*and*-zee-a) Named after Elias Til-Landz (1640-1693), Swedish botanist who was Professor of Medicine at the University of Abo in Finland.

Cultivation Similar to that of most other bromeliads. Position tillandsias in good indirect light or very gentle shade and maintain a min. temp. of 13°C (55°F). Let the compost dry out between waterings and spray occasionally with tepid water in summer. Feed once a month in summer and repot only when absolutely necessary in a peat-based compost. Good on bromeliad 'trees'. Propagation is by the removal of offsets.

THE SPECIES

Tillandsia lindenii (syn. **T. lindeniana**) (Peru) Blue-flowered Torch. Height and spread 1 ft. The narrow, channelled leaves are dull green and broadly overlapping at their bases, but it is the flower spike that presents the spectacle. The violet-pink blooms emerge in spring from a flattened spike of overlapping bright pink bracts that are creamy yellow at their bases. The flowers do not last very long but the spike itself is a bright sight for many weeks. *T. cyanea* is very similar but slightly smaller in stature.

Tillandsia lindenii

*Nidularium
innocentii*

Nidularium fulgens

Vriesea (*vree*-zee-a) Named in honour of William Hendrik de Vriese (1806-1862), Dutch botanist and Professor of Botany at Amsterdam and Leiden.

Cultivation These warmth-loving bromeliads need a winter min. temp. of 16°C (60°F) and a position out of direct sun but not in heavy shade. They enjoy good but indirect light. Water thoroughly only when the compost is quite dry, soggy compost will cause the roots to die. Spray daily with tepid water in summer. Keep the central 'vase' full of water at all times. Repot in spring using a peat-based compost only when the plant is so top-heavy that it falls over. Alternatively grow on a 'bromeliad tree' (see page 204). Propagation is by means of offsets which can be potted up individually after the old rosette has faded (inevitable after flowering).

THE SPECIES

Vriesea fenestralis (syn. ***Tillandsia fenestralis***) (Brazil) Netted Vriesea. Height and spread up to 1½ ft. The leaves arch gracefully and are leathery and green with a remarkably complex network of veins. The green to yellow flowers are carried in spring on a spike whose green bracts are spotted with brown.

Vriesea hieroglyphica (Brazil) King of Bromeliads. Height 1 ft, spread 1½ ft. The sturdy rosettes of leaves are pale green contrastingly banded with deep brown. The flowers are yellow and appear in summer. Extremely attractive.

Vriesea splendens (syn. ***V. speciosa, Tillandsia vittata, T. zebrina***) (Guyana, Venezuela, Trinidad) Flaming Sword. Height and spread 1-1½ ft. The leaves of this very popular species are rich green laterally banded with very dark brown, and they make a rather upright vase. From the centre of the rosette in late summer a sword-shaped flower spike may appear. Its bracts are bright red in colour and the flowers that emerge from it are yellow.

Vriesea hieroglyphica

Vriesea splendens

Vriesea fenestralis

Strelitziaceae   Bird of Paradise Flower Family

Four genera from Tropical America, the southern tip of Africa and Malagasy. All the plants within the family are grown as ornamentals.

Strelitzia   (strel-*it*-zee-a) Named in honour of Charlotte of Mecklenburg-Strelitz (1744-1818), Queen of George III of England.

Cultivation Keep strelitzia in good light all the year round, but give it protection from burning summer sun. A min. winter temp. of 10°C (50°F) should be aimed for, though the plant can tolerate 7°C (45°F) if necessary. Soak the compost whenever it feels dry between spring and autumn, but allow it to remain dry for a little longer in winter. Feed once a month in summer. Repotting in a standard soil-based compost should be carried out only when absolutely essential until the plant is in a 8- or 10-in pot, and then it should be left potbound to encourage flowering. Annual topdressings may be carried out in subsequent years each spring. Propagate by sowing seeds in a temp. of 21°C (70°F) in spring, or by dividing mature plants at the same time. Mealy bug and scale insects can be a problem.

THE SPECIES

Strelitzia reginae (South Africa) Bird of Paradise Flower. Height 3-4 ft, spread 2 ft. Brilliant orange and blue flowers emerge from the tops of sturdy stalks in spring and look like colourfully crested cranes. Each head of flowers lasts for many weeks, for as one bloom fades, another unfurls. The thick-stalked oval leaves are dull green and leathery. This is a plant for the patient indoor gardener, for it is reluctant to flower until it is about 5 years old. If it is repotted too frequently then the delay may be even longer.

Zingiberaceae   Ginger Family

A family of around 50 genera of rhizomatous plants native to the tropics. Many are cultivated for their economic value, yielding spices, dyes, perfumes and medicines; others are of ornamental interest.

Alpinia   (al-*pin*-ee-a) Named in honour of Prospero Alpino (1533-1616) an Italian professor of botany and author of *De Plantis Aegypti* (1592) – an Egyptian flora illustrated with woodcuts.

Cultivation Alpinia likes warmth, and a min. winter temp. of around 16°C (60°F) is desirable if it is to thrive. It enjoys good but indirect light and will tolerate gentle shade. Keep the compost moist at all times, and feed the plant fortnightly in summer. An occasional spray with tepid water will perk the plant up in warm weather. Repot into a standard soil-based compost with a little peat added when the plant has filled its existing container. Spring is the best time to do this, and also the best time to divide mature specimens to make new plants. Keep the offspring warm for a few weeks after separating them from the parent. Alpinia is a tricky but rewarding plant.

THE SPECIES

Alpinia **'Sanderae'** (New Guinea) Variegated Ginger. Height 3 ft or more, spread 2 ft. A beautiful foliage plant with upright stalks that are well clothed in oval green- and creamy-white-striped leaves. It is especially at home in terrariums, though it may quickly outgrow the space available.

Strelitzia reginae

Alpinia 'Sanderae'

Marantaceae Arrowroot Family

Tropical herbaceous plants in 30 genera. Although some are of commercial value (*Maranta arundinacea* produces arrowroot, and other species are used in basketware and for primitive roof repairs), their main importance is as ornamentals and these include the genera *Calathea*, *Ctenanthe*, *Maranta* and *Stromanthe*.

Calathea (cal-*ath*-ee-a) From the Greek: *kalathos* – a basket; an allusion to the arrangement of the flowers which sit in 'basket-like' sheaths, or a reference to the use of the leaves in the manufacture of waterproof baskets.

Cultivation These foliage plants are difficult to grow unless you can provide them with ideal growing conditions. A min. temp. of 18°C (65°F) is necessary for them to produce new leaves and they need a spot in light shade where their humidity-loving leaves will not be scorched by sunlight. Spray them daily with tepid water or stand them on a tray of moist gravel or peat. The smaller species do well in bottle gardens and terrariums where their foliage can luxuriate in the humid atmosphere. Cut off any leaves as soon as they fade or other parts of the plant may rot off with them. Try to keep the compost evenly moist at all times and just damp in winter. Feed monthly in summer and repot in spring when necessary, usually every 2 years or so, using a peat-based compost. Propagate by dividing the clumps in spring. The shorter-stemmed species can also be propagated by stem cuttings rooted in a propagator in spring or summer. Pests are seldom a problem. Dry air and low temperatures will cause leaf browning. Over-watering causes stem rot.

THE SPECIES

Calathea insignis (syn. *C. lancifolia*) (Brazil) Rattlesnake Plant. Height up to 3 ft in the home, spread 2 ft. Each long wavy-edged leaf is held on a stout stem. The upper surface of each leaf is mid-green with dark green elliptical markings arranged in a herringbone pattern on either side of the main vein. The underside of the leaf is mauve.

Calathea louisae (Origin unknown). Height 9 in, spread 1 ft. The leaves are wavy edged and unevenly mottled in different shades of green on the upper surface; they are green and purple on the undersides. Relatively easy to grow. (Not illustrated.)

Calathea makoyana (syn. *Maranta makoyana*) (Brazil) Peacock Plant. Height and spread 1-1½ ft in the home. Beautifully marked on the upper surface with cream stripes and dark green blobs. On the undersides the green changes to rich mauve.

Calathea ornata (Colombia, Guyana, Ecuador). Height and spread 2 ft or more. The oval dark green leaves are finely herringboned in white or pale pink stripes. The undersides of the leaves of this elegant plant are mauve.

Calathea zebrina (Brazil) Zebra Plant. Height and spread 1½-2 ft. The leaves have a velvety texture. The rich green ground colour is overlaid with bold smudges of purplish green. A greater predominance of purple is found on the undersides.

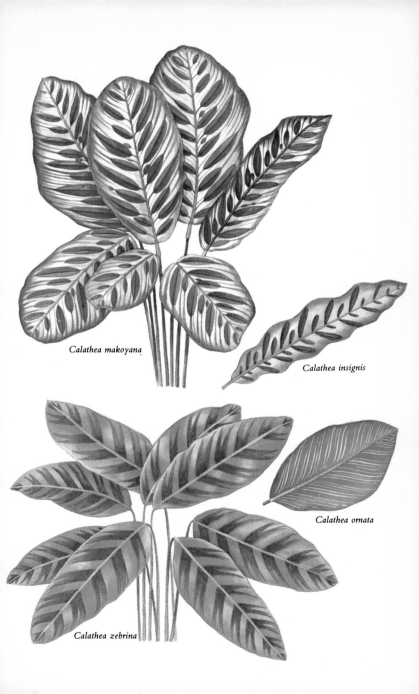

Calathea makoyana

Calathea insignis

Calathea ornata

Calathea zebrina

Ctenanthe (ten-*anth*-ee) From the Greek: *ktenos* – a comb; the bracts on the flower stalk stick out like teeth.
   Cultivation Exactly as for *Calathea* (see previous page).

THE SPECIES

Ctenanthe oppenheimiana 'Tricolor' (Originally Brazil) Never-never Plant. Height and spread 2 ft or more. The leaves are green and broadly marked in darker tones with a herringbone pattern on the upper surface, with additional irregular splashes of yellow. They are reddish on the undersides.

Maranta (ma-*ran*-ta) Named after Bartolommeo Maranti (c. 1559), a Venetian botanist.
   Cultivation Exactly as for *Calathea* (see previous page). Especially suited to bottle gardens and terrariums and often more successfully cultivated when watered from below (see *Saintpaulia*, page 168, for details).

THE SPECIES

Generally known as Prayer Plants because of their habit of folding their leaves upwards at night.
Maranta leuconeura var. _erythroneura_ (syn. **_M.l. erythrophylla, M. tricolor_**) (Brazil) Herringbone Plant, Red-veined Prayer Plant. Height 4–6 in, spread 1 ft or more. Beautifully marked leaves on which the midrib and main veins are rich in carmine pink. Several light green patches decorate the midrib from leaf base to tip, and darker smudges appear between the main veins.
Maranta leuconeura 'Kerchoviana' (syn. **_M. kerchoviana_**) Rabbit's Foot. Height 4 in, spread 1 ft. Probably the most popular maranta. The cool grey-green leaves are smudged with herringbone patterns of dark brown. Superb in group arrangements and terrariums if you can prevent the compost from getting too soggy.
Maranta leuconeura var. _leuconeura_ (syn. **_M. l. massangeana_**) (Brazil). Height 4–6 in, spread 1 ft or more. Similar in habit to the other two but this time the leaves have whitish blotches around the midrib and white veins. The areas between the veins are blackish green – really sooty – becoming paler towards the margin. This plant contrasts well with the other two marantas.

Stromanthe (stro-*man*-thee) From the Greek: *stroma* – a bed, and *anthos* – a flower; a reference to the form of the flowers.
   Cultivation Exactly as for *Calathea* (see previous page).

THE SPECIES

Stromanthe amabilis (Tropical America). Height and spread 1 ft. The vivid green leaves are marked with a darker tone in a clear herringbone pattern. The undersides are greyish green and the stems tinged with red. Well-grown plants always look fresh and healthy.

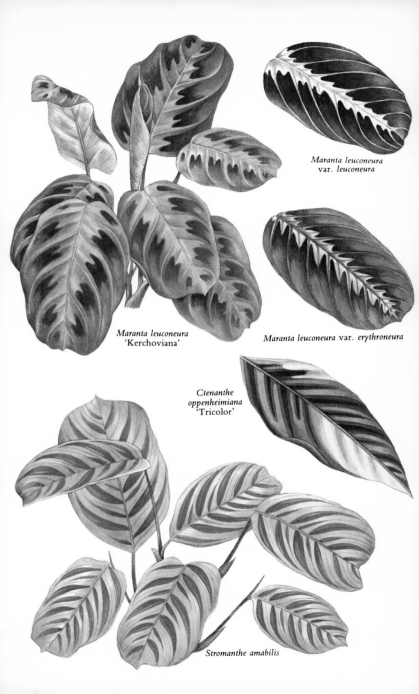

Maranta leuconeura
var. *leuconeura*

Maranta leuconeura
'Kerchoviana'

Maranta leuconeura var. *erythroneura*

Ctenanthe
oppenheimiana
'Tricolor'

Stromanthe amabilis

Palmae   Palm Family

Tropical and occasionally temperate trees with a long and ancient history. There are over 200 genera, many of which are cultivated for their economic value, producing coconuts, copra and coir fibre (*Cocos nucifera*), dates (*Phoenix dactylifera*), sago (*Metroxylon* sp.), palm oil (*Elaeis guineensis*), plus assorted fibres, canes, waxes, wine and other products. The greater proportion of the family is grown solely for ornament, and to the house-plant grower *Chamaedorea*, *Chamaerops*, *Howea*, *Microcoelum* and *Phoenix* are the most prized.

Chamaedorea (cam-ee-*dor*-ee-a) From the Greek: *chamai* – on the ground, and *dorea* – a gift; the plant is low growing and its fruits can be easily picked.

    Cultivation This little palm needs a spot in good but indirect light or in shade, and a min. winter temp. of 10°C (50°F) to grow well. It will survive lower temperatures but only reluctantly and its leaf tips may well turn brown. Cut off any leaves as soon as they fade (the lower ones die off from time to time). Keep the compost moist throughout the summer, watering it well as soon as the surface starts to feel dry. Never let it dry out completely in winter but keep it just damp. Dryness at the roots, cold air and sun scorch can all cause leaf burning. Stand the plant on a tray of moist peat or gravel to provide welcome humidity. Alternatively, spray it occasionally with tepid rainwater. Feed monthly in summer and repot in spring when necessary using a mixture of equal parts of standard soil- and peat-based compost; palms seem to like this open mixture. Propagation is by sowing seeds in a propagator in a temp. around 27°C (80°F). Red spider mite can be troublesome.

THE SPECIES

Chamaedorea elegans (syn. *Neanthe bella*) (Guatemala, Mexico) Dwarf Mountain Palm, Parlour Palm. Height to about 3 ft in the home, spread around 1½ ft. The dainty fronds arch from the central stem and are a fresh green in colour when young, darkening with age. Heads of yellow, spherical fruits are often produced. Good in bottle gardens and terrariums. It is suggested that the form most widely cultivated as a house plant is in fact *C.e.* 'Bella' which is considerably smaller in stature than the true *C. elegans*.

Chamaerops (cam-*ee*-rops) From the Greek: *chamai* – on the ground, and *rops* – bush; the plant is a low grower.

    Cultivation Exactly the same as for *Howea* (see overleaf).

THE SPECIES

Chamaerops humilis (Western Mediterranean) Dwarf Fan Palm, European Fan Palm. Height and spread up to 5 ft in the home. A statuesque palm which looks its best when given plenty of space to spread its arching fronds. The stalks are spiny and the glossy green leaflets radiate in a perfect fan formation. Many stems may shoot in favourable conditions, but they are usually very short. Yellow flower clusters may be produced.

Chamaerops humilis

Chamaedorea elegans

Howea (*how*-ee-a) Named after the palm's place of origin – Lord Howe Island to the east of Australia. It grows nowhere else.

Cultivation Contrary to popular belief, palms grown as house plants do not enjoy blazing sunshine as it scorches their leaf tips and generally dries them up. Position them instead in light shade (they will even tolerate quite dark corners). Maintain a min. winter temp. of around 10°C (50°F), although the palms may very occasionally tolerate less than this. They need a relatively humid atmosphere which will stop the frond tips from drying out so stand them in a large jardinière or on a shallow tray filled with moist gravel. An occasional spray with tepid rainwater will also be beneficial.

Cut off cleanly any leaves that turn brown (the lower ones will do so quite quickly from time to time). If the tips of healthy leaves turn brown check that the plant is not too cold, positioned in a draught, near a radiator, or that it is not too dry at the roots. Palms detest soggy compost but they will soon suffer from drought. Aim to keep the compost moist from spring to autumn and slightly drier in winter so it is just damp. Clean the leaves once a month with a moistened sponge. A monthly feed in summer will keep the plants healthy, and they can usually do with repotting every other spring into a mixture of equal parts standard soil- and peat-based potting compost. Propagate by seed sown in a temp. of 27°C (80°F) or remove suckers when repotting. Red spider mite is the only pest likely to be troublesome. Most problems are caused by faulty growing conditions. Gentle warmth and constant humidity, plus damp (rather than dry or soggy) compost are the secrets of success.

THE SPECIES

Howea belmoreana (syn. ***Kentia belmoreana***) (Lord Howe Island) Belmore Sentry Palm, Curly Palm, Kentia Palm. Height to around 6 ft or more in the home, spread 3 ft or more. A beautiful palm with long green stems that hold aloft arching fronds of dark, glossy green. One of the finest specimen house plants and surprisingly tolerant of room conditions. Brown leaf tips can be snipped off with a pair of scissors, but search for the cause to prevent future disfigurement.

Howea forsteriana (syn. ***Kentia forsteriana***) (Lord Howe Island) Forster Sentry Palm, Kentia Palm, Thatch Leaf Palm. Height and spread similar to *H. belmoreana*. In this species the fronds arch less spectacularly, but it is the more popular of the two being, if anything, a little easier to grow. Both species are expensive to buy (especially if they are of any size), but the effect they achieve makes the extravagance well worthwhile.

Microcoelum (my-cro-*see*-lum) From the Greek: *mikros* – small, and *koilos* – hollow; the endosperm (part of the food reserves within the seed) has a small hollow in it.

Cultivation Exactly as for *Howea*, but prefers good indirect light and a min. temp. of around 16°C (60°F).

THE SPECIES

Microcoelum weddellianum (syn. ***Cocos weddelliana, Syagrus weddelliana***) (Brazil) Dwarf Coconut Palm, Weddel Palm. Height and spread up to 3 ft in the home. The fronds are quite tough to the touch and very feathery in appearance. A good potted palm but not so graceful as the larger types. Do not expect any coconuts!

Microcoelum weddellianum

Howea forsteriana

Howea belmoreana

Phoenix (*fee*-nix) The Ancient Greek name used for the date palm by Theophrastus (c. 371-287 B.C.) the botanist and philosopher.

Cultivation Exactly as for *Howea* (see previous page).

THE SPECIES

Phoenix canariensis (Canary Islands and now elsewhere) Canary Island Date Palm. Height and spread to 6 ft or so in the home. A graceful and very feathery palm well suited to cool rooms. The fronds are glossy green and held rather upright. (Not illustrated.)

Phoenix dactylifera (Arabia, North Africa) Date Palm. Height up to 100 ft in the wild – usually considerably less in the home when both height and spread are 6 ft. The leaves are very finely divided and greyish green in colour. They arch right over and so the plant needs a considerable amount of space if it is to grow undisturbed by passers-by. Easily grown from date stones germinated in a pot of peaty compost in a polythene bag and kept at a temperature of 27°C (80°F) until germination has taken place. (Put the pot and bag in the airing cupboard.) Growth will be quite slow in normal room conditions and it is most unlikely that you will ever be able to pick your own dates.

Phoenix roebelenii (Assam to Vietnam) Dwarf or Miniature Date Palm. Height and spread usually around 3 ft in the home. This has a more open frond arrangement than the true date palm and it is considerably smaller (which makes it better suited to being grown as a house plant). The fronds are elegantly arched. This species does appreciate warmer conditions than the other two. Give it a min. temp. of around 18°C (65°F) if you can. Perhaps the best choice for centrally-heated rooms that are inclined to be stuffy – but remember to keep the atmosphere around the plant humid to prevent desiccation.

Phoenix dactylifera

Phoenix roebelenii

Pandanaceae Screw Pine Family

Trees, shrubs and climbers native to tropical and subtropical areas of the Old World. There are 3 genera, the best known of which is *Pandanus*. Some of the plants are ornamental, others are valued in basket making and thatching and some provide edible fruits.

Pandanus (pan-*dan*-uss) From the Malayan name for the plant, *pandan*.

Cultivation Keep this plant warm at all times, ensuring a min. winter temp. of around 13°C (55°F), and place it in good but indirect light. Soak the compost whenever it feels dry in spring and summer, but let it remain a little drier during autumn and winter. Spray the foliage daily with tepid water in summer. Feed fortnightly in summer and repot in a standard soil-based compost every other spring. Suckers that are produced from the base of mature plants can be removed with a portion of root if possible, or simply cut off and treated as cuttings. Remove them in spring. Do not cut off any aerial roots that form; instead encourage them to penetrate the surface of the compost to improve the anchorage.

THE SPECIES

Pandanus veitchii (Polynesia) Variegated Screw Pine. Height and spread 3 ft. A handsome specimen plant that forms a fountain of long, arching leaves heavily armed with spines. The leaves emerge in a spiral pattern from the stem (hence the common name) and are rich green edged with cream. Stand the plant where it will not be knocked by passers-by as it is easily damaged and can inflict painful scratches on bare skin.

Araceae Arum Family

A family of tropical and temperate herbaceous plants in over 100 genera. Many are ornamental and some are grown as food crops. The most widely known genera are *Arum*, *Monstera*, *Dieffenbachia*, *Philodendron*, *Anthurium*, *Arisaema*, *Acorus*, *Alocasia*, *Zantedeschia*, and *Dracunculus*.

Acorus (a-*cor*-uss) From the Greek: *akoron*, previously applied to the flag iris but now applied to the sweet flag *Acorus calamus* which has sweet-scented leaves formerly used for strewing on floors and in making cosmetics.

Cultivation A good plant for an unheated room where it will tolerate low temperatures. Acorus will grow well in good but indirect light or light shade, and should always be kept moist at the roots to prevent leaf browning. Feed once a month in summer and repot in spring when necessary using a standard soil-based compost. Propagate the plant by dividing it into several pieces in spring or summer and potting up the divisions in pots of a basic soil-based compost.

THE SPECIES

Acorus gramineus 'Variegatus' (Japan). Miniature Sweet Flag. Height and spread 1 ft. This attractive grass-like plant makes upright fans of cream-and-green-striped leaves. It is especially suitable for a terrarium or large bottle garden where it is never allowed to dry out.

Pandanus veitchii

Acorus gramineus 'Variegatus'

Aglaeonema (ag-lay-on-*ee*-ma) From the Greek: *aglaos* – bright or clear, and *nema* – a thread; the stamens are shiny.

Cultivation Good foliage plants for a semi-shady spot in a warm room. Keep them away from bright sunlight but try to avoid placing them in really dark corners where they may survive but not flourish. A winter min. of 13°C (55°F) will be tolerated but a little more warmth will be amply repaid by healthier growth. Water well as soon as the surface of the compost feels dry to the touch, but in winter keep the compost barely moist at all times or the plant may wilt – never to recover – it hates a cold, wet potful of compost. Feed monthly in summer and repot in spring when necessary (probably every second year) using a peat-based compost which the plant seems to prefer to a soil-based one. Spray the foliage regularly with tepid water, or, better still, stand the plant on a tray of moist peat or gravel so that the atmosphere around it is kept humid. Keep the plant out of draughts and propagate it by removing offshoots at repotting time. Tall and mature plants can be air layered (see page 22). Watch out for mealy bug.

THE SPECIES

These plants are collectively and individually known as Chinese Evergreens.
Aglaeonema commutatum (Moluccas, Philippines). Height up to 1 ft or so, spread 9 in. The typical aglaeonema leaves – oval and rather leathery to the touch – are mottled with irregular lateral bands of greyish-white. Each leaf lasts for a long time and white-spathed flowers may be produced in summer.
Aglaeonema commutatum **'Silver Spear'**. Height and spread similar to the true species. The leaves are mottled and splashed more generously with silvery grey. They are slightly narrower than those of the true species and much more decorative, thanks to their variegation.
Aglaeonema crispum **'Silver Queen'**. Similar in size to the other two, but the leaves are even more variegated. Green is in evidence only at the margins and as scattered speckling around the main veins; the rest of the surface is a clear silvery white with just a touch of cream. Like all highly variegated plants, this one needs reasonable (but indirect) light if it is to retain its strong colours.
Aglaeonema modestum (syn. *A. acutispathum*) (China, Philippines). Height and spread 1-1½ ft. The leaves of this species are a glossy plain green and held almost at right angles to the stalks. For that really dingy corner, this is the aglaeonema to choose, as it can put up with less light than the brightly marked forms.

Aglaeonema crispum
'Silver Queen'

*Aglaeonema
commutatum*

*Aglaeonema
commutatum*
'Silver Spear'

*Aglaeonema
modestum*

Anthurium (an-*thoo*-ree-um) From the Greek: *anthos* – a flower, and *oura* – a tail; reference to the tail-like spadix which protrudes from the flower.

Cultivation The warmer and more humid the atmosphere around these plants, the happier they will be. They tolerate a winter min. temp. of 16°C (60°F), but will prefer it a little higher. They need a place in light shade or indirect light; do not stand them in full sun where they will quickly dry out. Try to keep the compost moist at all times, never soggy but never dry. Spray the foliage daily with tepid rainwater and stand the plant on a tray or bowl of moist peat or gravel to increase humidity. Feed fortnightly in summer. Repot in peat-based compost every other year, taking care to make sure that the crown of the plant (the junction of the roots and shoots) sits on the surface of the compost; plant it below and there is a danger that the stems will rot. Propagate by dividing mature clumps at repotting time. Seeds can be sown in spring. Clean the leaves occasionally and keep a look out for scale insects and mealy bugs.

THE SPECIES

Anthurium andreanum (Colombia) Tailflower, Painter's Palette. Height and spread 2 ft or more. The bold, glossy green leaves of this species are shaped like fat arrowheads and are carried on sturdy stalks. The flowers are typical of the genus; they consist of a flat, colourful 'plate' known as a spathe, and from this protrudes a spadix which carries the tightly packed flowers. In the case of *A. andreanum* the heart-shaped spathe is bright rosy red and of a polished waxen texture. The spadix is yellow. The blooms appear at any time between spring and autumn and are very long lasting. As the plant grows and starts to produce aerial roots, wrap the stem in damp sphagnum moss, or provide a damp, moss- or foam-covered stick to which the roots can attach themselves and from which they can extract moisture. Not the easiest anthurium but certainly the most spectacular. Hybrids between this and other species are available with pink or white spathes but they are not easy to obtain.

Anthurium crystallinum (Peru, Colombia) Crystal Anthurium. Height and spread 2 ft. This species is grown solely for its foliage. The leaves are like massive arrowheads and are coloured a luscious deep green against which the creamy white veins stand out prominently. Good for a warm and moderately shady corner where (like *A. andreanum*) it should be provided with a moss bandage or a moss-covered stick when aerial roots start to appear. It is very much at home in jungle-like conditions – if you can provide them.

Anthurium scherzerianum (Costa Rica) Flamingo Flower. Height and spread 2 ft. The commonest anthurium in cultivation and also the easiest to grow. The leaves are long, oval and leathery and arch outwards from the growing point. The flowers consist of a curved red spathe (lacking the size and texture of that possessed by *A. andreanum*) and a twisted yellow spadix which has given rise to the common name. Forms are available with white, orange and even speckled spathes. The blooms appear between spring and late summer.

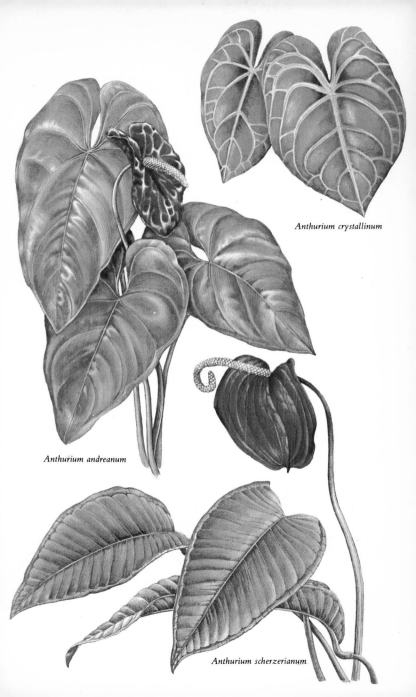

Anthurium crystallinum

Anthurium andreanum

Anthurium scherzerianum

Caladium (cal-*ay*-dee-um) The Latinized version of the Malay name for this plant – *kaladi*.

Cultivation As you would expect from the delicate appearance of the foliage, these plants need high temperatures and humidity, but only during the summer for they die down in autumn and remain dormant through the winter. Tubers or, more correctly, rhizomes (the root–like stems) are offered for sale in spring and can be planted just below the surface of peat-based potting compost in plastic pots. Keep the pots in a temperature of 24°C (75°F) at this stage and keep the compost moist, not soggy. As soon as growth is noticed, stand the pots in good but indirect light and maintain a temp. of between 18-21°C (65-70°F). As the plants grow they should be kept out of direct sunlight and the temp. should never fall below 16°C (60°F). As more leaves are produced the compost can be watered more freely and as soon as three leaves have fully expanded a liquid feed can be applied fortnightly. Spray the foliage daily with tepid water and stand the plants on a tray of moist peat or gravel. When the foliage starts to look tired in late summer and early autumn, let the compost slowly dry out until the leaves are crisp and dry. Knock the compost from the pot and salvage the rhizomes, storing them in damp peat in a temp. of 13°C (55°F). Keep the plants out of draughts at all times and do not place them where their fragile leaves may be knocked around. Propagation is by the removal and potting up of small rhizomes which are produced alongside the larger, older ones.

THE SPECIES

The plants are collectively and individually known as Angel's Wings and were originally native to tropical South America.

Caladium x *hortulanum* **'White Christmas'**. Height 1-1½ ft, spread 1½ ft. All the hybrids have generously proportioned arrow-shaped leaves which have a rubbery feel but are really quite thin; their translucency is part of their charm, for when viewed into the light the contrasting veination can be fully appreciated. This cultivar has creamy white leaves that are strikingly veined with a fresh green.

Caladium x *hortulanum* **'Carolyn Whorton'**. This cultivar has a rich rosy red centre which merges into a deep fresh green around the wavy leaf margins.

Caladium x *hortulanum* **'Doecile Anglaise'**. The veins are a deep pink and the majority of the leaf blade is marbled with soft pink, white and green.

Caladium x *hortulanum* **'White Wings'**. The leaf margin is deep green, merging through a mottled white marbling to pink veins in the centre. Like the other varieties, when grown with plain green perennial house plants the contrast is striking.

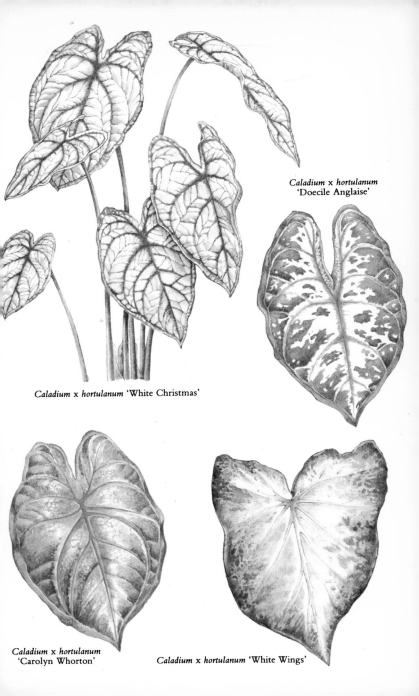

Caladium x *hortulanum* 'Doecile Anglaise'

Caladium x *hortulanum* 'White Christmas'

Caladium x *hortulanum* 'Carolyn Whorton'

Caladium x *hortulanum* 'White Wings'

Dieffenbachia (dee-fen-*back*-ee-a) Named after J.F. Dieffenbach (1790-1863) head gardener at the Palace of Schönbrunn in Vienna in the 1830's.

Cultivation Increasingly popular plants which need just a little extra care to keep them in really good condition. Good but indirect light is what they most enjoy, though a little light shade will do them no harm. What they do require is a fairly steady temp. regime, a min. of 16°C (60°F) is necessary and the plants must be kept out of draughts. In centrally-heated rooms they will do well provided that the air around them is kept humid. Spray the foliage daily with tepid water or stand the plant in a bowl of moist peat or gravel. Remove the lower leaves as they fade, peeling them away from the stem. In time a cluster of leaves will sit at the top of a tall stem and at this stage the plant can be cut back to within a few inches of compost level; the top section can be shortened and used as a cutting and the stump will produce new shoots if kept warm and the compost slightly moist. Do not overwater the dieffenbachia. If the compost around its roots is kept soggy its leaves will droop and shed tears. Wait until the surface of the compost is dry before watering well; let it remain slightly drier in winter but never totally desiccated. Feed monthly in summer, and repot in spring every year if necessary using a peat-based compost. Propagate by removing a section of stem and cutting it into 2-in long sections, each with a bud. Bed these into the surface of the rooting medium in a heated propagator and pot up the young plants that arise. Suckers can be removed from older plants in spring and potted up on their own. The sap of all these plants is poisonous and can cause inflammation of the tongue, so be sure to wash your hands thoroughly after taking cuttings or removing leaves and keep the sap away from your mouth at all times.

THE SPECIES

Dieffenbachia amoena (Tropical America) Giant Dumbcane. Height 5 ft, spread 2 ft. Large, pointed, oval green leaves of a thin but leathery texture are speckled with yellow around the main veins. Not the most spectacular species but one of the most shade tolerant. The arum lily-like flowers of this and the other species mentioned are rarely noticed due to their insignificant appearance.

***Dieffenbachia picta* 'Exotica'** (Originally Brazil) Leopard Lily. Height 2-3 ft, spread 1½ ft. In this cultivar the green leaves are heavily spotted and speckled with creamy yellow. Due to its ease of culture this is the most widely grown of the group, and deservedly so, for it is extremely handsome too.

***Dieffenbachia picta* 'Rudolph Roehrs'** (syn. *D. p.* 'Roehrsii'). Height 2-3 ft, spread 1½ ft. The most brightly marked of the four. Here the leaves are a fresh green only around the edges and along the midrib. The rest of the surface is butter yellow and, if kept in reasonable light, retains its fresh appearance all the year round. Like all heavily variegated plants it is rather more tricky than its plainer relations.

***Dieffenbachia picta* 'Superba'**. Height 2-3 ft, spread 1½ ft. Midway between *D.p.* 'Exotica' and *D.p.* 'Rudolph Roehrs' in the amount of variegation on its foliage. Plentiful splashes of creamy white decorate the leaf area between the midrib and the margin. Smart and stately as a single specimen.

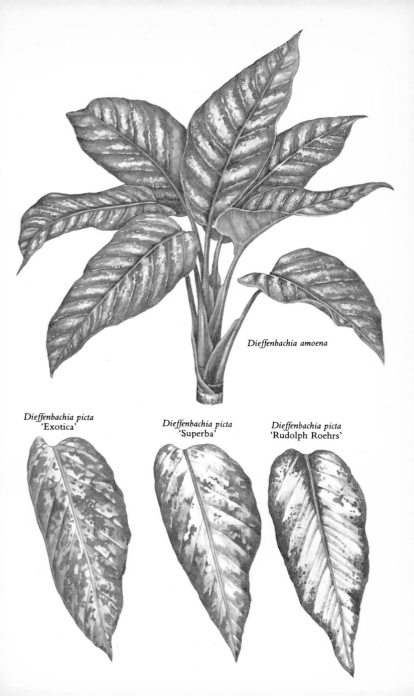

Dieffenbachia amoena

Dieffenbachia picta
'Exotica'

Dieffenbachia picta
'Superba'

Dieffenbachia picta
'Rudolph Roehrs'

Epipremnum (ep-ee-*prem*-num) From the Greek: *epi* – upon, and *premnon* – trunk; the plants are epiphytes and cling to trees for support.

Cultivation These must be kept warm to thrive; ensure a min. temp. of 13-16°C (55-60°F) and keep in good but indirect light. Water freely in summer as soon as the surface of the compost feels dry, but let it remain barely moist in winter; stem rot may result if the compost is kept soggy. Peel off any leaves that fade. Feed monthly in summer and provide the plant with some support (a moss-covered stick is best). It may dehydrate if grown as a trailing plant as it needs humid atmosphere, so spray frequently with tepid water. Repot in spring in a peat-based compost only when potbound. Propagate by taking cuttings comprising a leaf and a small portion of stem. Pinch out the shoot tips in the early stages to promote branching.

THE SPECIES

Epipremnum aureum (syn. ***Scindapsus aureus, Pothos aureus***) (Solomon Islands) Devil's Ivy, Golden Pothos, Taoro Vine. Height and spread 6 ft or more, depending on the size of the support system. A bright foliage plant with vine-like stems clad in heart-shaped green leaves splashed with bright yellow. Aerial roots should be trained into a mossed stick. Pot-grown plants seldom flower.

Epipremnum aureum **'Marble Queen'** (syn. ***Scindapsus aureus*** **'Marble Queen'**). Dimensions and general appearance as the true species but the foliage variegation is much more pronounced and creamy white in colour. Rather more difficult and needing just a little more light, heat and humidity.

Monstera (*mon*-ster-a, not mon-*steer*-ee-a) Probably from the gigantic size and monster-like appearance of the slashed and perforated leaves.

Cultivation Make sure that the temp. never falls below 10°C (50°F) and keep around 18°C (65°F) during the day if the plant is to make growth. Give it good light or slight shade. Push the tips of the aerial roots into a moss stick or the surface of the compost, never cut them off or the plant will be weakened. Pull off completely any faded leaves. Feed weekly in summer and water the compost thoroughly whenever it feels dry on the surface. Keep it just damp in winter. Spray daily with tepid water and clean the leaves with rainwater once a month. Repot annually in equal amounts of a standard soil- and peat-based compost. Keep the plant warm, out of draughts, away from radiators, and do not overwater. Brown leaves (unless they are just old) indicate dry air or starvation; yellow leaves indicate starvation or over-watering (the latter also causes water to drip from the leaf edges). If the leaves are not perforated then the plant may be too young (they usually split after 3 or 4 years), underfed, in too small a pot or in poor light. Propagate by stem cuttings, leaf-bud cuttings or by air layering tall plants (page 22).

THE SPECIES

Monstera deliciosa (syn. ***Philodendron pertusum***) (Central America and Mexico) Ceriman, Swiss Cheese Plant, Mexican Breadfruit, Shingle Plant, Split-leaf Philodendron. Height and spread around 6 ft when grown as a house plant. The huge heart-shaped leaves carried on this thick-stemmed scrambler are deep green, leathery and usually perforated and slashed. The young leaves are fresh green and unroll from the top of the stem. The creamy-white, pineapple-scented arum flowers rarely appear.

Monstera deliciosa

Epipremnum aureum

Epipremnum aureum
'Marble Queen'

Philodendron (fil-o-*den*-dron) From the Greek: *phileo* – to love, and *dendron* – tree; the plants love to climb trees.

Cultivation Varied plants in many shapes and sizes but with similar requirements when it comes to growing conditions. All prefer indirect light to bright sunshine which scorches the fleshy leaves, and one in particular, *Philodendron scandens*, will tolerate heavy shade. The latter can also put up with lower temperatures than most – around 10°C (50°F) – the others preferring a min. of 13-16°C (55-60°F). Train the stems of the climbing kinds around a supporting framework or, better still, up a moss stick where they can sink their aerial roots into the moist material. Peel off any faded leaves as soon as they are noticed. Spray the plants daily with tepid water, or stand them on a tray of moist peat or gravel to improve atmospheric humidity. Clean the leaves once a month with a damp sponge. Water thoroughly in summer whenever the compost feels dry, but keep it only slightly damp in winter to prevent stem rot. Feed monthly in summer and repot every other spring into a peat-based compost. Propagation is by means of stem cuttings taken in spring and summer and rooted in a heated propagator or by air layering older plants at the same time of year.

THE SPECIES

Philodendron bipennifolium (syn. *P. panduriforme*) (Brazil) Fiddle Leaf, Panda Plant. Height 6 ft or more, spread dependent upon support system. The glossy green leaves of this species are shaped nothing like a fiddle despite their common name. They vary in shape according to age and where they occur on the plant. These are very attractive and well displayed by their fleshy climbing stem.

Philodendron bipinnatifidum (Brazil) Panda Plant, Tree Philodendron. Height 5 ft or more, spread 6 ft. A philodendron for a large room where it can spread without encroaching too much on the living space. The large leaves are deeply cut into round-ended lobes and radiate on stout stalks from a central stem. Shrubby rather than climbing.

Philodendron domesticum (syn. *P. hastatum* of gardens) (Origin unknown) Elephant's Ear, Spade Leaf. Height 6 ft or more, spread dependent upon support system. Glossy green arrow-shaped leaves are carried quite thickly on a fleshy climbing stem. Relatively easy to grow up a moss stick. *P.* x 'Burgundy' is similar but has dark green leaves and deep maroon leaf stalks.

Philodendron bipinnatifidum

Philodendron bipennifolium

Philodendron domesticum

Philodendron (continued)

Philodendron scandens **var.** *oxycardium* (syn. *P. oxycardium*) (Tropical America) Sweetheart Plant, Parlour Ivy, Heart-leaf. Height and spread dependent upon support system. The neat heart-shaped leaves are mid-green and glossy, tinged with coppery bronze when first unfurling from their pink sheaths. The true *P. scandens* has leaves tinged with pink on their undersides, but it is this variety which is most commonly offered. Climbing stems display the leaves well and they can be garlanded around shelves and bookcases. The plant also does well in suspended pots and is remarkably tolerant of poor growing conditions and neglect. Pinch out the shoot tips occasionally to keep it in trim. A reliable plant for any novice. (Not illustrated.)

Philodendron scandens **'Variegatum'**. As the true species but the leaves are splashed with cream. Rather more difficult to grow so keep it slightly warmer and in reasonable light conditions rather than heavy shade.

Philodendron selloum (Brazil) Lacy Tree Philodendron. Height 5 ft or more, spread 6 ft. Rather like *P. bipinnatifidum* (but the foliage is much more finely cut. The long leaf lobes are wavy edged and so have a lacy appearance. If anything slightly more difficult than *P. bipinnatifidum* and needs just as much space.

Scindapsus (sin-*dap*-suss) Greek name for an ivy-like plant.

Cultivation Exactly as for *Epipremnum* (see page 234) to which it is closely related (the two were at one time grouped in the same genus).

THE SPECIES

Scindapsus pictus **'Argyraeus'** (Indonesia, Malaysia) Ivy Arum, Silver Vine. Height and spread dependent upon support system. The leaves are heart shaped and not unlike those of *Epipremnum aureum* in general outline, but instead of being heavily variegated in bright yellow they are lightly blotched with silvery grey in a roughly circular pattern. This cultivar is said to be a juvenile form of the true species which has blotching of a more greeny colour. Not the easiest climbing house plant to grow as it needs plenty of heat and humidity to do well.

Scindapsus pictus 'Argyraeus'

Philodendron scandens var. *oxycardium*

Philodendron selloum

Spathiphyllum (spath-ee-*fill*-um) From the Greek: *spathe* – a spathe, and *phyllon* – a leaf; the broad spathes are leaf like.

Cultivation These are plants for a slightly shady situation in a warm room. They demand a min. winter temp. of 13°C (55°F) and resent draughts and fluctuating temperatures. Stand them on a tray of moist peat or gravel to increase humidity levels. Try to keep the compost moist at all times during the growing season, but barely damp in winter. Never let it dry out completely. An occasional spray over with tepid water will be appreciated. Feed fortnightly in summer and repot in spring using a peat-based compost. Clean the leaves with a damp sponge once month. Propagation is by division of the clumps at repotting time.

THE SPECIES

Spathiphyllum wallisi (Colombia) Peace Lily, White Sails. Height and spread up to 1½ ft. The dark green leathery leaves are pointed and crimped along the edges and they arch outwards from the central growing point. The flowers may appear from spring to autumn and consist of a large greenish-white spathe (which becomes purer white as it ages) centred with a spiky spadix. Each bloom lasts for many weeks. Suitable for large mixed plantings.

Syngonium (sin-*go*-nee-um) From the Greek: *syn* – together, and *gone* – reproductive organs; the ovaries are joined together.

Cultivation Cultivation is exactly the same as that for the climbing *Philodendron* species (see page 236). Syngonium likes a min. temp. of 16°C (60°F), a spot in indirect light, a moss stick up which to be trained and a humid atmosphere. Removal of the climbing stems as they form will keep the plant bushy. As the plant ages its leaves will change shape – they start off as simple arrowheads and eventually become five-lobed.

THE SPECIES

Syngonium podophyllum (syn. ***Nephthytis liberica*** and ***N. afzelii*** of gardens) (Mexico to Panama) African Evergreen, Arrowhead Vine, Goosefoot Plant. Height to 3 ft or more in the home, spread dependent upon support system. The fresh green leaves are flushed with creamy white around the veins. Bushy in the early stages of growth, the climbing habit develops with age. (Not illustrated.)

***Syngonium podophyllum* 'Emerald Gem'** (syn. ***Nephthytis* 'Emerald Gem'**). Height to 3 ft or more, spread dependent upon support system. Here the leaves are broader than in the true species and there is less creamy-yellow marking. The entire leaf surface is a really bright green.

***Syngonium podophyllum* 'Imperial White'** (syn. ***Nephthytis* 'Imperial White'**). Height to 3 ft or more, spread dependent upon support system. The most freely variegated cultivar. Only the leaf margin is rich green, the rest is creamy white with a speckled zone where the two colours meet. Very spectacular but needing reasonable light at all times if the variegation is not to lose its lustre.

Spathiphyllum wallisii

Syngonium podophyllum
'Imperial White'

Syngonium podophyllum
'Emerald Gem'

Zantedeschia (zan-ted-*esh*-ee-a) Named after the Italian botanist Francesco Zantedeschi (1797-?).

Cultivation Good plants for spacious, cool rooms where the light intensity is good. Maintain a min. temp. of 7°C (45°F) for *Z. aethiopica* and a minimum of 13°C (55°F) for *Z. elliottiana*. A spot in good but indirect light is preferred. Plant the fleshy rhizomes singly in 6-in pots of a standard soil-based compost in late summer so that they rest only 1 in below the surface. Give a good watering and then apply no more until growth is noticed, then keep the compost amply moist at all times. Feed fortnightly from spring to early summer and give an occasional spray with tepid water. After flowering gradually allow the compost to become quite dry so that the leaves turn yellow. Pull away the faded leaves and repot the rhizomes in late summer to start the process all over again. Alternatively *Z. aethiopica* can be kept in gentle growth all the time if water is not withheld. Propagate by division of clumps at repotting time.

THE SPECIES

Zantedeschia aethiopica (syn. ***Z. africana, Richardia aethiopica***) (South Africa and now elsewhere) Arum Lily, Common Calla, White Calla Lily. Height and spread around 3 ft. A bold and succulent plant with lustrous green arrow-shaped leaves carried on fat, juicy stalks. The white arum flowers with their wrap-around spathes and yellow spadices are exceptionally elegant and quite long lasting if kept cool. Superb in cold conservatories and sunrooms.
Zantedeschia elliottiana (syn. ***Richardia elliottiana***) (South Africa) Golden Calla Lily, Yellow Arum Lily. Height 2-3 ft, spread 2 ft. Smaller in stature than *Z. aethiopica* but still statuesque. The thick green arrowhead leaves are speckled with silver grey and the flowers are a rich chrome yellow flushed with green at the base. Just a little more difficult than the white arum lily.

Zantedeschia aethiopica

Zantedeschia elliottiana

Liliaceae   Lily Family

A large cosmopolitan family of herbs, succulents and one or two climbers. Many have swollen underground storage organs, and a good proportion of the 250 genera are cultivated for their economic value, among them asparagus, leeks, onions and garlic. Other species have medicinal uses but the majority are cultivated as ornamentals including lilies, tulips, hyacinths and fritillarias. The following genera are widely grown as house plants; *Aloe*, *Asparagus*, *Aspidistra*, *Beaucarnea*, *Chlorophytum*, *Haworthia*, *Lachenalia* and *Veltheimia*.

Aloe (*a*-loe) Derived from the original Arabic name.

Cultivation Easy plants for sunny windowsills where they will tolerate a min. temp. of 5°C (40°F) provided they are not kept too damp. During summer water the compost thoroughly whenever it feels dry, but in winter allow it to remain drier, watering once every six weeks or so to prevent shrivelling as the plants will have stored plenty of water in their fleshy leaves during the summer. Feed occasionally in summer and repot in spring only when the existing container is too small to accommodate the rosette of leaves, using equal parts standard soil-based compost and coarse sand to ensure really sharp drainage. Propagate by removing offsets at repotting time, or by taking off these sideshoots during spring and summer, letting them dry off for a few days and then rooting them in sandy compost. Mealy bugs may be troublesome.

THE SPECIES

Aloe arborescens (South Africa) Candelabra Plant, Tree Aloe. Height up to 3 ft in the home but to 10 ft if allowed; spread 2 ft. The tall, often unbranched stem produces arched grey-green leaves one on top of another. Each leaf may be up to 2 ft long, and although the curved spines look lethal they are relatively soft. Peel off any leaves that fade, and provide support for tall plants before they topple. Clay pots are more efficient than plastic ones at keeping old plants upright. Red flower clusters may be produced in winter.

Aloe aristata (South Africa) Lace Aloe, Torch Plant. Height 4 in, spread 6 in. A rosette-forming aloe with plump but elongated leaves of fresh green. Little 'teeth' appear all over the leaves to give them a coarse feel, and there is usually a shrivelled wispy end to each leaf tip. Offsets are produced in abundance. A north-facing windowsill is best for this species to prevent discoloration. Red flowers may appear on long stalks in summer.

Aloe humilis (South Africa) Hedgehog Aloe. Height 3-4 in, spread 6 in. Another ground-hugging rosette form similar in appearance to *A. aristata* but a more glaucous green. The leaves are once more speckled with little white teeth and this time the flowers (green and red in colour) appear in winter.

Aloe variegata (South Africa) Partridge-breasted Aloe. Height 6 in, spread 4 in. This species makes an upright cockade of leaves with smudged markings of dark green, light green and silver grey. The pinkish green tubular flowers are carried on 1-ft high stems in spring.

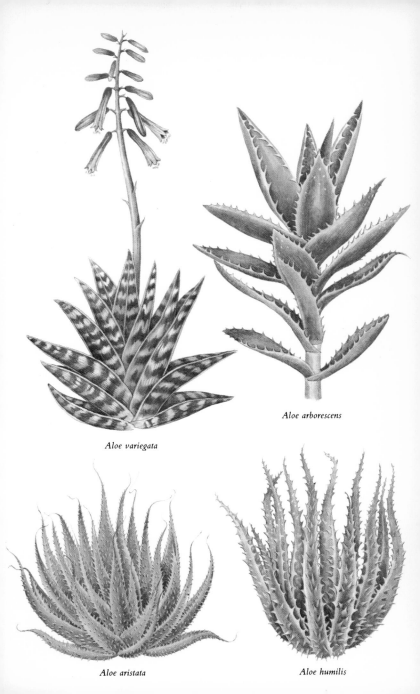

Aloe variegata

Aloe arborescens

Aloe aristata

Aloe humilis

Asparagus (asp-*a*-rag-uss) The ancient name for the plant.

Cultivation Excellent foliage plants for cool rooms where their thin 'leaves' (really leaf-like stems known as cladodes) will not be dried out by excessive heat. They will tolerate temps. as low as 7°C (45°F) if they have to, and prefer a position in indirect light or light shade (sun will scorch them). Cut off completely any stems whose leaves have turned yellow, and trim away untidy growth in spring. Water thoroughly when the surface of the compost feels dry, but keep it barely moist in winter. An occasional spray over with tepid water will perk up the foliage, and a fortnightly feed in summer will keep the plants in peak condition. Repot every spring in a standard soil- or peat-based compost. Propagate by division at repotting time, or by seeds sown in gentle heat in spring.

THE SPECIES

All are generally known as Asparagus Ferns.

Asparagus densiflorus (syn. ***A. sprengeri***) (South Africa). Height 1 ft, spread to 3 ft. A graceful arching plant with soft fuzzy foliage that makes a perfect background for more dazzling plants. Nevertheless *A. densiflorus* is still worth growing on its own as a hanging-basket specimen or in suspended or wall-mounted pots. If grown as a climber it can be trained up a support system for 6 ft or so. Easy to manage and tolerant of a fair amount of neglect. Clusters of small white flowers may be produced. Watch out for the tiny thorns.

Asparagus densiflorus* 'Myersii'** (syn. ***A. meyeri, A. myersii). Height 2 ft, spread 3 ft. Surely the most handsome of the asparagus ferns, this cultivar holds its ferny foliage in tubular 'bottle-brushes' of bright green. Long lasting and well suited to cool conservatories and sunrooms.

Asparagus setaceus (syn. ***A. plumosus***). Height 4 to 6 ft, spread up to 4 ft. This is the wedding buttonhole asparagus fern and whilst the true species scrambles to 6 ft or so, there is a much more compact form *A.s.* 'Nanus' (syn. *A.p.* 'Nanus') which grows to 1 ft with a spread of 2 ft. The feathery triangular fronds must be kept cool and away from heat sources if they are not to be shed. Flowers are seldom produced.

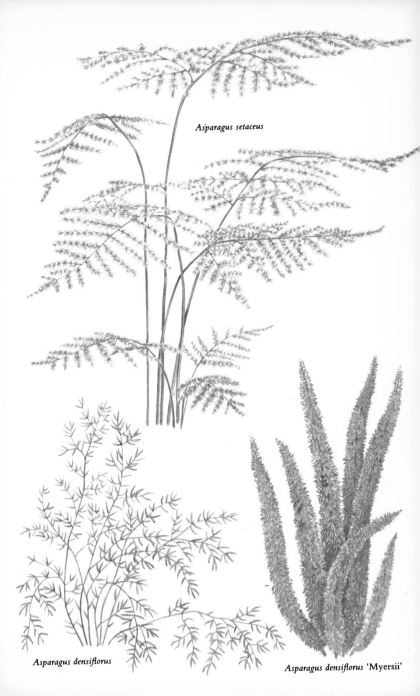

Asparagus setaceus

Asparagus densiflorus

Asparagus densiflorus 'Myersii'

Aspidistra (ass-pid-*iss*-tra) From the Greek: *aspidion* – a shield; the stigmas are shield-shaped.

Cultivation The aspidistra really does thrive on neglect – only overwatering and excessive root disturbance will cause it to curl up and die. It will tolerate temps. as low as 5°C (40°F) with no sign of hardship, but it may suffer in rooms that are excessively hot and dry, though not where the central heating is adjusted to a reasonable level; around 21°C (70°F). Keep it out of bright sunlight at all times or the leaf tips will scorch. It will tolerate as much shade as you care to give it. Any leaf tips that do turn brown can be neatly snipped off with a pair of scissors. Water thoroughly in summer only when the compost has become dust dry. Give less water in winter, a soggy compost at this time of year will harm the plant. Feed monthly in summer and repot only when absolutely necessary when the plant is really pushing itself out of its pot. Use a container only 2 in larger than the previous one and a standard soil-based compost. Clean the leaves once a month with a damp sponge. Propagate by division of clumps at repotting time. Red spider mites and mealy bugs may be a problem.

THE SPECIES

Aspidistra elatior (syn. *A. lurida*) (China) Cast Iron Plant, Parlour Palm. Height and spread 1-2 ft. The leathery dark green leaves are long and pointed and quite a fresh shade of green when they first emerge. Each leaf will last for several years (usually at least five) and with any luck the pot will eventually become filled with a crowded cluster of foliage. Ridiculously easy if you don't kill it with kindness. Most striking when grown against a pale background. Purplish stemless flowers may be produced at soil level but you will have to look closely to see them. They are pollinated by slugs.

Aspidistra elatior 'Variegata' (syn. *A. lurida* 'Variegata'). In this cultivar the leaves are striped with creamy white and dark green. It is a little more difficult to cultivate than the true species, demanding slightly higher temperatures and good but indirect light. A striking pot plant when well grown.

Beaucarnea (bo-*car*-nee-a) Named by Victor Lemoine, (1823-1911) a French nurseryman, after Monsieur Beaucarne a 19th century Belgian public notary.

Cultivation A good plant for centrally-heated rooms and where a temp. of 10°C (50°F) can be guaranteed in winter. Position the plant in good light, it will even tolerate some direct sunshine. Peel off any leaves as they fade. Water the plant thoroughly but only when the surface of the compost is dry as it resents overwatering but can happily tolerate a little dryness. Feed monthly in summer and repot in spring when necessary using a soil-based compost. Propagate by means of offsets which can be removed and potted up in spring. Seeds can be sown in a temp. of 18°C (65°F) in spring.

THE SPECIES

Beaucarnea recurvata (syn. *Nolina recurvata*) (Mexico) Bottle Palm, Pony-tail Plant. Height up to 6 ft or more in pots, spread about 2 ft. An oddity with a pony tail-like tuft of linear green leaves at the top of a tall, woody stem. The base of the stem is swollen rather like a turnip which adds to the bizarre appearance. A good talking point if nothing else.

Aspidistra elatior

Aspidistra elatior 'Variegata'

Beaucarnea recurvata

Chlorophytum (clor-o-*fy*-tum) From the Greek: *chloros* – green, and *phyton* – a plant; most species are green, rather than variegated.

Cultivation An easy plant to grow if given a rich diet. It demands little in the way of heat, tolerating 7°C (45°F) in winter and preferring good ventilation during the warmer months of the year, and it likes a spot in really good light. Water the compost really thoroughly as soon as it is dry on the surface in summer. In winter keep it barely damp, but never let it dry out at any time of year or the leaf tips will turn brown. Similar symptoms will result if the plant is starved so make sure that it is fed once a fortnight in summer and that it is repotted every spring into a larger container of standard soil- or peat-based compost. Occasional misting with a hand sprayer will do no harm at all and helps to keep the plant's lustre. Plantlets will form on older plants that are not starved. Propagation is simple; just remove and pot up the small plantlets individually, or coax them to produce a few roots first by standing them in small jar of water.

THE SPECIES

***Chlorophytum comosum* 'Mandaianum'** (South Africa) Spider Plant. Height 1½ ft, spread 2 ft. The nomenclature surrounding this plant is very confused but this name should represent the common Spider Plant with arching fountains of channelled leaves centred with creamy white and margined with rich green. Tall creamy-yellow flower stems are produced by mature plants and, as well as bearing tiny white blooms, they also carry the plantlets which can be detached and grown on. Excellent in hanging baskets where the leaves and young plants will cascade over the edge of the container.

Haworthia (ha-*wor*-thee-a) Named after Adrian Hardy Haworth (1768-1833), an Englishman who was an authority on succulents and butterflies and moths. He published a monograph on *Mesembryanthemum* in 1794.

Cultivation Exactly as for *Aloe*, (see page 244).

THE SPECIES

Haworthia margaritifera (South Africa) Pearl Plant. Height 3-4 in, spread 4 in or more. A plump-leaved rosette-forming succulent with mid-green leaves banded with little white warty outgrowths that are known as tubercles. Many offsets are produced, making propagation easy.

Haworthia reinwardtii (South Africa) Wart Plant. Height 6 in, spread 1 in or more. A columnar haworthia with deep blue-green succulent leaves that are tightly clustered together in a helical pattern. Shade this plant from brilliant sunshine in the summer to prevent it from becoming desiccated. The white tubercles give the plant its common name. It will often produce heads of flowers in winter. This species should be given a little water in winter, unlike *H. margaritifera* which can be left almost bone dry.

Chlorophytum comosum
'Mandaianum'

*Haworthia
reinwardtii*

*Haworthia
margaritifera*

Lachenalia (lack-en-*ay*-lee-a) Named after Werner de la Chenal (1736-1800), Professor of Botany at Basle, Switzerland.

Cultivation Easy and unusual bulbs well worth growing in a cool room where the temp. remains over 7°C (45°F). The plants like full light and even bright sun. Pot up the bulbs at the rate of five to a 5-in pot of standard soil-based compost in late summer or early autumn; the 'noses' of the bulbs should be just below the surface of the compost. Water the bulbs in and then do not water again until growth is observed. Once the leaves appear, water the compost well whenever the surface feels dry. When plenty of growth has been made, feed the plants at fortnightly intervals until the flowers open. After flowering water as instructed for several weeks, then allow the compost to dry out completely. Knock the bulbs from the dry compost in early autumn and start them into growth as before. Propagate by removing and potting up offsets. Greenfly may be a problem.

THE SPECIES

Lachenalia aloides (syn. *L. tricolor*) (South Africa) Cape Cowslip. Height and spread 1 ft. The strap-shaped arching green leaves are spotted with liver brown and the flower stems rise up amongst them from late winter to spring. The tubular yellow flowers hang like elongated bells and are yellow tinged with green and red.

Veltheimia (vel-*time*-ee-a) Named after August Ferdinand von Veltheim (1741-1801), a German patron of botany.

Cultivation These bulbs prefer a slightly warmer situation than lachenalia but they still dislike hot and stuffy rooms. Maintain a winter min. of 10°C (50°F) and avoid temps. above 18°C (65°F). The plants like a position in good but indirect light. Plant in autumn at the rate of one bulb to a 5-in pot of standard soil-based compost, leaving half the bulb exposed. Water in and then do not water again until growth is visible, then water well as soon as the surface of the compost feels dry. Feed fortnightly once plenty of growth has been made, stopping only when the flowers fade. Keep the compost around *V. bracteata* moist after flowering (it does not need a resting period) but allow the compost around *V. capensis* gradually to dry out completely. The bulbs can be salvaged from the old compost and repotted in autumn. Propagate by removing the offsets and potting these up individually to grow on to flowering size. Greenfly are the only pest likely to be troublesome.

THE SPECIES

Veltheimia bracteata (syn. *V. viridifolia*) (South Africa) Forest Lily, Winter Red-hot Poker. Height up to 1½ ft, spread 1 ft. The purplish flower stalk rises up from the lustrous broad green leaves in winter and opens its rich pink, green-tinged blooms over a period of several weeks.
Veltheimia capensis (syn. *V. glauca, V. roodeae*) (South Africa). Height up to 1½ ft, spread 1 ft. Altogether a more dainty looking plant. The glaucous-green leaves arch gracefully and possess wavy margins. The flower stalk is purplish and the tubular bells are pink and rather shorter than those of *V. bracteata*; they appear about a month earlier. Forms are available with flowers of differing shades and with colourful spotting. (Not illustrated.)

Lachenalia aloides

Veltheimia bracteata

Amaryllidaceae Daffodil Family

Evergeen and deciduous plants usually with swollen underground storage organs. The 75 genera occur mainly in warm temperate areas but also in the subtropics and tropics.

Clivia (*kly*-vee-a and sometimes *kliv*-ee-a) Named after the granddaughter of Clive of India, in whose garden the plant first flowered.

Cultivation Place in a cool, well-lit room with a temp. as low as 7°C (45°F). Plants will suffer in high summer temperatures and bright sunshine. Water well when the surface of the compost feels dry during spring and summer, but keep it much drier in winter, only watering when the plant feels limp. This resting period will help to promote flower production. Feed monthly in summer and repot in autumn only when essential using a standard soil- or peat-based compost; the plants flower better when potbound. Clean leaves monthly with a damp sponge. Divide established clumps in autumn.

THE SPECIES

Clivia miniata (syn. *Imantophyllum miniata*) (South Africa) Kaffir Lily. Height and spread 2-3 ft. Thick flower stalks push up between the dark green strap-like leaves in spring and summer bearing a cluster of orange flowers marked with yellow in the throat. Keep the plant cool and never move in bud or bloom or the flowers may be shed.

Haemanthus (hee-*man*-thuss) From the Greek: *haima* – blood, and *anthos* – a flower; the blooms of most species are red.

Cultivation These bulbous plants should be grown in a sunny spot in a warm but well-ventilated room with a min. temp. of 10°C (50°F) and around 18°C (65°F) when in active growth. Pot the dormant bulbs in a basic soil-based compost, individually in a 4-in, or 3-in pot, with the noses exposed. Keep barely moist until growth shows then water only when the surface of the compost feels dry. Never overwater. Feed once when the blooms are open and again after they have faded. Continue to water for a few weeks, then gradually let the compost become drier, drying out completely when the leaves begin to yellow. Start them into growth by watering again a year after purchase. Repot every third year in standard soil-based compost. Propagate by seeds or by removing offsets at repotting time.

THE SPECIES

Known as Blood or Torch Lilies, Cape Tulips and Paint Brushes.

Haemanthus albiflos (South Africa). Height and spread 1 ft. An evergreen which needs a monthly trickle of water during its resting period. The bracts are greenish white and surround a bunch of stamens tipped with bright yellow pollen. The dull green leaves are thick and leathery.

Haemanthus coccineus (South Africa). Height 9 in, spread 2-4 ft. The flowers, a tuft of yellow-tipped stamens surrounded by bright red bracts, are held on a red-spotted stem. They emerge before the leaves.

Haemanthus katherinae (Natal, East Transvaal, Malawi). Height and spread 1-2 ft. The 1-ft long leaves are green, quite broad but not succulent. The bright red starry blooms are carried in clusters and emerge in summer on a 1-ft stalk.

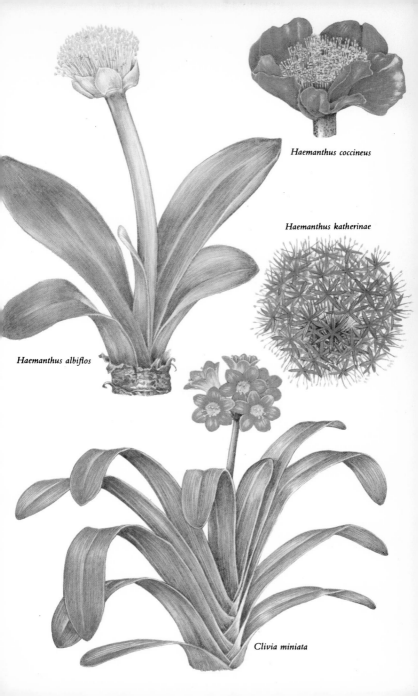

Haemanthus coccineus

Haemanthus katherinae

Haemanthus albiflos

Clivia miniata

Hippeastrum (hip-ee-*ass*-trum) From the Greek: *hippos* – horse, and *hippeus* – rider; when the scales that cover the flower stand upwards before the bud opens they resemble a horse's ears and the bud represents the horse's head.

Cultivation Hippeastrums are purchased as dry bulbs in autumn. Pot up each bulb singly in a 6-in pot of a basic soil-based compost. Use moist compost and leave the upper half of the bulb exposed to view. If the compost is moist at potting time there will be no need to water it until the flower spike is well in evidence; it emerges before the leaves. Stand the pot in a well-lit spot out of direct sunlight and maintain a temp. of around 18°C (65°F) with a min. of 13°C (55°F). During its flowering period the bulb will produce very few roots and if the compost is kept too wet the base of the bulb may rot, so water with care until the flowers fade. Cut off the stalk once the blooms have gone, and water whenever the compost feels dry. Feed at fortnightly intervals as the leaves grow. In late summer allow the compost to dry off completely and remove the leaves when they are quite crisp. Bulbs that are kept growing all the year round seldom flower as well as those that are rested. Do not repot every year. Instead scrape away the top 2 in of compost in autumn and replace it with fresh, watering gently to encourage growth. Bottom heat is helpful in encouraging flower development. This topdressing will give the bulb a boost without causing root disturbance. Propagate by sowing seeds in a temperature of 18°C (65°F). Pot up the seedlings individually in 2-in pots and keep the compost moist all the year round to encourage continuous growth (it can remain slightly drier in winter). Grow the young plants like this for 3 years, potting them on as necessary. They can then be treated like mature bulbs and given an annual rest. Offsets can be removed from large bulbs at repotting time. Mealy bugs may infest the growing point.

THE SPECIES

Nowadays all the hippeastrums grown as house plants are:

***Hippeastrum* cultivars** (Raised as a result of crossing *H. aulicum, H. elegans, H. reginae, H. reticulatum* and *H. striatum.*) (Originally natives of Central and South America) Amaryllis. Height up to 2 ft, spread 1½ ft. Two to four spectacular flowers emerge on a fat pale green stalk sometimes flushed with red. The massive blooms have 6 tepals (petal-like sepals) which may be crimson, scarlet, orange, pink or white, often suffused with a darker or lighter colour. The blooms usually open in spring but 'treated' bulbs bought from a specialist merchant can be flowered in winter. The green, leathery leaves are strap shaped and arch elegantly.

Hippeastrum cvs.

Vallota (val-*oe*-ta) Named after Pierre Vallot (1594–1671), a French botanist and physician who wrote of Louis XIII's gardens in 1623.

Cultivation A colourful plant for a bright spot, especially a windowsill. Maintain a min. winter temp. of 7°C (45°F) and preferably a little more. The bulbs are evergreen and never die down completely but they can be bought while relatively dormant in summer. Pot up the bulbs individually in 5- to 6-in pots of a standard soil-based compost and water very carefully at first until growth is underway. Feed at monthly intervals when leaves form but stop after the flowers fade or in late autumn. Water with care in winter, keeping the compost barely moist until early summer. Repot every three years or when pots are overcrowded with bulbs. Topdress every year, removing some compost from the surface and replacing it with fresh. Do this in summer. Propagation is by the division of mature clumps of bulbs in summer.

THE SPECIES

Vallota speciosa (syn. ***V. purpurea***) (South Africa) Berg Lily, George Lily, Scarborough Lily. (The English common name has arisen as a result of some bulbs being washed ashore from a wrecked Dutch ship at Scarborough on the Yorkshire coast in about 1800, though the plant was first introduced to Britain some 30 years earlier.) Height and spread up to 1½ ft. The narrow green leaves arch elegantly from the soil and are present at the same time as the flower spikes which rise up among them. The flowers (up to 10 in number) are orange-red star-shaped blooms with 6 tepals (petal-like sepals). The red stamens are tipped with golden anthers. The flowers open in late summer and autumn. Forms are available with pink or white flowers and these are usually given the names of *V. s.* var. *delicata*, and *V. s.* var. *alba* respectively.

Vallota speciosa var. *delicata*

Vallota speciosa var. *alba*

Vallota speciosa

Agavaceae Sisal Hemp Family

A family of woody, rhizomatous plants and a few climbers native to arid regions of the tropics and subtropics. There are around 20 genera and many of them are grown for their economic value. Two of the *Agave* species produce sisal hemp, and *Phormium tenax* is the New Zealand flax. Other species are also grown for their fibres, and one or two are used as a source of alcoholic drinks (*Agave americana* produces tequila). From the house-plant grower's point of view the family is very important, for it includes *Agave*, *Cordyline*, *Dracaena*, *Sansevieria* and *Yucca*.

Agave (a-*gar*-vee, but often incorrectly *a*-gayve) From the Greek: *agauos* – admirable; the plant is a handsome sight when in flower.

Cultivation These are easy plants to grow provided they are given bright light, even direct sun, at all times of the year. They will tolerate the natural rise of temperature in summer and will put up with a min. of 5°C (40°F) in winter provided they are kept much drier at the roots. In summer water freely when the surface of the compost feels dry but in winter be much less generous. Peel off any of the lower leaves that wither and turn brown. Feed once a month in summer. Repot in spring using a standard soil-based compost with some extra sharp sand added if possible to ensure really good drainage. Do not repot every year but only when the plant has obviously filled its existing container with roots and exhausted the available nutrients. Agaves look good outdoors during the summer and the fresh air will improve them before they are returned to the house in early autumn. The plants seldom flower in pots which in some ways is an advantage, for the old rosette of leaves usually dies when the flowers fade. Seeds can be sown in a heated propagator in spring, or offsets can be removed and potted up on their own at repotting time. Beware of mealy bugs and scale insects.

THE SPECIES

Agave americana (Mexico and now Mediterranean areas) American Aloe, Century Plant, Maguey. Height and spread 3 ft or much more but usually around 1-2 ft in pots. The spiny-edged fibrous leaves are slightly blue grey and edged with crimson spines. The rosette formation is rather open and very handsome. The flower stem may be up to 25 ft high and the juice which is extracted from it and fermented is tequila. Do not build up your hopes of making this though, because the common name of Century Plant (although a slight exaggeration) indicates how long it takes for the plant to flower.
Agave americana **'Medio-picta'**. As the true species but each leaf is centred with a broad creamy-yellow stripe.
Agave americana **'Variegata'** (syn. *A. a.* **'Marginata'**). This cultivar has bright butter-yellow stripes along the margins of the leaves.
Agave victoriae-reginae (Mexico) Queen Agave. Height 6 in, spread 9 in. A distinctive succulent plant with multi-faceted leaves that are lined with white and tipped with black spines. The appearance is rather like that of a globe artichoke prepared for eating, though the scales are much fatter and more three-dimensional. An important succulent for the collector.

Agave americana
'Medio–picta'

Agave americana

Agave victoriae-reginae

Agave americana 'Variegata'

Cordyline (cor-dee-*ly*-nee, and often incorrectly *cor*-dee-line) From the Greek: *kordyle* – a club; the roots of some species are very thick and club-like.

Cultivation Stately plants for cool, well-lit rooms, the two species illustrated on the page opposite are the easiest cordylines to grow. They both tolerate fairly low temperatures in winter and *C. australis* will even survive slight frost and is grown outdoors in sheltered parts of Britain. *C. indivisa* is best provided with a winter min. of 7°C (45°F). Grow both in bright light at all times and put them outdoors in summer where they will enjoy the sunshine and showers. Both plants are frequently used as specimen tub or urn plants and as dot plants in bedding schemes. Water the compost freely in summer when it shows signs of drying out on the surface (the plants are great drinkers in warm weather). In winter keep the compost only just moist. Clean the leaves once a month with a damp sponge when the plant is indoors. Feed fortnightly in summer and repot in spring every year if necessary using a rich soil-based compost. Clay pots will help to keep the plants upright. Peel off the lower leaves when they fade. Propagate by sowing the seeds in spring at a temp. of 18°C (65°F).

THE SPECIES

Cordyline australis (syn. ***Dracaena australis***) (New Zealand) Cabbage Tree. Height up to 5 ft in pots, spread 3 ft. Easy 'palms' to grow from seed. They are plants which become even more handsome with age as the leaves radiate in a full sphere from the top of the steadily extending stem. The foliage is narrow and green with each leaf being perhaps 1 in wide at most and 3 ft long.

Cordyline indivisa (syn. ***Dracaena indivisa***) (New Zealand) Mountain Cabbage Tree. Height and spread as for *C. australis* which this species greatly resembles. However, it is not quite so hardy and will also prefer good indirect light to bright sunshine indoors.

Cordyline indivisa

Cordyline australis

Cordyline (continued)

The following *Cordyline* species are best treated as for *Dracaena* (see cultivation details on page 266).

Cordyline terminalis (syn. ***Dracaena terminalis***) (Tropical Asia, Polynesia) Dragon Tree, Ti Tree. Height 2-3 ft in pots, spread 1-1½ ft. A splendidly showy, if rather difficult plant for a warm room. The broad, pointed leaves are stalked at the base where they wrap partially around the finger-thick stem. The leaves are glossy and dark green with stripes and splashes of maroon and carmine. The coloration may vary from plant to plant. Clusters of small whitish flowers may be produced but these are rather insignificant.

***Cordyline terminalis* 'Rededge'** (syn. ***Dracaena terminalis* 'Rededge'**). As *C. terminalis* in shape and stature, but here the leaves are deep burgundy edged with carmine. It is a very showy cultivar but needs warm, humid conditions and good light at all times (but never direct sun) if it is to do really well. Like all the dracaenas in this group the plant produces a single woody stem as it ages and the fountain of leaves sits on the top. A spectacular specimen plant.

***Cordyline terminalis* 'Tricolor'** (syn. ***Dracaena terminalis* 'Tricolor'**). The leaves of this cultivar are a real painter's palette of colour. They are a mixture of rich green, butter yellow and cream with splashes of rosy red. Not the most subtle of mixtures but a good plant for a warm, well-lit corner that needs bringing to life.

Cordyline terminalis
'Rededge'

Cordyline terminalis

Cordyline terminalis
'Tricolor'

Dracaena (dra-*see*-na) From the Greek: *drakaina* – a female dragon; so named either because *Dracaena draco* produces dragon's blood (a red resin), or after Sir Francis Drake who supplied Clusius, the Flemish botanist, with plants.

Cultivation These need a min. temp. of 13°C (55°F) in winter and between 18 and 21°C (65 and 70°F) in summer. They thrive in indirect light or slight shade. Peel off dead leaves as soon as they wither; this should only happen to the bottom ones, if the upper ones turn brown the plant is either in a draught, too near a heat source or a sunny window, too cold, or too wet or dry at the roots. Water freely in summer as soon as the compost feels dry on the surface, but in winter keep it barely moist but never bone dry. Spray the foliage daily with tepid rainwater, or stand the plant in a tray or bowl of moist peat or gravel to increase humidity. Repot in spring when necessary, usually every other year, using a standard soil-based compost. Feed fortnightly in summer. Remove the insignificant flower heads as soon as they are seen.

Propagate by sowing seeds or from 'toes' (thick fleshy root tips), 2-in lengths of which can be bedded right way up in the rooting medium of a warm propagator. Older plants which outgrow available space can be decapitated and the top 6 in of stem rooted in a propagator. The stump left behind may sprout new shoots. Sometimes mature plants produce suckers and these can be removed and potted up at repotting time. Tall-stemmed plants can be air layered (page 22) and 2-in long sections of mature stem can be inserted into a rooting medium in a propagator and potted up when shoots and roots have appeared. Keep a look out for mealy bug and scale insects.

THE SPECIES

All are known as Dragon Lilies or Dragon Trees, although the latter name belongs to *Dracaena draco*.

Dracaena concinna (syn. **D. marginata 'Tricolor'**, **D.m.** var **concinna**) (Malagasy, Mauritius) Rainbow Plant. Height 3 ft or more, spread 1-1½ ft. The thin leaves open from the stem in the usual fountain pattern. The leaves have a central stripe of green, banded on either side by creamy yellow; the margins are a rich rosy pink. Difficult to grow, it needs humidity to prevent the leaf tips from turning brown. Do not keep the plant too shaded or the colouring will become lacklustre. It is more susceptible than most species to overwatering. Spray regularly with tepid rainwater or the opening leaves may stick together and force the growing point to snap off. If you want a single-stemmed plant keep spraying; if you want a bushier specimen content yourself with standing the plant on a tray of moist gravel. The plant offered as *D. marginata* has narrow, glossy dark green leaves edged with rosy red, but it lacks the yellow stripes.

Dracaena deremensis 'Bausei' (Originally Tropical Africa). Height 3-10 ft in the home, spread around 2 ft. This cultivar has pointed leaves that have one or two broad, creamy-white stripes down the centre.

Dracaena deremensis 'Roehrsii' (syn. **D.d. var. rhoersii**). Similar to 'Bausei', but this variety has two white stripes which are quite narrow and centred with a broader stripe of fresh green.

Dracaena deremensis 'Warneckii'. Almost a combination of the previous two cultivars, with many narrow white stripes running down the leaf.

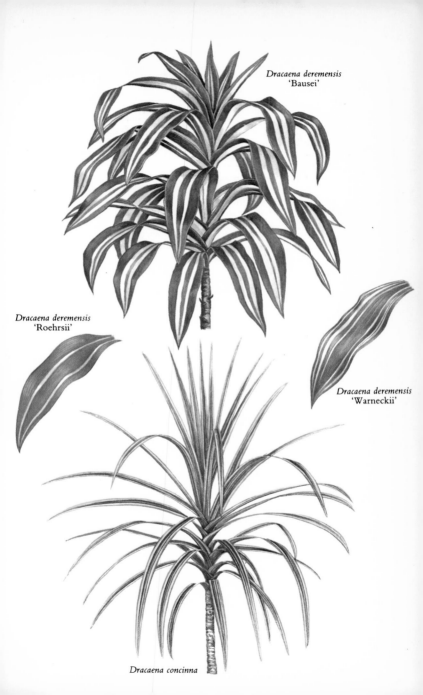

Dracaena deremensis
'Bausei'

Dracaena deremensis
'Roehrsii'

Dracaena deremensis
'Warneckii'

Dracaena concinna

Dracaena fragrans **'Lindenii'** (Originally Tropical Africa) Corn Plant. Height 2-3 ft when grown in pots, spread 1-1½ ft. A feature of all cultivars of *D. fragrans* is their really broad foliage. The leaves are like razor strops, a full 2 in or more across, and they arch so much that they almost turn under at the ends. Keep them in good condition with plenty of warmth and humidity and they will make spectacular specimen plants, though they often seem to do best when plunged in their pots in a group planting scheme – the presence of larger quantities of moisture in the atmosphere both from the plants and the extra compost works wonders. This particular cultivar has leaves which are broadly margined with yellow, and the yellow streaking seems to run through the central green zone as well. Reasonable light (but not scorching sunlight) will be necessary to retain the strength of variegation.

Dracaena fragrans **'Massangeana'** (Sometimes sold as *D. massangeana*). Similar in stature to *D. f.* 'Lindenii'. Here the leaves are a rich and lustrous green, striped in the centre with bright yellow, through which run smaller stripes of green. Another excellent foliage plant.

Dracaena reflexa **'Variegata'** (syn. *Pleomele reflexa* **'Variegata'**) (India, Sri Lanka) Song of India. Height 3 ft or more, spread 1½ ft but slow growing. A fine specimen plant often with more than one stem (unlike most of the dracaenas). It is more sensitive to overwatering than most and needs repotting only once in three years in average room conditions. The leaves radiate from a central stem and stick out quite stiffly, so the plant does not possess quite as much grace as those species whose leaves arch and cascade like a vegetative waterfall. Each leaf is margined with bright acid yellow which turns to cream with age. Good in group arrangements as well as being a worthy specimen plant.

Dracaena fragrans 'Lindenii'

Dracaena fragrans
'Massangeana'

Dracaena reflexa 'Variegata'

Dracaena (continued)

Dracaena sanderiana (Central Africa) Belgian Evergreen, Ribbon Plant. Height up to 6 ft but usually half this in the home, spread 1 ft. Perhaps the most slender and dainty of the dracaenas, this one is at its best while quite young, for then the entire stem is clad in 1-in wide leaves that are just 6-9 in long. The leaves are green in the centre and margined with creamy-white stripes. Pots of *D. sanderiana* sold in nurseries and garden centres often contain three plants. Singly the plants are useful for rooms where space is restricted, but grouped together they provide a better potful. Use the stem tips as cuttings when the plants become tall and spindly. The old stumps may well sprout again.

Dracaena surculosa (syn. ***D. godseffiana***) (Central Africa) Gold Dust Dracaena. Height and spread up to 3 ft. This dracaena is quite a slow grower and different in appearance to all the rest. It looks like a tropical version of the spotted laurel *Aucuba japonica* and has broad oval leaves spotted with pale creamy yellow. The plant is branched, unlike most other dracaenas which possess a single stem. The cultivar known as *D. s.* 'Florida Beauty' is particularly heavily spotted. Both plants do best in group plantings in larger containers.

Furcraea (fer-*cree*-a) Named in honour of Antoine François Fourcroy (1755-1809) French naturalist and professor of chemistry who also busied himself in the French Revolution.

Cultivation Generally as for *Dracaena* (see page 266). The important thing to remember about these plants is that they resent overwatering more than anything else. They will tolerate centrally heated rooms better than most plants and are certainly not so fussy about atmospheric humidity as dracaenas.

THE SPECIES

***Furcraea foetida* 'Aureo-striata'** (Originally Tropical America) Variegated False Agave. Height 1½ ft, spread up to 4 ft. A spreading plant with a rosette of long, smooth-edged leaves which are attractively variegated in cream and shades of green. Furcraeas need a reasonable amount of space in the house but can be stood outside during the summer.

Dracaena sanderiana

Dracaena surculosa

Furcraea foetida 'Aureo-striata'

Sansevieria (san-sev-*eer*-ee-a) Named after Raimond de Sansgrio, Prince of Sanseviero (1710-1771); an Italian patron of horticulture.

Cultivation Ranking with the aspidistra for ease of culture, these plants are best pleased if you stand them on a sunny windowsill, though they will also tolerate some shade. Maintain a winter min. temp. of 10°C (50°F) and the plants will come to no harm. Water only when the surface of the compost feels quite dry, the only way you can possibly kill this plant (short of setting fire to it or freezing it) is by overwatering. In winter be even more careful and keep the compost very much on the dry side, watering simply to prevent shrivelling. Feed monthly in summer, and sponge the leaves with tepid water at the same time. Repot only when the plant starts to grow out of its existing container, or when it cracks the sides. Repot in spring using a standard soil-based compost and a clay pot for added stability. Propagate by division at repotting time, or by rooting 2-in sections of leaf in a propagator in spring and summer.

THE SPECIES

Sansevieria trifasciata (South Africa) Bowstring Hemp (a name applied to most species), Mother-in-law's Tongue, Snake Plant. Height and spread up to 3 ft or more. The tall, spiky leaves of this plant are thick and fibrous and twist gently as they ascend. The ground colour of the leaf is deep green but this is overlaid with zones of grey and glaucous green to make a pattern that resembles snakeskin. The leaves are carried on thick rhizomes and these can be severed for propagation purposes. Whitish-green flowers may be produced on mature plants.

Sansevieria trifasciata **'Hahnii'** (syn. ***S. hahnii***). Height 6-9 in, spread up to 1 ft. This dwarf cultivar has much shorter, broader leaves and makes more of a rosette. The same attractive markings are present.

Sansevieria trifasciata **'Hahnii Variegata'** (syn. ***S. t.*** **'Golden Hahnii'**, ***S. hahnii*** **'Variegata'**). As *S. t.* 'Hahnii' in stature, but here the leaves are longitudinally banded with broad butter yellow stripes.

Sansevieria trifasciata **'Laurentii'**. Similar in stature to the true species, but much more spectacular for the leaves are margined with broad butter-yellow stripes. Propagate by division, for the striping is lost when plants are raised from leaf cuttings.

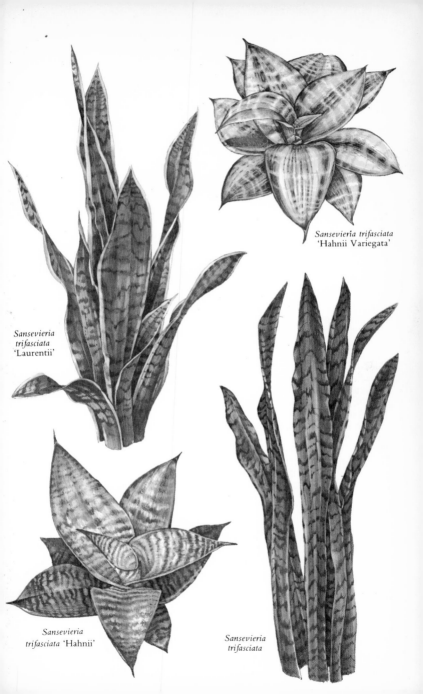

Sansevieria trifasciata
'Hahnii Variegata'

*Sansevieria
trifasciata*
'Laurentii'

*Sansevieria
trifasciata* 'Hahnii'

*Sansevieria
trifasciata*

Yucca (*yuk*-a) The Carib name for a plant in another family (*Manihot esculenta* in the *Euphorbiaceae* – better known under its common name of tapioca).

Cultivation Easy and popular plants valued for their relatively low selling price, ease of culture and distinctive appearance. As long as they have a spot in bright light yuccas will stay in good shape. Keep them cooler in winter than in summer if possible, and maintain a min. temp. of 7°C (45°F). Water the compost well whenever it feels dry during summer, but keep it barely moist in winter. An occasional spray over with tepid rainwater will do the plant good, and it benefits from being stood outdoors in summer in a warm spot sheltered from winds which may topple it over. Feed fortnightly in summer and repot every other year in spring. Use a standard soil-based compost rather than a peat-based compost as its weight will help to hold the plant upright. A clay pot will give additional stability. Propagation is by the removal of offsets at repotting time; pot these up in smaller containers of a basic soil-based compost. Lengths of mature stem around 2-3 in in diameter can be stuck into pots of moist compost and (provided they are the right way up) roots will be produced at the base and shoots at the top. This is how plants are raised commercially and it explains their rather unusual appearance. Mealy bug and scale insects can be a problem.

THE SPECIES

Yucca aloifolia (West Indies, South Eastern U.S.A.) Spanish Bayonet, Ti Tree (see also *Cordyline terminalis*). Height 6 ft or more, spread 1½ ft. An oddity rather than a beauty, this plant is sold not in its youth, when it has an appearance similar to a dracaena, but grown specially from logs. This gives it the appearance of a sawn-off tree from which young green plants are sprouting. The foliage is long and narrow and arranged in a rosette. The leaf colour is mid-green and the leaf tips are armed with spikes. Flowers may be produced on older specimens that are healthy and happy. The clusters of bloom appear in early summer and are creamy white.

Yucca elephantipes (syn. *Y. guatemalensis*) (Central America) Spineless Yucca. Height 3-6 ft in the home, spread 2 ft or more. Usually sold as a more shapely plant with a fountain of arching leaves that are twice as long as those of *Y. aloifolia* and not armed with spikes. Flowers are rarely produced but they are cream and open in summer. Easier than dracaena for the novice to grow.

Yucca elephantipes

Yucca aloifolia

BIBLIOGRAPHY

Baker, H. A., and Oliver, E. G. H., *Ericas in Southern Africa*, Purnell, Cape Town, South Africa, 1967

Beckett, Kenneth, A., *Greenfingers A–Z of Gardening*, Orbis Publishing Ltd, London, 1977

Blunt, Wilfrid, *The Art of Botanical Illustration*, Collins, London, 1971 reprint

Clifford, Derek, *Pelargoniums*, Blandford Press, 1970 (second edition)

Davidson, William, and Rochford, T.C., *The Collingridge All-Colour Guide To House Plants, Cacti & Succulents*, Hamlyn, London, 1976

Gardeners' Chronicle, *Pronunciation of Plant Names*, London 1909

Hadfield, M., Harling, R., Highton, L., *British Gardeners, A Biographical Dictionary*, A. Zwemmer Ltd/Condé Nast Publications Ltd, London, 1980

Hellyer, A. G. L., *The Collingridge Encyclopaedia of Gardening*, Hamlyn, London, 1976

Hessayon, D. G., *The House Plant Expert*, PBI Publications, 1980

Heywood, V. H., (Ed.) *Flowering Plants of the World*, Oxford University Press, Oxford, 1979 Reprint

Mathew, Brian, *Dwarf Bulbs*, Arco Publishing Company, Inc., New York, 1973

Mathew, Brian, *The Larger Bulbs*, B. T. Batsford, London, 1978

Rienits, Rex & Thea, *The Voyages of Captain Cook*, Paul Hamlyn, London, 1968

Rose, Peter Q., *Ivies*, Blandford Press, Poole, 1980

Royal Horticultural Society *Dictionary of Gardening*, (ed. Chittenden), Oxford University Press, Oxford, 1956 (Second Edition)

Royal Horticultural Society *Journal*, London, 1947–1966

Smith, A. W., Stearn, W. T., Smith, I. L. L., *A Gardener's Dictionary of Plant Names*, Cassell, London 1971

Sotheby & Co., *The Library of the Stiftung Für Botanik, Liechtenstein*, Parts 1, 2, & 3, London 1975–1976 (sale catalogues)

Synge, Patrick M., *Collins Guide to Bulbs*, Collins, London, 1971 (second edition)

Willis, J. C., *A Dictionary of the Flowering Plants and Ferns*, (rev. Airy Shaw), Cambridge University Press, Cambridge, 1973 (eight edition)

Wright, Robert C.M., and Titchmarsh, Alan, *The Complete Book of Plant Propagation*, Ward Lock Ltd., London, 1981

INDEX

Page numbers in bold type refer to illustrations